T0318243

Routledge Revivals

Economic Growth in Britain and France 1780-1914

First published in 1978, Professor O'Brien's *Economic Growth in Britain and France 1780-1914* is an original and pioneering exercise in comparative and quantitative economic history. It finds a controversial place in the debate on the question of French retardation in the 19th century and as a brave and important contribution towards the understanding of economic growth in Western Europe.

The author attempts to comprehend and evaluate the economic performance of France through explicit comparisons with Britain, while considering British economic history from a French perspective. Challenging the orthodox view that France lagged behind Britain in economic terms, the book argues that there were two paths of economic growth to the 20th century, with France's path seen as a more humane and no less efficient transition to industrial society.

Economic Growth in Britain and France 1780-1914

Two Paths to the Twentieth Century

Patrick O'Brien
and
Caglar Keyder

Routledge
Taylor & Francis Group

First published in 1978
by George Allen & Unwin Ltd.

This edition first published in 2011 by Routledge
2 Park Square, Milton Park, Abingdon, Oxon, OX14 4RN

Simultaneously published in the USA and Canada
by Routledge
605 Third Avenue, New York, NY 10017

Routledge is an imprint of the Taylor & Francis Group, an informa business

A Library of Congress record exists under ISBN: 0043302882

ISBN 13: 978-0-415-68234-3 (hbk)
ISBN 13: 978-0-203-80281-6 (ebk)
ISBN 13: 978-0-415-68498-9 (pbk)

ECONOMIC GROWTH IN BRITAIN AND FRANCE 1780–1914

For Cassy

Economic Growth in Britain and France 1780-1914

Two Paths to the Twentieth Century

PATRICK O'BRIEN
St Antony's College, Oxford
and
CAGLAR KEYDER
Middle East Technical University, Ankara

London
GEORGE ALLEN & UNWIN
Boston   Sydney

First published in 1978

British Library Cataloguing in Publication Data

O'Brien, Patrick
   Economic growth in Britain and France,
   1780–1914
   1. Great Britain – Economic conditions
   2. France – Economic conditions
   I. Title   II. Keyder, Calgar
   339.5'0941   HC255

ISBN 0–04–330288–2

Printed in Great Britain in 10 on 11 point Times by
Hazell Watson & Viney Ltd, Aylesbury, Bucks

Contents

List of Tables

Introduction and Acknowledgements

Reason is the enumeration of quantities already known;
imagination is the perception of the value of those quantities,
both separately and as a whole.
> Shelley, *In Defence of Poetry*, 1821.

Comparative economic history is conducted on the assumption that systematic comparisons of economic development across countries might help historians and economists to understand modern economic growth. Thus the contrasting history of British and French industrialisation over the nineteenth century has attracted considerable attention from scholars in Europe and America. There exists a rich and growing historiography and, what is more important, a serious controversy around the subject. This study, which is an exercise in measurement, is offered primarily as a contribution to that debate. It was inspired by the work of Jean Marczewski and his associates in France and the work of Deane, Cole and Mitchell on the quantitative history of Britain. It forms a preface to our own continuing research into productivity levels in European economies.*

The book is divided into three parts. Part One contains a historiographical survey of recent writings on the comparative economic development of France and Britain from 1780 to 1914 which leads conveniently into a discussion of the methods employed in this essay to measure the relative retardation of the French economy compared to that of Britain. Part Two offers two indicators of French 'backwardness': domestic output per head and commodity flow per head, and explores hypotheses designed to explain the unexpectedly small gap in per capita incomes (or 'welfare') between the two countries. Part Three is concerned to measure and compare the productivity of labour employed in industry and agriculture and to account for the relatively low productivity of workers engaged in French agriculture and the superior productivity of employees in French industry that, to our surprise, persisted for most of the nineteenth century.

Throughout this study we deliberately attempted to comprehend and evaluate the economic development of France through explicit comparisons with Britain. The comparative approach also brings with it a 'French' perspective on British economic history. Our main chapters

---

*J. Marczewski, 'Le produit physique de l'économie française de 1789 à 1913 (comparaison avec la Grande Bretagne)', *Cahiers de l'Institut Statistique Economique Appliqué*, AF, 4 July 1965.

(2–6) are statistical exercises followed by inferences drawn from numbers that seek to modify the orthodox view that, in economic terms, France definitely lagged behind Britain over the period 1780–1914. Our conclusions (Chapter 7) are set in the context of the historiographical debate (surveyed in Chapter 1) on French retardation. There we also widen the discussion to evaluate the two very different paths of development to industrial society taken by Britain and France over the nineteenth century.

While conducting research for this monograph, we have been fortunate to benefit from the congenial and stimulating environment provided by the Warden and Fellows of St Antony's College, Oxford, and financial assistance from a Social Science Research Council grant. Our intellectual debt to Marc Bloch and Simon Kuznets will be obvious. A long list of busy academics took time and trouble to discuss ideas with us and several commented in detail upon an earlier draft of this manuscript. We are pleased to thank Rondo Cameron, François Crouzet, Phyllis Deane, Peter Dickson, Mark Elvin, Juan Esteban, John Habakkuk, Max Hartwell, Tom Kemp, Pierre Leon, Maurice Lévy-Leboyer, Peter Mathias, William Parker, Richard Roehl, Berrick Saul, Herman Van der Wee, Angus Walker and John Wright for the improvements and additions that their suggestions made to the final text. That 'perfect colleague', Stan Engerman, merits a special word of thanks for persistent help and encouragement. Daniel Heath's research on the agricultural chapter is gratefully acknowledged both here and in the joint paper, published with him in the *Journal of European Economic History*. Finally we are indebted to Mrs Siang Ng and Miss Susan Symes for excellent research assistance and to Mrs Elizabeth Stevens who typed up and retyped our illegible pages and drafts with such speed, accuracy and cheerfulness. Our publisher, Michael Holdsworth, has been more than usually patient.

Part One
HISTORIOGRAPHY, DATA AND METHODS

Chapter 1

Definitions and Historiography of Retardation

According to the *Oxford English Dictionary*, retardation means lateness, slowness or delay compared to some expectation based upon previous progress or to some other independent norm. In assessments related to the performance of economies over the long run, retardation implies either deceleration in rates of economic progress or slow growth compared to other economies deemed appropriate for comparison. The first meaning of the word is predicated upon assumptions about a supposed potential for development at constant or accelerating rates of growth, and when the actual record of a given country is considered in terms of potential for growth that potential is usually defined in terms of a comparison with other countries. Failure or poor economic performance means opportunities missed, leads lost and output foregone because of a neglect of best economic practice. But a slower rate of growth provides a rather inadequate index of the failure of a country to exploit new technology or other inputs that might raise productivity. In comparative terms, condemnation of performance based upon relative rates of growth assumes that producers in two countries faced equal, or roughly equal, opportunities to expand production – in this particular comparison, that the growth of domestic and international demand for the products of French industry and agriculture expanded at the same rate as the demand for British output. Clearly this was not true, but terms like retarded or relatively backward may still be warranted if it can be shown that French producers made less of their opportunities than their rivals in Britain. On the other hand, it could be the case that opportunities offered to British businessmen between 1780 and 1914 were greater but that French businessmen exploited their more limited markets more effectively.

But like other historians we propose to concentrate upon the comparative sense of the term 'retardation', while recognising that countries should (if possible) be studied in terms of some unique capacity for development at different stages of their history.

When he first surveyed the problem, nearly two decades ago, Rondo Cameron found the French 'rate of growth for all relevant variables substantially below that of other Western industrial nations' and considered the disparity in performance puzzling because of the obvious advantages possessed by France.[1] He admitted, however, that on a per capita basis the French record looked better and in a later study of European banking tabulated some crude estimates of French and British per capita incomes which show how the differential between the two countries narrowed from 52 per cent in 1801 to 27 per cent by 1872.[2] More recently, after citing data which indicated that for the half-century before 1914 the rate of growth of real per capita output in France was above the rate for the United Kingdom and only slightly below the German rate, Cameron seemed inclined to abandon terms like 'retardation' in favour of something called 'slow growth'.[3] His own research has, moreover, always been concerned to emphasise the positive achievements of the French economy and the substantial contributions made by France to economic development in the rest of Europe.[4]

Kindleberger set out to compare economic development in Britain and France for a century after 1850 and since he had 'no doubt that income per capita in France was well below that of Britain in 1851' his analysis is directed to explaining the persistence of French backwardness.[5] But his first chapter, which purports to be an outline of economic growth in Britain and France (and which should presumably specify the problem and delimit it chronologically), merely separates periods of expansion from periods of contraction in the two economies. Relative backwardness is nowhere defined or measured in terms that indicate changes over time in differential per capita incomes in the two countries. Kindleberger's failure to specify the explicandum means that his analysis of various factors (such as coal, capital formation, population, entrepreneurship, technology, scale and agriculture) behind the British and French rates of growth from 1850 to 1950 is an interesting exercise in the *mechanisms* of economic development but less satisfactory as quantitative economic history.

'Retarded' is not only applied to a country's inferior record in the rate of growth of real per capita income, but is also taken to connote some incapacity for structural change. The argument runs like this: since over the long run structural change and the growth of output are correlated, the indicators of structural change can be used to rank countries along a scale of economic development. Thus one country has been described as backward or retarded because the share of industrial output in its national product is below that of (or increasing more slowly than that of) another country.

A less acceptable form of this equation of development with industrialisation is one that focuses upon the structure of industry itself. Thus countries have been described as backward because their coal and iron and cotton production are relatively low. Of course, the examples selected for emphasis are not chosen arbitrarily since the development of industries like iron, steel, coal and textiles has been at the centre of earlier examples of industrialisation, particularly the English pattern. But there is more than one strategy for growth, and idealisation of the English model does not provide unambiguous indicators for all national development.

Kemp's extensive writings on French economic history exemplify the notion that backwardness can be defined and analysed in structural terms. According to Kemp, 'the origins of the problem of French industrial lag may be said to be found [under the *ancien régime*]' when 'agriculture stagnated and industrial development proceeded along traditional lines'.[6] He asserted that in per capita terms no improvement took place over the eighteenth century and the kind of growth that occurred 'was not accompanied by the preparation of conditions for structural change'.[7]

Although Kemp is not engaged in comparative history, there is no doubt that his judgements on the performance of the French economy over the nineteenth century are permeated by implied references to British standards. Thus he recognised that although 'growth was taking place it fell short of what was required to bring the economy into line with the best results elsewhere'.[8] Kemp perceived that economic development in France adapted to the availability of local resources, to the characteristics of local and European markets and to the international division of labour that emerged after Waterloo. But he had no doubt that better results could have been achieved if resources had been allocated from agriculture to industry so that the contribution of agriculture to national output declined more rapidly.[9]

Kemp also saw the principal defect of French *industrial* development in structural terms as a failure 'to turn over earlier and more completely to large scale production or to mass production methods'.[10] 'Large sections of French industry underwent little change in technique or structure during this whole period' and 'the continued vitality of the old forms of artisanal production and small scale organisation in consumer goods industry' is seen throughout his books and articles as a source of backwardness derived from a failure to assimilate British technology and the factory system.[11] Thus even the silk industry 'despite some technical improvements continued to represent old style capitalism' and the survival of domestic textile industry in Normandy over the first half of the nineteenth century 'may be taken as an adaptation to French peculiarities which inhibited growth'.[12]

Established correlations between levels of per capita income and the share of the economy's labour force employed in agriculture and the share of agriculture in total output are derived from international comparisons taken from samples of countries and are related to the modern period. It is also the case that the long-run improvement in the level of per capita income observed from the historical records of

20–30 countries, now affluent, is associated with the relative decline of the agricultural sector.[13] Nevertheless, no presumption can be derived from the literature on structural change that transformation should proceed with equal speed in all countries over any finite historical period. The reallocation of labour and other resources from agriculture to industry and services is efficient only if its marginal productivity is higher outside primary production. There can be no easy assumption that a relatively large agricultural sector is 'abnormal' or demonstrably suboptimal.[14]

Finally there is far less theoretical validity and very little statistical support for his proposition that small-scale artisanal forms of industry should have been superseded as early as possible in the nineteenth century by larger-scale factories in all forms of industrial enterprise. An efficient allocation of resources cannot be equated with one form of industrial organisation or indeed with any one technique of production. Economic theory lends no support to assumptions, present all too often in writings on French backwardness, that there is one definable and optimal path to higher per capita incomes and still less to the implicit notion that this path can be identified with British industrialisation as it proceeded from 1780 to 1914.

Such assumptions are even more obvious in the technological approach to French retardation. In its cruder forms, that approach assumes that only certain forms of technology produce structural change and economic growth and tends to confine the history of economic development to a history of inventions and their diffusion. Retardation in this framework means a failure or slowness to adopt techniques and forms of organisation of the country or countries already industrialised.

There is no doubt that *The Unbound Prometheus* is the best study of retardation conceived in technological terms, and the book has had a deep influence on European economic history ever since its early publication as an essay in the *Cambridge Economic History of Europe*.[15] Of course the author is too sophisticated to accept any simple equation of material progress with mechanisation. Nevertheless, paragraph after paragraph in Landes's famous study suggests that the economic history of Western Europe for the century can be understood as the diffusion of techniques of production (machines and chemical processes) and forms of industrial organisation (factories) from the first industrial nation, Britain, to more backward economies on the European mainland. For Landes the central problem in European economic history is to explain Britain's early start and the relatively slow diffusion of British methods into Belgian, French and German industry.

Chapter headings in *The Unbound Prometheus*, 'The Industrial Revolution in Britain', 'Continental Emulation' and 'Closing the Gap', proclaim Landes's approach to industrial history. But his text is even more eloquent. 'By the mid 18th century', he wrote, 'it was already obvious that British industrial technique had advanced significantly beyond the rest of the world.' 'In view of the enormous superiority of these innovations, one would expect the rest to have followed automatically . . . but even the quickest nations marked time until the third and fourth decades of the 19th century.' 'Their industrial revolution was substantially slower than the British. Although they were able to study the machines and engines . . . they were generations in absorbing them and even longer in catching up to British practice.'[16]

Landes does cite (without critical comment) some estimates of per capita income expressed in sterling for the 1860s which indicate levels in the United Kingdom 35 per cent ahead of France and 60 per cent ahead of Germany.[17] But throughout the book progress is conceived largely in technological terms as 'the substitution of machines for labour, the substitution of inanimate for animate sources of power and the use of new and abundant raw materials. These inputs are the industrial revolution. They yielded an unprecedented increase in man's productivity and with it a substantial rise in income per head.'[18] Landes assumes that the best technology, organisation and scale of industrial production could be found in Britain and that backwardness can be recognised as a failure or slowness to emulate British methods.

An alternative definition of retardation (derived from a famous stage theory) envisages the growth of output through industrialisation as a process of discontinuous development and ranks economies according to their time of arrival at the point of discontinuity or take-off. Rostow's schema cuts the historical record of countries into segments, in order to periodise their development along a growth curve from traditional society to an age of high mass consumption. Advanced economies pass through the take-off stage before backward or retarded follower countries.[19] Rostow's stage theory is now recognised as taxonomy with very limited general validity even in its retrodictions.[20] French historians have certainly demonstrated that it could not be used to rank France along any scale of relative backwardness because the long run development of the French economy exhibited no discontinuities of the kind posited by Rostow. In Marczewski's words, 'there was no true take-off in France at all: the growth of the French economy was very gradual and its origins lie far in the past'.[21] Nor apparently can a take-off stage in France (or indeed in Britain, the first industrial nation) be dated in terms of discontinuities in the rate of capital formation or the emergence of leading industries which in Rostow's theory push the economy on to a path of sustained growth.[22]

Gerschenkron's more illuminating typology suggests that countries in the process of creating modern industry exhibit well-defined characteristics that differ systematically not merely between earlier and later industrialisers, but, more significantly, between economies that began to industrialise from different levels of economic development. In his scheme the relative backwardness of a country's economic system can be inferred by observing methods adopted for industrialisation. Such methods, or strategy, provide indicators of the degree to which a country had developed preconditions for the creation of modern industry. Thus the more backward the economy at the onset of industrialisation, the greater will be the acceleration or spurt in the rate of growth of industrial output. The more backward an economy the greater will be the stress on producers' goods industries, larger-scale plant and monopolistic forms of industrial organisation. Furthermore, countries proceeding from positions of relative backwardness will tend to deploy centralised methods for the finance of capital formation – such as industrial banks in Germany, and the State in less developed economies like Russia, farther east. Such capital formation tends to be accompanied by stronger pressure on consumption levels and a more pronounced ideology in favour of industrialisation. Finally, the more backward the economy the smaller the contribution made by the agricultural sector as a market for industrial goods.[23]

It is not our intention to review Gerschenkron's sophisticated approach to European industrialisation, but only to see if the relative backwardness or retardation of the French economy, compared to that of Britain, could be inferred from the pattern of French industrialisation. A more comprehensive exercise along these lines has, however, been undertaken in a recently published paper by Richard Roehl.[24] There is, moreover, no presumption that Gerschenkron would claim that such an inquiry (conducted within the framework of his typology) would yield the kind of insights he derived from comparisons between Russian and German industrialisation or from contrasts between Austria and Hungary.

But the limitation of the typology becomes all too apparent when applied to Britain and France. The available evidence is thin and ambiguous. There is, for example, no discernible spurt in French industrial output. Industrialisation in France probably did not proceed with greater emphasis on producers' goods, larger-scale plant or monopolistic forms of industrial organisation.[25] There is no proof that the agricultural sector in France consumed a lower proportion of industrial output than was the case across the Channel. In fact in terms of an acceleration in the rate of growth of industrial output, Marczewski suggested France as the 'leader' and Britain as the 'follower' country.[26]

Gerschenkron finds confirmation of relative backwardness in the role played by industrial banks under the Second Empire, compared with England where 'industrialisation had proceeded without any substantial utilization of banking for long term investment purposes'.[27] But we simply do not know if the shares of fixed capital formation in the industrial sector financed through loans from banks differed in the two countries and there is no longer a presumption that British banks played an insignificant part in the finance of long-term investment.[28] Furthermore, it is possible to see the emergence of industrial banks not as a symptom of backwardness but as a response to constraints imposed on the French system by the Banque de France which made English-style country banking impossible in France.[29] It is also equally possible to explain the reluctance of the French government to embrace an English-style *laissez-faire* strategy in economic management as the product of a long and quite different tradition of economic regulation. In any case the differences in the extent of state intervention in the two economies is really rather slight.

Gerschenkron is, moreover, disposed to see the articulation and influence of the ideas of Saint-Simon under the Second Empire as the kind of ideology for industrialisation that emerges in conditions of relative backwardness, where 'the businessman needs a more powerful stimulus than the prospect of high profits. What is needed to remove the mountains of routine and prejudice is faith – faith in the words of Saint-Simon, that the golden age lies not behind but ahead of mankind.' By way of contrast he sees the characteristic English ideology of free trade as 'rational arguments in favour of industrialization policies' which did not need to 'be supplemented by quasi religious fervour'.[30] Not only has the influence of Saint-Simonist ideology been exaggerated in French economic development, but these passages come close to familiar beliefs that the Europeans embraced ideologies and the English rational ideas, though a reading of the controversy over the spread of free trade ideas in England will dispel any notion that they constituted anything less than an ideology, articulated, propagated and held with all the fervour of religious ideals.[31]

Our central point is that something called relative backwardness cannot be inferred from characteristic features of French industrialisation, even where they could be shown to differ from the British pattern. Industrialisation in France simply took place in a different legal, political and cultural tradition and it does not seem to be illuminating to single out elements of that process as symptoms of relative backwardness, particularly when there seems to be a normative assumption in the typology that the 'English way' constitutes not merely initial but best or normal practice.

Of course Gerschenkron recognised that adjectives like backward or retarded can only be applied to those nations that have failed to provide standards of material consumption for the population at large equivalent to higher standards found elsewhere in the world. There is no reason to suppose that backwardness in this sense can be inferred from differences in the timing or strategy of industrialisation among European nations in the nineteenth century, and in recent tests both Barsby and Roehl showed such correlations to be rather weak.[32] We would certainly dispute any presumption of French backwardness based upon loosely specified comparisons with the English model.

By using one, or more commonly a combination of these definitions and criteria, historians, usually of Anglo-American origin, have categorised the French economy from the late eighteenth century to the First World War as retarded or relatively backward compared to that of Britain. Nevertheless, it is always difficult to use such terms precisely and in ways that will command widespread acceptance. For example, in economics there has never been a presumption that a set of machines, chemical processes or forms of industrial organisation found to be efficient in one country should be adopted by another with the shortest possible time-lag.[33] The comparison of British and French technology does not provide unambiguous indicators of a potential for development over the long run and still less of levels of development at particular periods of time. Nor can the typologies propounded by Rostow and Gerschenkron be employed to validate adjectives like retarded because the evidence is either not available or contradictory. Even if more facts could be found, the typologies themselves rest upon foundations that seem to generate notions of backwardness that may, in the end, mean that France industrialised a bit later than Britain and conducted that process in a different way.

Growth rates of real per capita output seem more helpful, but all recent evidence suggests that, given the usual margins of statistical error as well as the inherent problems of index numbers, the long-run performances of the French and British economies appear to be too similar to warrant the derogatory adjectives usually applied to France.[34] In any case rates of change do not inform us about absolute levels of per capita output and consumption in the two countries.

In the light of this survey of the historiography we wish to suggest that the gap between British and French per capita incomes provides the least ambiguous and perhaps the only viable statistical basis for introducing or focusing historical discussion related to the retardation of the French economy between 1780 and 1914.

There is no need to repeat arguments against the employment of per capita income as an indicator of national development. But with all its conceptual and computational drawbacks it remains the best single measure available, if only because all other suggested indicators of economic and social progress (such as calorie and protein intake per head, literacy rates, life expectancy and cubic feet of accommodation per family) seem to be highly correlated with it.[35]

We propose to use per capita output as the index for comparisons between Britain and France in order to say something about relative levels of material consumption attained by residents of the two countries across the nineteenth century. Comparisons of welfare which use statistics of this type are not, however, on firm ground and must make the assumption that production in the two societies took place within a comparable framework of values and objectives, which implies that the output of commodities was perceived in both Britain and France as something to be maximised in order to increase the satisfaction of consumers. Thus tastes and needs are regarded as roughly similar on both sides of the Channel so that higher output in one country could not, for example, be perceived as a response to the deprivation imposed by a harsher climate or the propensities of one set of consumers to eat far more food than the other. Such comparisons usually ignore differences in the quality of the two national products as well as diseconomies associated with the more rapid growth of output that came with industry and urbanisation. In this same context Frenchmen and Englishmen are regarded as consumers, not as workers, and the indices also ignore possible differences in conditions of work in the two countries. Thus it could be the case that the English labour force produced a higher level of output per head than its French counterpart by working harder, longer and in conditions of employment that French workmen preferred not to tolerate.[36] Finally, to make another familiar point, income per capita is an average which ignores differences in the distribution of income in the two countries.[37]

But unless statisticians are willing to make such assumptions and to posit comparable conditions of work, environment, and income distribution in the two countries, it will be impossible to rank one situation as preferable to another in terms of per capita income.

Some of the complexities of comparing levels of average welfare across countries can be avoided by employing output per worker as an index of productive capacity, that is, as a measure of the relative potential of an economy to provide its nationals with goods and services. For example, when the indicator suggests that output per worker was higher in Britain than France that implies that the productive capacity available in Britain could provide a volume of output which, relative to population, was larger than that of France. Or, in other words, the British workers could supply their families with a bundle of commodities exactly equivalent to the bundle supplied by French workers, and more. Thus output per worker is also an index of productivity which measures the capacity of an economy to produce goods and services for its population, and such goods could be used for consumption, capital formation, defence, the relief of poverty or in any way a society chooses.[38] In this book we propose to begin with the numbers and compare levels of welfare in Chapter 3 and labour productivity in Chapters 4–6, where we also discuss all the problems connected with variations in tastes, differences in the quality of output, income distribution and preferences for urban and rural styles of living in the two countries.

NOTES TO CHAPTER 1

1 R. E. Cameron, 'Economic Growth and Stagnation in France, 1815–1914' in B. E. Supple (ed.), *The Experience of Economic Growth* (New York: Random House, 1963), p. 329.
2 R. E. Cameron, *Banking in the Early Stages of Industrialization* (New York: Oxford University Press, 1967), p. 101.
3 R. E. Cameron, 'L'économie française: passé, présent, avenir', *Annales E.S.C.* (*Economie Societe, Civilisation*), September–October 1970, pp. 1424–7.
4 R. E. Cameron, *France and the Economic Development of Europe, 1800–1914* (Princeton: Princeton University Press, 1961).
5 C. P. Kindleberger, *Economic Growth in France and Britain, 1851–1950* (Cambridge, Mass.: Harvard University Press, 1964), p. 9.
6 T. Kemp, *Economic Forces in French History* (London: Dobson, 1971), pp. 41 and 46, but see also ch. 2 of his most recent book, *The French Economy, 1913–39: The History of a Decline* (New York: St Martins Press, 1972).
7 Kemp, *Economic Forces*, pp. 70–1.
8 ibid., p. 223.
9 T. Kemp, 'Structural Factors in the Retardation of French Economic Growth', *Kyklos*, XV (1962), 2, and *Industrialization in Nineteenth Century Europe* (London: Longmans, 1969), ch. 3.
10 Kemp, *Economic Forces*, p. 287.
11 ibid., p. 247.
12 ibid., pp. 115–16.
13 S. Kuznets, *Economic Growth of Nations* (Cambridge, Mass.: Harvard University Press, 1971), chs 3–6.
14 Kemp, 'Structural Factors', pp. 333–9; also Cl. Fohlen, 'France 1700–1914' in C. M. Cipolla (ed.), *The Fontana Economic History of Europe*, vol. 2 (London: Fontana, 1973), p. 29, and P. Deane and W. A. Cole, 'The Growth of National Incomes' in *The Cambridge Economic History of Europe*, vol. VI, part I, ed. H. J. Habakkuk and M. Postan (Cambridge: CUP, 1966), pp. 44–8.
15 D. S. Landes, *The Unbound Prometheus* (Cambridge: CUP, 1970). For example, see F. Crouzet, 'Western Europe and Great Britain: Catching-up in the First Half of the 19th Century' in A. J. Youngson (ed.), *Economic Development in the Long Run* ((London: Allen & Unwin, 1972); Cl. Fohlen, 'France 1700–1914', and A. Milward and S. B. Saul, *The Economic Development of Continental Europe, 1780–1870* (London: Allen & Unwin, 1973), chs 3–5.
16 Landes, *The Unbound Prometheus*, pp. 125–6.
17 ibid., p. 224.
18 ibid., p. 41.
19 W. W. Rostow, *The Stages of Economic Growth* (Cambridge: CUP, 1971), chs 2–4.

20 W. W. Rostow (ed.), *The Economics of Take-off into Sustained Growth* (London: Macmillan, 1963). See in particular chs 1, 2, 4, 9 and 14; see also A. Fishlow, 'Empty Economic Stages', *Economic Journal*, March 1965.

21 J. Marczewski, 'The Take-off Hypothesis and French Experience' in Rostow (ed.), *The Economics of Take-off*, p. 129; see his 'Discussion of the Paper by Habakkuk' in E. A. G. Robinson (ed.), *Problems of Economic Development* (London: Macmillan, 1965), pp. 132–3.

22 ibid.; and see M. Lévy-Leboyer, 'La croissance économique en France au XIXe siècle. Résultats préliminaires', *Annales E.S.C.*, July–August 1968, and F. Crouzet, 'Essai de construction d'un indice annuel de la production industrielle française au XIXe siècle, *Annales E.S.C.*, January–February 1970.

23 A. Gerschenkron, *Economic Backwardness in Historical Perspective* (Cambridge, Mass.: Harvard University Press, 1966). See chs 1, 2, 6 and the Postscript, and his *Continuity in History and Other Essays* (Cambridge, Mass.: Harvard University Press, 1968), ch. 4.

24 R. Roehl, 'French Industrialization. A Reconsideration' in *Explorations in Economic History*, vol. 13 (1976), pp. 233–81.

25 M. Lévy-Leboyer, 'Les processus d'industrialisation: le cas de l'Angleterre et de la France', *Revue Historique*, 1968, 2.

26 J. Marczewski argues that if there was a take-off in France it might have occurred 'around 1750'. See his article in Rostow (ed.), *The Economics of Take-off*, p. 129.

27 Gerschenkron, *Economic Backwardness*, p. 14, and Roehl, 'French Industrialization', pp. 253–6.

28 P. Mathias, 'Capital, Credit and Enterprise in the Industrial Revolution', *Journal of European Economic History*, Spring 1973.

29 Cameron, *Banking*, ch. 4.

30 Gerschenkron, *Economic Backwardness*, p. 25.

31 L. Brown, *The Board of Trade and the Free Trade Movement* (Oxford: OUP, 1968), and N. McCord, *The Anti-Corn Law League 1838–1846* (London: Allen & Unwin, 1958).

32 S. L. Barsby, 'Economic Backwardness and the Characteristics of Development', *Journal of Economic History*, September 1969, and Roehl, 'French Industrialization'.

33 This argument is fully developed in R. M. Hartwell's and R. Higg's review of Landes's *The Unbound Prometheus* in *American Historical Review*, April 1971, pp. 471–4.

34 F. Crouzet, 'French Economic Growth in the Nineteenth Century Reconsidered', *History*, June 1974, pp. 167–79, which is a shorter version of his paper in *Revue du Nord*, July–September 1972. See also Cameron, 'L'économie française', and Roehl, 'French Industrialization', pp. 4–7.

35 See, for example, part 1 in A. N. Agarwala and S. P. Singh, *The Economics of Underdevelopment* (Oxford: OUP, 1958), and *Journal of Development Studies*, April 1972. For an argument in favour of per capita income, see A. Emmanuel, 'Myths of Development versus Myths of Underdevelopment', *New Left Review*, May–June 1974, p. 64.

36 W. Beckerman, *International Comparisons of Real Incomes* (Paris: OECD, 1966), ch. 1. Hill's investigations show that even for the modern period, normal margins of error exceed differences between highest and lowest rates of change: T. P. Hill, *The Process of Economic Growth* (Paris: OECD, 1971).

37 M. Lévy-Leboyer suggests that income distribution in France might have been more skewed: 'Les processus', p. 281.

38 H. Leibenstein, *Economic Backwardness and Economic Growth* (New York: Wiley, 1963), ch. 2.

Chapter 2

Data and Methods

2.1 DATA

Of course the fundamental problem was to find suitable data, and our statistical exercises rest upon years of painstaking work, by Deane, Cole and Mitchell for England and Marczewski, Toutain and Markovitch for France, devoted to the construction of national accounts for both countries.[1] Without their research, quantitative economic history and cross-country comparisons of the kind attempted here would be impossible.

There seems to be no need to survey the sources they employed in detail because deficiencies in the quality of the statistics that make up British and French national accounts have been analysed by their compilers and reviewed by historians interested in the long-run development of the British and French economies.[2] Furthermore, we hold that data widely regarded as suitable for the measurement of growth and structural change in the two countries should also be immune from deep scepticism and regarded as adequate for the comparison of levels of development between them. Nevertheless, it is necessary to explore likely directions of bias, inherent in the quality of basic sources and in the reconstruction of national accounts, biases which inevitably become relevant whenever comparisons of per capita output or output per worker are undertaken.

Estimates for Britain were built up from income flows to labour and property. Deane and Cole reconstructed the wage and salary bills for different sectors of the economy from the censuses of population and other sources which provided them with rough estimates for the allocation of labour. Their wage data is possibly more crude, and tax returns supplied information on flows of rent, interest and profits to the owners of productive assets. They checked their results against contemporary estimates of national income.[3]

Deficiencies in the British estimates mentioned by one critical review include: gaps in the data, particularly for small-scale domestic industry, the low quality of the statistics employed to allocate the labour force among industries, and the difficulties encountered in distinguishing between wages and profits.[4] There has been no comparable critique of tax returns as a historical source and Deane and Cole have not published either a full evaluation of their sources or anything like the detail required to conduct a proper appraisal of the data they used.[5] For France, the estimates were constructed from flows of output. Data for agricultural production derive from censuses conducted at various times throughout the century and from interpolations based upon growth rates for particular crops for inter-census years.[6] The estimates for industry came essentially from customs and other statistics related to inputs of raw materials and are more reliable where a single and homogeneous input (such as raw cotton or wood) could be used to estimate output for the relevant industry.[7]

Marczewski collated and amended Toutain's figures for agriculture and the Markovitch estimates for industry into national commodity output.[8] He concluded that even with much more research the results could have been improved only slightly and the ISEA estimates for the nineteenth century have not been seriously challenged by French historians, whose reviews of the data deal with the feasibility of using such figures over long spans of time and with the treatment of France, the political unit, as a meaningful unit for economic history.[9]

Thus French debate has centred to some extent around Toutain's controversial estimates for agricultural production for the eighteenth century but is more concerned with familiar problems of index numbers and interpretations of countrywide averages. Except for Wright's criticism, reviews of Deane and Cole's research also concentrated on the interpretation of statistics rather than on the validity of the figures employed. For both countries historians have conceded that, with all their shortcomings, the estimates have been properly constructed and are the best available for the time being.[10]

Our problem in comparing national accounts across countries is first of all to ascertain coverage. *A priori*, one can argue that wage and tax data, used for Great Britain, will probably not include as high a percentage of total productive activity as French output figures, reconstructed from raw material inputs and official censuses of production. Thus the sources and methods employed for the compilation of French estimates would seem to bias levels of output upwards compared with the British figures. Furthermore, Deane and Cole also underestimated the proportion of commodity output in national product, because they admit that their labour force distribution probably allocated many small producers and craftsmen into the service sector;[11] while the Markovitch estimates for French industry, which do not rely on the allocation of labour or the composition of output, will include almost all commodity output.

As far as the measurement of labour productivity in industry and agriculture is concerned, the Deane and Cole method seems more accurate because, if there is a bias, it tends to be in the same direction for both labour inputs and sectoral outputs; whereas for France the size of the industrial labour force is certainly understated, owing to the inclusion of workers employed in domestic industry as part of the agricultural work force. Of course, this also implies an overstatement of the French labour force employed in agriculture.

We can do no better than summarise Marczewski's assessment of potential biases in comparisons of per capita outputs and labour productivities between Britain and France.[12] In his view the productivity of labour in industry in France could be exaggerated, owing to the underestimation of the industrial labour force in France. On the other hand, output per worker in French agriculture is underestimated because of the inflated figures for the labour force employed in that sector. Thirdly, the level of industrial output in Britain may be understated for the reasons set out above. Total commodity output in Britain will also be understated to a lesser degree because of the overestimation of the labour force employed in British agriculture. Finally, since the British coverage refers to Great Britain and not to the United Kingdom, the omission of Ireland (a relatively backward region discussed under Table 3.5, p. 65) will 'bias' the comparison against France.[13]

While it is clear that the British estimates have been constructed from income flows and the French estimates from the output side, the standard concepts underlying their presentation have not been made sufficiently explicit. The British figures refer to gross national income or gross national output valued at factor cost and the French estimates are designed to approximate to a concept of gross national product at *prix à la production*.[14] *Prix à la production* means farm and factory gate prices – that is to say, prices which exclude markups for transport costs, distribution charges and indirect taxes. Although the methods used by the economists at ISEA to calculate *prix à la production* are not set out in detail, it is clear that both Toutain and Markovitch see their estimates of *produit brut* 'as corresponding to the income of these industries at factor cost. This is equivalent to wages, profits, interest and rent realized in these activities.'[15] Thus both sets of estimates can be described as gross national output at factor cost. 'Gross' implies the familiar qualification that neither set of estimates excludes an allowance for depreciation on capital used up in the course of production.

In the last resort, since there is no way of correcting for biases in the data, we simply propose to refer to them whenever we offer generalisations based upon the far from perfect estimates for the national incomes and work forces of Britain and France.

2.2   SERVICES AND COMMODITY OUTPUT

The term 'output' employed in our comparisons of British and French development from 1780 to 1914 refers throughout to *commodity output.* Output here means physical commodities, including agricultural and other primary produce, minerals, industrial goods and the products of the construction sector. It is simply tangible goods used for consumption or capital formation. Services are excluded from consideration. Thus we have not compared the two economies in terms of their national incomes or products, defined in the standard way.

ISEA has not yet published estimates for the output of the French service sector, except for transport.[16] Nevertheless, given the dubious nature of the statistics normally offered as measures of production in services, and (what is more important) given the assumptions typically employed to define final output in the service sector, the limitation imposed by the absence of adequate data for France is perhaps not serious. On the contrary, there are good arguments for confining comparisons across countries, at least for the nineteenth century, to the volume of physical commodities produced and made available to the citizens of those countries.

For example, the output of services in the national accounts of Britain, the United States, France and Germany is often defined as equivalent to the wage and salary bill of the labour force employed in that sector. Such a definition fails to capture all or large parts of the income accruing to property utilised in the sector, and although capital output and capital labour ratios for services are lower than they are for commodity production, the provision of services, in branches like transport, does require considerable quantities of fixed capital.[17] Furthermore, the development of modern industry and commercial agriculture, particularly in its early stages, requires considerable investment in circulating capital for the distribution of output across time and space.[18]

But even if comprehensive and reliable estimates could be obtained of total returns to all factors of production engaged in services, special conditions must operate if the claims made by those factors on the national incomes of Britain and France are to be regarded as equivalent to the contribution of services to their respective national products. Briefly, and this provision applies to agriculture and industry as well as services, there must be full employment, perfect competition in factor and commodity markets and an absence of tariffs and external economies.

Such conditions are perhaps less likely to obtain for the service economy than for agriculture and industry. For example, government and domestic servants, workers in repair shops, laundries, hotels and restaurants, and the more numerous groups of males, females and children engaged in wholesale and retail trade and the liberal professions, are not likely to be employed in the kind of market framework where wage rates are pushed towards a convergence with marginal products. On the contrary, almost everything written by social historians about occupational groups engaged in services over the nineteenth century suggests that their recruitment as well as their methods and levels of remuneration departed markedly from the conditions specified for the operation of competitive labour markets. Thus, at the top, professional occupations like doctors, lawyers, merchants and civil servants commanded fees and salaries that included a significant element of monopoly rent, and at the other end of the pay scale large segments of the urban poor received transfer payments from the rest of the productive labour force.[19] Urban services in the conditions of accelerated population growth and internal migration that accompanied industrialisation in Britain and France became, for many workers, a residual employment category. With low ratios of capital to output and flexible ratios of capital to labour, the sector attracted family enterprise, self-employed workers, females and others with low opportunity cost. They relied partly on the jobs they performed and partly upon the social and political institutions of the capitalist system to maintain their standards of pay and consumption not too far below the average wage paid to unskilled labour in agriculture and industry.[20] Classical economists regarded all service occupations as parasitic, and Malthusians saw them as evidence of population pressure. Without adopting either of these extreme positions and while recognising the real contribution of services to the growth of national income over the nineteenth century, we remain extremely sceptical of any method that measures that contribution in terms of the total remuneration received by those employed in the service sector.

There is another, and possibly more telling, objection to the inclusion of services in the comparison of economic development in Britain and France. Before 1914 in both countries, a considerable share of production in services consisted of work that approximated more to intermediate than final output. For example, much of government activity, transport, trade and financial services can be perceived as inputs designed to assist the production and distribution of commodities for final consumption. The growth of local government, legal services, police and public health, as well as trade and transport, can be seen as intermediate production that developed with and in response to the needs of an urban industrial economy. Clearly, not all growth in the service economy can be regarded as derived from the growth of commodity production or from changes in its composition and location. For example, the growth of demand for professional services from doctors, teachers, entertainers, artists and transport for travel, increased final output just as much as any addition to the supply of food or clothing. But in so far as the growth of a good deal of activity conventionally defined as final output in the service sector is arguably a reflection of greater specialisation, derived from the development and location of modern industry, to include it as final output in the comparison of per capita incomes in Britain and France would introduce an element of double counting, biased in favour of the more urban and industrialised British economy.[21]

In addition, if there are significant differences in the quality of those services performed in direct response to consumer demand, distortions again enter comparisons of per capita incomes across countries since wages rates in the service sector would not reflect the decline in quality. For example, changes in the quality of services performed for consumers resident in towns could be inversely related to the rate of internal migration. Professional and skilled services are not usually in elastic supply and any rapid increase in the demand for doctors, lawyers, educators, or trained and diligent officers for local government could lead to falls in the quality of services performed, at least over the medium term. At the same time the shift in demand and increased productivity and incomes from commodity production would preclude any fall in professional fees and remuneration. Income and output from services would appear from the statistics to go up, but the figures would be silent about any fall in quality.

Over the nineteenth century structural change and urbanisation proceeded much further in Britain than in France.[22] Thus in Britain services (defined to include trade, transport, government and domestic service, housing and income from abroad) accounted for 44 per cent of gross national output in 1801, 45 per cent in 1851 and 54 per cent in 1901; while in France the share of the service sector (defined as all non-commodity output) amounted to 28 per cent in 1788, 26 per cent in 1852 and 24 per cent in 1902–3. This differential in terms of the percentage of national output contributed by the tertiary sector was also reflected in the distribution of the labour force. Labour engaged in the British service sector amounted to 34 per cent of the work force in 1801, 45 per cent in 1851 and 1901; while in France the labour force share engaged in the non-commodity sector was 27 per cent in 1781–90, 22 per cent in 1855–64 and still only 29 per cent in 1895–1904.[23]

To us it is plausible to argue that the inclusion of output from services (a sector which, relative to commodity output, grew far more rapidly in Britain) would lower per capita incomes in France compared to Britain. In an exercise designed to discover how relative levels of welfare and productivity may have changed between the French Revolution and the First World War, it appears reasonable to confine measurement to flows of commodities. Services have been excluded not merely because we were reluctant to fall back upon unsatisfactory statistics for France but mainly because the measurement of service output in terms of labour income is a dubious procedure and because the inclusion of an output that is to a large degree intermediate or derived from industrialisation and possibly subject to relative decline in quality over time, introduces an unknown but probably important bias against France.

We are *not* arguing like the classical economists that services are unproductive, and in any case see the force of Nietsche's remark that 'the strength of a civilization is to be measured by the number of parasites it can support'. Furthermore, services are *not* excluded entirely from the calculations set out above because the benefits of services like transport, distribution, commerce, finance and even government will affect the prices of physical commodities. This means that, in so far as Britain enjoyed advantages from a more efficient service sector, agricultural and industrial prices will be lower compared to prices in France, where (in value terms) the markup for services would probably be higher. Lower prices in Britain operated to raise the purchasing power of sterling compared to francs and will be reflected in the exchange rate established between the two currencies. Our attempt to calculate purchasing power parity exchange rates (see Section 2.4) should to some extent capture the relative contribution made by services to welfare and productivity in the two countries.

We are also aware that part of the output of the British service sector consisted of banking, insurance and mercantile services performed for foreigners and which should be included in international comparisons. That problem is, however, dealt with explicitly under a discussion of import surplus (see Section 3.3). For the rest we prefer to compare levels of welfare and productivity in terms of commodity output and do not expect our departure from standard procedure in social accounting to seriously qualify our analysis and conclusions,

2.3   PERIODISATION AND CYCLES

Since the concern of this study is to identify long-term changes in the movement of per capita commodity output and labour productivity it is appropriate to present figures calculated as decennial averages. Our time span is a 'long' nineteenth century which begins in 1781 and ends with the First World War. The secular trend refers to movements through twelve sub-periods which are contiguous except for gaps around times of revolution and war in France, from 1793 to 1815. This periodisation is based upon research conducted at the ISEA, an ongoing investigation into French national accounts from the eighteenth century to the twentieth. To adjust the ISEA figures to any other periodisation less dependent on particularities of French history would have been forbiddingly difficult. For this reason we utilised the sub-periods which the ISEA found appropriate and which are acceptable, provided the time spans do not introduce biases into the comparison. With arbitrary time divisions, there is always a danger that a particular cycle or cycles of economic activity may be unequally distributed between two periods in the two countries. Only if the timing of economic cycles in France and Great Britain was roughly the same, would the periodisation be free from bias. But since cycles in the international economy are transmitted with time-lags, a particular sub-period may end when the peak of an upswing has been reached in one country whereas the second economy may still be in the phase of intensifying productive activity. Ideally the *absence* of bias from the periods used in this study would imply that within any given sub-period both countries experienced comparable fluctuations in the timing and amplitude of economic activity.

We investigated this type of bias and used Lévy-Leboyer's index of commodity output to locate peaks and troughs for French business cycles.[24] The cycles were then ranked according to their amplitude. These data were compared with a similar table for Britain in Aldcroft and Fearon, which lists nineteenth-century cycles with peak-to-peak dates, troughs, duration and amplitude.[25] Then for both countries we selected the three most important cycles (cycles where downswings exhibited the greatest amplitude) and juxtaposed our periodisation along these cycles.

France experienced more violent fluctuations in economic activity in the second half of the century, whereas the British economy passed through downswings of the highest amplitude before 1860. For England, the most 'severe' cycles occurred during 1836–9, 1839–46 and 1846–56. The first cycle falls within our sub-period 1835–44, except for its final years. But in France there was a similar upswing which ended in 1845. In both countries the trough came in 1843. Thus our periodisation could be described as slightly biased in favour of Britain because the sub-period 1845–54 includes two years of an upswing for Britain, but only one year for France. Fortunately, the cycle from 1836 to 1839 lies totally within a sub-period. France experienced a similar cycle between 1838 and 1841, again totally within the period. The 1846–56 cycle in Britain is, however, more problematic. The last two years of the upswing are included in our 1855–64 period. However, France also experienced an upswing which ended in 1858. France went through a trough in 1854, while England was at a low point in 1850. Therefore, the comparison for our period 1855–64 is biased in favour of France.

To look now at the most important French cycles, which occurred in 1869–75, 1875–82 and 1882–92: the first comes entirely within a sub-period, with a corresponding British cycle from 1865 to 1874. The second cycle again falls within a sub-period, and a British cycle occurred over almost exactly the same years, namely from 1874 to 1883. The 1882–93 cycle in France corresponded to the 1883–90 cycle across the Channel, and does not introduce any bias into a cross-country comparison.

Towards the end of the nineteenth century the years of upswing and downswing became more similar, although in France the amplitude of cycles exhibited greater intensity. From all our periods, some recognisable bias in comparisons, due to the dissimilar phasing of business cycles, comes in 1855–64. Thus we do not expect biases from the phasing and amplitude of cycles in Britain and France to be sufficiently important to require significant correction of the figures. Since our analysis pertains to trends from 1780 to 1914, we can safely ignore any biases introduced by cycles of economic activity.

2.4   THE RATE OF EXCHANGE

Since we wished to compare levels of commodity output in Britain and France, we had to devise a method of making estimates expressed initially in francs and sterling comparable. Unfortunately there is no ideal solution to this familiar exchange rate problem.

To convert francs into sterling at the official rate that operated for dealings in foreign exchange markets would be misleading because at best this rate represents the equilibrium price for the two currencies which in turn reflects demand and supply for goods and services *traded* by Britain and France. Since neither the commodity composition nor the prices of traded goods represent the entire structure of production and consumption in the two countries, the foreign exchange rate is not the 'true' purchasing power parity between francs and sterling. It is an unsuitable ratio to employ in exercises designed to compare levels of material welfare and productivity across countries.[26]

For this purpose the ideal method would be that adopted in recent studies by the OECD where national products of different nations were broken down into a large number of composite products and services and then valued in a single unit of account.[27] For a two-country comparison the same formulae would be:

$$\frac{\text{British products} \times \text{British prices}}{\text{French products} \times \text{British prices}}$$

or

$$\frac{\text{British products} \times \text{French prices}}{\text{French products} \times \text{French prices}}$$

Serious difficulties still arise because statisticians are compelled to make assumptions about the similarity of commodities produced in different countries. Nevertheless, the method does confront the index number problem which emerges whenever historians offer indicators which purport to measure growth over time or income levels across countries. Just as there is no ideal index for the measurement of long-term changes in national output, there is equally no unambiguous measure of relative levels of output based upon a set of prices prevailing in one economy. Prices are socially determined weights, and pricing the products of Britain and France first in one set of prices and then the other avoids the conceptual difficulty of a unilateral comparison. Equally valid comparisons can be made in francs or sterling. Differences between them reflect British and French preference patterns, which in turn reflect tastes, needs, income levels and income distribution, productive efficiency and, to complete the circle, the structure of relative prices in the two societies which in turn affects and is influenced by the composition of demand.[28]

An exercise employing OECD methods would not be feasible for the nineteenth century because available estimates for British and French national outputs simply cannot be broken down into composite commodities. Many have been estimated from income flows or factor payments and cannot be decomposed into value added in different sectors of industry and agriculture.

But this summary of the ideal method is a useful introduction to our own compromise method because it brings out the essential properties of the 'true' purchasing power parity rate of exchange required to make international comparisons. The purchasing power parity of the pound sterling in terms of the franc can be defined as the number of francs required to buy, in France, a basket of goods 'representative' of British expenditure patterns which cost £1 to purchase in Britain. Alternatively the purchasing power parity of the franc in terms of the pound is the amount of British currency required to buy in Britain a bundle of commodities, representative of French expenditure patterns, which cost 100 francs to buy in France. The 'true' ratio of exchange between francs and pounds can be derived from the following formulae:

(a) $\dfrac{\text{British products valued at British prices}}{\text{British products valued at French prices}}$

or

(b) $\dfrac{\text{French products valued at French prices}}{\text{French products valued at British prices}}$

The ratio between the two sums expressed in sterling and francs required to purchase *all* the commodities produced either in Britain or France represents the appropriate exchange rates between the two currencies. Notice that there are two exchange rates: the first based on the structure of production in Britain, valued first at British and then at French prices, and the second based upon the composition of output in France valued first at French and then at British prices. Unless the structure of production and relative prices happen to be similar in the two countries the calculations generate two different (but equally valid) rates of exchange for the conversion of francs into sterling. Thus the conversion of French national income into its sterling equivalent at the first rate of exchange is designed to compare per capita output in Britain and France in terms of the patterns of expenditure or the structure of production in Britain. It conceptualises the French economy from a British standpoint. The alternative rate of exchange conducts the comparison from a French viewpoint.

Some economists use an arithmetic average of the two results, if they are not too wide apart, and a geometric average if they are. In fact the problem is similar to averaging rates of growth measured first on a Paasche and then on a Laspeyres index. Unless it seems convenient to present a single figure, the comparisons of income levels across countries should be presented as two alternatives: one where the conversion of currencies into a single unit of account employs an exchange rate based upon the pattern of production or expenditure in Britain, and an alternative which uses an exchange rate based upon the composition of production and consumption in France.

For France and Britain in the nineteenth century such complete information on commodities and prices is impossible to obtain. Our conversion technique is a modified version of the ideal method and was certainly influenced by the availability of data. First we broke down national output in the two countries into six 'representative' sectors, two from agriculture and four from industry. Then we selected just one commodity to represent each of these sectors and assumed that prices of all commodities included in a given sector moved in line with the price of the representative commodity. For example, we selected wheat as the commodity to represent arable farming and assumed that prices of other grains and vegetables included in that sub-sector of the economy moved proportionately to the price of wheat. For certain years between 1780 and 1914 we estimated the share of each sector to commodity output as a whole. These ratios were then recalculated as relative weights and augmented to add up to unity.

These assumptions provided us with a 'representative basket of goods' which contained wheat, beef, coal, cotton yarn, pig iron and flour as proxies for the value of output in six corresponding sectors of the economy, namely arable farming, animal agriculture, mining, textiles and clothing, metallurgy and engineering, and processed food. Our first exchange rate could then be calculated as the ratio between the sterling required to buy a French basket of goods sold in France for a total of 1,000 francs and composed of six commodities, weighted in relation to the importance of their corresponding sectors to the overall total of commodity output for a given year. This calculation produced a set of exchange rates based upon the structure of French output and expenditure patterns as they evolved from 1781 to 1913. The same exercise, using an English basket of commodities, yielded exchange rates based upon English patterns of production and consumption as they altered over the nineteenth century. The results of this exercise are graphed below (Figure 2.1, p. 40) and compared with the trading rate of exchange. But the actual rates and a detailed account of the methods and sources employed are contained in Appendix A at the end of this chapter.

Our method is a compromise forced upon us by the paucity of price data and there are several necessary assumptions built into the exchange rates. Perhaps the most critical is the deployment of 'representative' commodities and prices for broad sectors of industry and agriculture. Unfortunately it is just not possible to test that assumption systematically. The data are not available, and particular commodities were selected primarily because price quotations happened to be published in the sources cited in Appendix A, but also because the commodities utilised are fairly homogeneous with respect to quality. For example, flour was preferred to bread or cakes to represent the processed food industry because the quality of flour is less likely to vary significantly from one side of the Channel to the other; and the same argument applies to wheat, beef, coal, cotton yarn and pig iron. But we did correlate movements in the prices of just a few commodities with the prices of some other goods in the same sub-group. The results of this test revealed nothing to invalidate our hypothesis that the variance for price movements among broad groups of similar commodities is not sufficient to invalidate the deployment of 'representative commodities and prices' (see Appendix C at the end of this chapter).

Prima facie, the commodities selected as 'representative' also appear open to the objection that, while they are comparable in terms of quality, they tend to be at the primary end of the production process. This objection has far greater force for industrial than for agricultural products and seems to apply more to pig iron and cotton yarn than to flour and coal which were sold directly to consumers as final outputs.

In any case the problem is the potential direction of bias involved in using flour, not bread, to represent processed food, cotton yarn rather than cotton cloth to represent textiles, and pig iron rather than metal goods to represent metallurgy. Since the overall rate of exchange is a ratio between British and French prices, the issues comes down to the ratios between British and French prices within different sectors of industry. How might the ratios of yarn, pig iron, flour and coal prices differ from the ratios for cloth and metal goods and other finished goods? The answer is that they would differ only if labour and capital costs varied significantly between the industries as production proceeded from the raw material to the finishing end of the manufacturing process.

Although wage rates were definitely lower in France, capital costs seem to have been higher and capital–labour ratios not dissimilar from those in Britain. There is evidence to support the argument that the differential in industrial prices probably narrowed in favour of France towards the finishing end of manufacturing. The productivity comparisons assembled in Tables 6.3 and 6.4, pp. 152 and 157 below, suggest that British industry possessed greater natural and technological advantages in industrial raw materials (like coal) and in the manufacture of intermediate goods (like pig iron). Thus our particular selection of 'representative' industrial goods used to calculate the exchange rate operates to reduce the level of industrial prices in Britain relative to France and compared also to some alternative and more representative sample of commodities, which would ideally include a higher proportion of finished manufactured goods.

There is no way of correcting for this bias. The commodity samples utilised were determined by the availability of statistics and by the need to select homogeneous products. There is a definite bias that tends to cheapen the franc in terms of the pound and thus to reduce the value of French industrial output when converted to sterling at the rates of exchange set out in Table A.5 (p. 47).

Just how dependent these purchasing power parity rates of exchange are upon the particular sample of commodities and price quotations used for their construction is difficult to say. They do not diverge significantly from the rates of exchange established for foreign trade. Furthermore, provided deviations and movements from the 'true' levels of agricultural and industrial prices are to some extent offsetting, there is no reason to assume that our analysis and conclusions will be seriously distorted by potential or probable shifts in the exchange rates employed to convert francs to sterling. On the contrary, our sensitivity test for 1856 (see Appendix B at the end of this chapter) suggests that rather large and implausible variations in relative prices would be required to produce the kind of revisions to exchange rates that could seriously affect our analysis and conclusions.

To conclude: comparisons of levels of welfare and productivity across countries which convert at the trading rate of exchange between the two currencies assume some identity of consumption and production to patterns of trade, which rarely exists. Our method for the conversion of francs into sterling does not make that assumption, but allows us to express per capita incomes in sterling in terms of consumption and production patterns that prevailed in both countries, decade by decade, from 1780 to 1914.

Thus a comparison of per capita incomes in terms of the French basket will tell us what an individual earning the equivalent of English per capita income could buy in England if that person spent his money in accordance with modal patterns of commodity output (expenditure) in France. If an 'average Englishman' could buy all the goods purchasable in a year by the 'average Frenchman' and still have cash to spare, this enables one to say that per capita incomes were higher in England, by French standards.

The alternative exchange rate is calculated in terms of a basket of goods representative of English output patterns and compares the income required in France to provide a Frenchman with a basket of commodities representative of the British output pattern. If the sum required exceeds per capita income in France, it can then be argued that French per capita income is low by English standards.

Since relative prices reflect output patterns in the two countries, the conversion of francs into sterling in terms of an English basket of goods (exchange rate *b*) will make an average income in France converted to sterling seem relatively low compared to England. This is because commodities that are relatively cheap in Britain (because of their greater availability) will be given greater weight. The conversion in terms of a French output pattern (exchange rate *a*) will bias a comparison the other way. Bias is, however, the wrong word. There are simply two possible exchange rates: one based upon British consumption patterns and prices and an equally valid alternative based upon French standards and prices.

The results of this exercise are also interesting in their own right. For example, in so far as Britain and France were for most of the nineteenth century two economies with roughly similar price levels and incomes and where the structure of relative prices within each country were not far apart, we expected our method to yield exchange rates which did not diverge wildly for any given decade. We do not place much confidence in the rates of exchange calculated for the period 1803–12, when price structures, particularly in France, were gravely distorted by the effects of war and blockade. Nevertheless, it seems that the two economies were sufficiently similar in their economic structures, and a cross-country comparison of outputs based upon either French or English patterns of demand did not produce estimates of the same degree of divergence that statisticians find in comparing incomes between developed and undeveloped economies at the present time. Furthermore, the two exchange rates converge towards the end of the period, which suggests that the composition of output and structures of relative prices became more similar over time. Finally, a comparison with the rate of exchange established for foreign trade between Britain and France suggests an overvaluation of the franc during the latter half of the century, indicating that estimates of per capita incomes based upon that particular rate of exchange will tend to overstate levels of income and welfare in France compared with Britain (see Figure 2.1).

Figure 2.1   *Purchasing Power Parity and Trading Rates of Exchange*

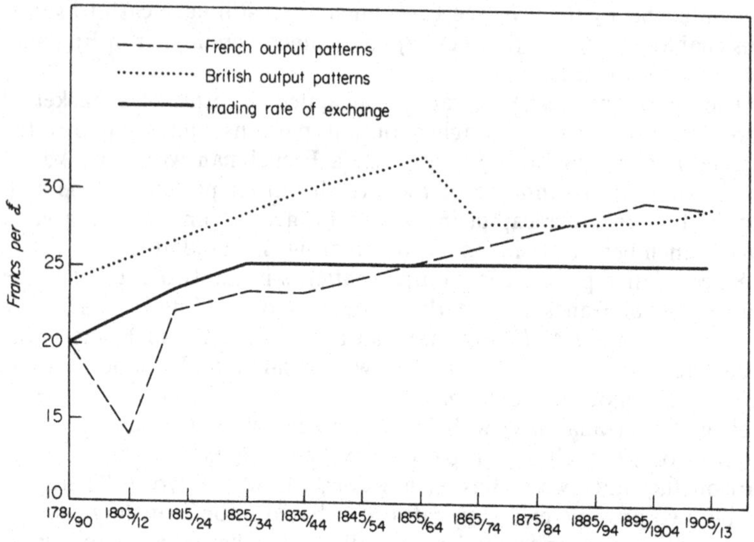

APPENDIX A: THE EXCHANGE RATES

The procedure employed to find the 'exchange rates' derives from the theoretical and practical considerations enumerated in the text. A similar method was used by Marczewski who divided the output of France and England into two sectors: agriculture and manufactures. He transformed agricultural output to wheat equivalents and manufacturing output to pig iron equivalents by dividing the value of production in each sector by the prices of wheat and pig iron which converted value estimates into physical units. Secondly, he valued the outputs of both countries, first in French and then in English prices for the two commodities. This allowed him to identify the differences involved in making a comparison based on either of the relative price sets.[29] But since the price vectors consisted of only two prices Marczewski's method introduced an indeterminate bias into the comparison. Marczewski made no attempt to derive an exchange rate from this exercise. His concern was to compare levels of output. Our method increased the output and price vectors to six elements by using six sectors to represent the economy rather than two. We also calculated purchasing power parity exchange rates for the century as a whole which can be used by other researchers involved with nineteenth-century comparisons between Britain and France.

For French data we relied exclusively on the ISEA estimates. For the division of total commodity output into agriculture and manu-factures we used Marczewski's correction of the Markovitch figures on manufacturing output, and Toutain's figures on agricultural output.[30] Once this division was established, we divided the manufacturing output into four sectors based upon the Markovitch estimates for the structure of value added in industry.[31]

Several industries were combined to form the mining sector: solid combustible minerals, metal extraction, construction materials ex-traction, other mining. Next the categories of metal production and transformation of metals were added together to form the metallurgy and engineering sector. The textiles sector included textiles and clothing and cloth production. For the food industry we used Markovitch's own category for alimentation industries plus tobacco. For agriculture, we derived the structure of production from Toutain's figures on animal and non-animal output.[32]

All industrial prices for France came from the Markovitch data.[33] Agricultural prices were slightly more difficult to obtain, because Toutain presents composite indices of cereal prices and meat prices.[34] This gave us beef prices for the second half of the century, and prices for the first half were derived from Toutain's composite index. For the latter part of the century where Toutain provided data on the value of output and prices for oats, barley and wheat, his figures were used to calculate a single price for cereals which is a more representative figure than the simple price of wheat.

For Great Britain the collection of data presented a much greater problem. Most of our figures had therefore to be based on assumptions and interpolations. We began by estimating the composition of com-modity output in 1907. This was done directly by using estimates for gross output, then we employed figures from the census of production to estimate the contribution of agriculture and manufacturing. The 'net value' of production in selected industries was also calculated from the census. Basically we used the following sources: Deane and Cole, Feinstein, Matthews, and Report on the 1907 census.[35] Matthews collected figures for 1856, 1873 and 1899 which showed the percentage share of agriculture, mining, manufacturing, construction, gas–electricity–water, and services in gross domestic output. Using these figures we first calculated the share of physical commodity output in

Gross Domestic Product, and then estimated the share of agriculture and mining directly from the figures. We used Deane and Cole to estimate the share of the other two industries, namely textiles and metallurgy. For the food industry, we found a ratio from the census of 1907.[36] We assumed that the relative share of food industry in total manufacturing output showed the same downward trend as occurred in France. Thus all the figures for the share of food industry with the exception of the figure for 1907 have been derived by interpolation. But for the earlier part of the century we tested our assumption by comparing our estimates with contemporary estimates. The share of animal products in agricultural output was also a problem, since we found only one direct estimate for 1907.[37] Another estimate, which came from Deane and Cole, found animal output to be about 50 per cent of total agricultural output around mid-century. We interpolated between these two figures and assumed that the decline in the share of non-animal output in agricultural output as a whole has been uniform.

An independent estimate by Pebrer for 1831 (as reconstituted by Deane, and used by Deane and Cole) gave us an estimate for the share of the staple industries in the national income.[38] Proportions were established between the share of an industry in the national income and the proportion of value added to material output, which is the figure that interested us. The ratio of agricultural to manufacturing output was taken from Pebrer's figures, and the share of animal to vegetable output in agriculture was again found by straight line extrapolation. The weight or share for the food industry was again estimated by the method mentioned above, that is by using the French trend as indicative of English development.

We used Colquhoun's estimate (reconstructed by Deane) for the share of particular industries in English output.[39] Assuming that Colquhoun's and Pebrer's figures referred to the same categories, we took the progression from Colquhoun to Pebrer as representing an actual trend and the magnitude of change. Hence we could use the growth rates derived from a comparison of Colquhoun and Pebrer with the figures we had established for 1831. Thus we found a new set of figures for 1812, with the share of the food industry again based on extrapolation. 1805 was taken to 'represent' the decade 1803–12; and for 1781–90, 1785 was selected as a representative year. For 1805 we used Deane and Cole's estimates for the shares of textiles, coal and iron, and extrapolated for food industry.[40] An additional source for 1805 and for 1785 was P. K. O'Brien's unpublished manuscript on the terms of trade between agriculture and industry for the eighteenth century which contains estimates for wholesale commodity flows for the period. O'Brien's estimates were utilised in conjunction with figures from Deane and Cole.

Our estimates for 1785 are based on Young's estimates for 1770, and an assumption of straight line growth between 1785 and 1805.[41] For these last two dates we were interested only in relative values of the sectors, so we did not approach the problem of shares from the gross value of all commodity output. Indeed, we attempted to find the relative values of sectors as against each other. In other words, for these last two sets of figures we could only derive pure weights rather than ratios of the output of one sector to total output which is the basis for weighting. For 1785 we also used the growth data in Deane and Cole for certain industries in the eighteenth century.[42] Thus coal deliveries data were used to indicate the mining output, and metals were used for metallurgy.

Tables A.1 and A.2 set out our estimates of the share of value added by six sectors from 1780 to 1914.

Estimates for the structure of English commodity output for seven benchmark years across the century had to be made comparable with the French data. We simply assumed that the years for which we had estimates for the structure of output were reasonably representative for the relevant decades. For example, the output structure of 1905–13 was assumed to be identical to the figure for 1907. For 1895–1904, we accepted 1899; for 1865–74, we accepted 1873; for 1855–64, we accepted 1856; for 1825–34, 1831; for 1803–12, 1805; and for 1781–90, 1785.

We next searched for 'representative' prices for the six 'representative' commodities, averaged around the benchmark years to compare with the French price data which are based on decennial averages. Our British data came from the *Report on Prices* by the Board of Trade,[43] Mitchell,[44] Sauerbeck,[45] Ashton,[46] and *The Economist*.[47] When actual prices were not obtainable, we used an appropriate index to extrapolate the price for a given commodity. For example, beef prices for the early part of the century were obtained by using the index of prices for animal products in Mitchell together with actual price figures in the *Report*.[48] In the same vein, since the cotton yarn figures in Ashton were not comparable to the figures we had used for the later part of the century we used Ashton's figures to construct an index and then used this index to derive comparable cotton yarn prices.[49] Wheat and coal prices were taken from Mitchell and the *Report on Prices*.[50] Beef prices were derived from *The Economist* and Mitchell's index. Cotton yarn prices came from the *Report* and our index derived from Ashton. Flour prices came from Sauerbeck and the *Report*,[51] and for the early period from an index derived from bread prices, published by Mitchell. O'Brien's unpublished price index for metals was used to estimate pig iron prices for 1785; prices for the rest of the century were found in Mitchell.

Table A.1 British Commodity Output Structure 1785–1907, in Percentage Shares of Sectors

	1785	1805	1831		1856		1873		1899		1907	
	Weights	Weights	Actual share	Weights	Actual share	Weights	Actual share	Weights	Actual share	Weights	Actual share	Weights
Agriculture												
Animal	23	20	20	20	20	19	16	16	11	11	13	13
Arable	38	27	24	24	19	19	13	13	6	6	6	6
Industry												
Mining	4	8	7	9	10	11	12	14	16	20	13	21
Metallurgy	7	13	8	11	14	16	21	24	16	20	17	27
Textiles	17	21	18	23	21	23	18	21	19	25	10	17
Food	12	10	10	13	10	11	11	12	13	17	10	16
Total	100	100	87	100	94	100	91	100	81	100	69	100

Note: For the industrial sectors, from 1831 on, there are two figures: the first refers to the actual share of the industry in total physical output; the second is the figure used for the purposes of this exercise, i.e. it has been augmented so that the sum of all shares is 100 per cent. For 1785 and 1805, we have only these figures which have been derived from the relative values of the sectors to each other. The weights may not add to 100 due to rounding.

Sources: See text, pp. 41–3.

Table A.2   French Commodity Output Structure 1781–90 to 1905–13

	Animal	Non-animal	Mining		Metals		Textiles		Food	
1781–90	17·2	40·2	0·7	1·0	3·7	5·1	23·6	32·4	14·5	19·9
1803–12	16·1	37·4	0·8	0·9	6·0	6·8	25·4	28·9	14·3	16·2
1815–24	16·4	38·4	0·8	1·0	3·2	4·1	26·8	34·1	14·4	18·3
1825–34	14·8	36·4	0·8	1·0	3·4	4·3	31·2	39·6	13·4	17·0
1835–44	14·4	30·6	1·0	1·1	4·1	4·7	36·7	41·9	13·2	15·1
1845–54	14·4	30·5	1·0	1·1	4·3	4·8	35·6	39·9	14·3	16·0
1855–64	14·0	32·8	1·7	1·8	6·2	6·6	30·3	32·4	15·1	16·1
1865–74	15·5	31·4	2·0	2·2	7·0	7·8	28·6	31·8	15·5	17·3
1875–84	17·1	26·4	2·6	2·9	9·2	10·1	30·1	32·9	14·3	15·6
1885–94	17·3	23·8	3·1	3·2	9·0	9·2	32·0	32·5	14·7	15·0
1895–1904	16·9	22·3	4·0	4·0	13·2	13·1	28·3	28·6	14·9	14·8
1905–13	17·1	22·7	3·8	4·1	14·1	15·1	29·3	31·4	13·0	14·0

Note: For the manufacturing sectors, the first figure represents the share of the industry in total manufacturing. The second figure has been used in our calculations, and this figure is added to the actual share of agriculture in order to equal 100 per cent. The weights may not aggregate to 100 due to rounding.

Sources: See text, pp. 41–3.

Table A.3 English Prices in Current Shillings 1785–1907

	1785	1805	1831	1856	1873	1899	1907
Wheat (qr = 216 kg)	48	87	56	45	43	28	31
Beef (cwt)	27	50	37	44	66	39	68
Coal (ton)	24·2	43·0	7·2	9·5	13·0	11·8	11·9
Pig iron (ton)	92	123	69	68	61	48	55
Cotton yarn (lb)	2·9	2·7	1·4	0·9	1·4	0·8	1·0
Flour (sack = 280 lb)	44	82	50	45	46	21	29

Notes and sources: see text.

Table A.4 French Prices in Current Francs 1781–90 to 1905–13

	1781–90	1803–12	1815–24	1825–34	1835–44	1845–54	1855–64	1865–74	1875–84	1885–94	1895–1904	1905–13
Wheat (qn)	20·7	24·7	26·9	25·5	25·5	26·8	28·8	30·9	27·3	22·8	20·8	24·8
Beef (kg)	0·6	1·0	0·9	0·9	0·9	1·0	1·3	1·7	1·7	1·0	1·4	1·6
Coal (metric ton)	10·7	9·8	10·3	9·8	9·7	9·9	11·9	13·2	13·3	11·5	12·9	15·0
Pig iron (metric ton)	262·4	350·0	380·0	200·0	161·1	167·6	135·3	106·8	89·9	60·7	62·6	72·0
Cotton yarn (kg)	11·8	14·0	4·0	5·5	4·7	3·3	4·9	5·8	3·2	2·8	3·2	4·9
Flour (kg)	0·2	0·2	0·3	0·3	0·3	0·3	0·3	0·3	0·3	0·2	0·2	0·2

Notes and sources: see text, pp. 41–3, footnotes to Tables A.3 and A.4.

This exercise yielded seven pairs of exchange rates based on the French and British output for benchmark years (Table A.5).

Table A.5   *Rates of Exchange Between Francs and Sterling 1781–1914*

	French output	English output	Rates of exchange for trade
	(ratio of francs to £)	(ratio of francs to £)	(ratio of francs to £)
1781–90	20·18	24·22	29·19
1803–12	14·34	25·94	22·49
1825–34	23·93	28·75	25·46
1855–64	25·44	32·57	25·58
1865–74	26·37	28·44	25·62
1895–1904	29·66	28·25	25·38
1905–13	29·04	29·76	25·25

For the remaining decades we interpolated and assumed linear rates of change. Thus, for example, between 1865–74 and 1875–84 we assumed that the French basket exchange rate increased uniformly from 26.37 to 27.47.

	French output	English output	Rate of exchange for trade
	(ratio of francs to £)	(ratio of francs to £)	(ratio of francs to £)
1815–24	22·28	27·34	24·30
1835–44	23·93	30·02	25·70
1845–54	24·63	31·29	25·59
1875–84	27·47	28·38	25·47
1885–94	28·57	28·31	25·46

Sources: The sources for the trading rate of exchange are: *Select Committee on the Expediency of the Bank Resuming Cash Payments*, British Parliamentary Papers 1819 (IV), p. 239 and *Select Committee on Banks of Issue*, BPP 1840 (IV), p. 196ff. and BPP 1841 (I), p. 2. We are indebted to Dr Brian Mitchell for sending us photocopies of the data for 1788–1847. Thereafter our source was *Journals of the Royal Statistical Society*, vols 22–73. The exchange rate for 1855–64 was distorted by cyclical depression and for 1803–12 by war: see Section 2.3.

APPENDIX B: SENSITIVITY ANALYSIS FOR 1856

In 1855–64 the exchange rate (based upon the French output structure) was calculated to be: 25·44 francs = £1. We conducted a test to ascertain how this exchange rate could vary for given deviations between selected prices and commodities utilised in our sample and a hypothetical set of 'more representative' prices and commodities. The test proceeded on the following assumptions, and we also held French prices constant.

Assumption	Recalculated exchange rate (Actual rate: 25·44 francs = £1)
1 All British prices were 10% higher	23·12
2 Grain prices were 10% higher	24·36
3 Processed food prices were 10% higher	24·88
4 Metal prices were 10% higher	25·32
5 Metal prices were 50% higher	24·97
6 Processed food prices were 50% higher	22·84
7 Grain prices were 50% higher	20·88
8 All British prices were 10% lower	28·25

Of course, French prices utilised in this exercise could also diverge in either direction from a more representative and realistic sample of prices and commodities and could reinforce as well as countervail deviations on the British side. But the calculations in Table B.1 do show that the influence of price variations depended not only upon the degree of divergence from 'true' price level but also upon the weight of a given commodity in the sample. For any single commodity the degree of deviation from the 'real' price had to be of considerable magnitude in order to significantly alter the exchange ratio between francs and sterling. Thus the conversion of estimates for French per capita incomes and labour productivities from francs into sterling will probably not generate data that are particularly sensitive to the limited selection of 'representative' commodities and prices used in our samples.

APPENDIX C: PRICE CORRELATIONS

For the construction of purchasing power parity rates of exchange we disaggregated the commodity outputs of France and Britain into six sectors: two from agriculture and four from industry. We then selected price movements for a single commodity to 'represent' long-term movements for the prices of all commodities within a sub-sector. The prices used included: wheat to represent arable farming; beef to represent animal agriculture; cotton yarn to represent textiles; coal to represent minerals; pig iron to represent metallurgy; and flour to represent processed food.

In theory the degree to which the prices of these commodities are representative can be tested by correlating price movements of the selected commodity with price trends of other commodities within the same group. Unfortunately the price data at our disposal did not allow us to conduct systematic tests across a wide range of commodities. The data available related for the most part to similar commodities where price trends were likely to be comparable.

Thus the results of our regressions tabulated in summary form below do not provide evidence that the commodities selected were representative. On the other hand, they do not invalidate the sample selected.

Correlations for France	*Correlation coefficient*
1 Animal agriculture*	
(a) Beef with veal poitrine (1846–85)	0·92
(b) Beef with veal loin (1846–85)	0·92
(c) Beef with lamb poitrine (1846–85)	0·91
(d) Beef with eggs and dairy produce (1846–85)	0·87
2 Arable agriculture	
Wheat with rye (1846–85)	0·86
3 Processed food	
(a) Flour with bread (1781–1913)	0·77
(b) Farinaceous products with a basket of groceries and wine (1846–85)*	0·75
4 Metals	
(a) Pig iron with cast iron (1781–1913)	0·80
(b) Pig iron with metal goods (1781–1913)	0·85
(c) Pig iron with copper (1820–57)	0·37

5   Textiles
   (a) Spun with woven cotton (1781–1913)   0·91
   (b) Spun cotton with cotton clothing (1781–1913)   0·90
   (c) Spun cotton with cotton linen (1781–1913)   0·74
   (d) Spun cotton with woollen clothes (1781–1913)   0·56
   (e) Spun cotton with leather (1820–57)   0·34

Correlations for Britain

1   Animal products
   (a) Beef with mutton (1846–85)   0·92
   (b) Beef with pork (1846–85)   0·60
   (c) Beef with bacon (1846–85)   0·83
   (d) Beef with butter (1846–85)   0·89

2   Arable agriculture
   (a) Wheat with barley (1846–85)   0·66
   (b) Wheat with oats (1846–85)   0·70
   (c) Wheat with potatoes (1846–85)   0·47

3   Metals
   (a) Pig iron with iron bars (1846–85)   0·93
   (b) Pig iron with tin (1846–85)   0·51
   (c) Pig iron with lead (1846–85)   0·61
   (d) Pig iron with copper (1846–85)   0·45

4   Processed food†
   (a) Flour with biscuits (1878–1902)   0·68
   (b) Flour with jam (1878–1902)   0·45
   (c) Flour with bread (1846–85)   0·90
   (d) Flour with stout (1878–1902)   0·09

Notes and sources:
   All data for France are from T. J. Markovitch, 'L'industrie française de 1789 à 1964', *Cahiers de l'ISEA*, AF 4, July 1965, tables 5(a) and 5(b), unless marked*. All data for Britain are from A. Sauerbeck, 'Prices of Commodities, 1907', *Journal of the Royal Statistical Society*, vol. 71 (1908), unless marked †.
   *J. Singer-Kerel, *Le coût de la vie à Paris de 1840 à 1954* (Paris: Presses Universitaires de France, 1961), and J. Fourastié, *Documents pour l'histoire et la théorie des Prix* (Paris: Colin, 1962).
   †B. R. Mitchell and P. Deane, *Abstract of British Historical Statistics* (Cambridge: CUP, 1962), and *Parliamentary Paper*, 1903 (LXVIII).

NOTES TO CHAPTER 2

1 P. Deane and W. A. Cole, *British Economic Growth, 1688–1959* (Cambridge: CUP, 1962); B. R. Mitchell and P. Deane, *Abstract of British Historical Statistics* (Cambridge: CUP, 1962); J. C. Toutain, 'Le produit de l'agriculture française de 1700 à 1958', *Cahiers de l'ISEA*, AF 1, July 1961, and AF 2, July 1961; T. J. Markovitch, 'L'industrie française de 1789 à 1964', *Cahiers de l'ISEA*, AF 4 July 1965, 'Analyse des faits', AF 5, May 1966, 'Analyse des faits (suite)', AF 6, June 1966, 'Conclusions générales', AF 7, November 1966; J. C. Toutain, 'La population de 1700 à 1959', *Cahiers de l'ISEA*, AF 3, January 1963; and J. Marczewski 'Le produit physique de l'économie française de 1789 à 1913 (comparaison avec la Grande Bretagne)', *Cahiers de l'ISEA*, AF 4, July 1965.

2 J. R. T. Hughes, 'Measuring British Economic Growth', *Journal of Economic History*, 1964, 1, pp. 60–82, and J. F. Wright, 'British Economic Growth, 1688–1953', *Economic History Review*, August 1965, 2, pp. 400–4.

3 Deane and Cole, *British Economic Growth*, pp. 164–8.

4 Wright, 'British Economic Growth'.

5 P. K. O'Brien, 'British Incomes and Property in the Early Nineteenth Century', *Economic History Review*, August 1959, 2, pp. 258–61, evaluates tax data. See also Deane and Cole, *British Economic Growth*, appendix II, and J. F. Wright's review of the second edition of P. Deane and W. A. Cole, *British Economic Growth, 1688–1959* (Cambridge: CUP, 1969) in *Economic History Review*, April 1970, p. 189.

6 Toutain, 'Le produit de l'agriculture', AF 1, ch. 1.

7 T. J. Markovitch, 'L'industrie française', especially part 2; M. Lévy-Leboyer, 'La croissance économique en France au XIXe siècle. Résultats préliminaires', *Annales E.S.C.*, July–August 1968; F. Crouzet, 'Essai de construction d'un indice annuel de la production industrielle française au XIXe siècle', *Annales E.S.C.*, January–February 1970. The last two articles also discuss the methods used by Markovitch.

8 Marczewski, 'Le produit physique', pp. XVII–XX. Marczewski's correction consists of subtracting 'l'autoconsommation paysanne de produits industriels' from 'industry' and adding them to 'agriculture'.

9 See reviews by P. Vilar in *Revue Historique*, April–June 1965, p. 293; P. Chaunu in *Cahiers Vilfredo Pareto*, 1964, 3, p. 165; M. Morineau in *Revue Historique*, 1968, vol. 239, p. 299; F. Furet in *Annales E.S.C.*, 1971, vol. 26, p. 63.

10 On Toutain's estimates for agricultural output over the eighteenth century see E. Le Roy Ladurie, *Le territoire de l'historien* (Paris: Gallimard, 1973), pp. 253–70 and 278–80. For example, see S. Pollard and D. W. Crossley, *The Wealth of Britain 1085–1966* (London: Batsford, 1968), pp. 7–9.

11 Deane and Cole, *British Economic Growth* (1962), p. 141.

12 Marczewski, 'Le produit physique', pp. XLIX–L.

13 See sources to Table 3.2, where we discuss the share of Ireland in the national income of the UK.

14 Deane and Cole, *British Economic Growth* (1969), appendix 3.

15 Toutain, 'Le produit de l'agriculture', AF 1, pp. 14–16; Markovitch, 'L'industrie française', pp. 42–4.

16 F. Perroux, 'Prises de vue sur la croissance de l'économie française, 1780–1950' in *Income and Wealth*, Series V. Perroux's estimates for services are regarded by Marczewski as 'first approximations'. See his 'The Take-Off Hypothesis and French Experience' in W. W. Rostow (ed.), *The Stages of Economic Growth* (Cambridge: CUP, 1971), p. 122; J. C. Toutain, 'Les Transports en France de 1830 à 1965', *Cahiers de l'ISEA*, AF 9, September 1967.

17 V. R. Fuchs, *The Service Economy* (New York: NBER, 1968), ch. 3 and pp. 198–9; R. E. Gallman and T. J. Weiss, 'The Service Industries in the Nineteenth Century' in V. R. Fuchs (ed.), *Production and Productivity in the Service Industries* (New York: National Bureau of Economic Research, 1969), pp. 287–381; R. M. Hartwell, 'The Service Revolution: The Growth of Services in Modern Economy' in C. M. Cipolla (ed.) *The Fontana Economic History of Europe* (London: Fontana, 1973), vol. 3, pp. 358–94.

18 P. T. Bauer and B. Yamey, 'Economic Progress and Occupational Distribution', *Economic Journal*, December 1951; and their 'Further Notes on Economic Progress and Occupational Distribution', *Economic Journal*, March 1954.

19 K. Marx, *Grundrisse* (London: Penguin, 1973), p. 272; S. Kuznets, *Modern Economic Growth* (New Haven: Yale University Press, 1966), pp. 414–20.

20 D. Usher, *The Price Mechanism and the Meaning of National Income Statistics* (Oxford: Clarendon Press, 1968), ch. 8.

21 M. A. Katouzian, 'The Development of the Service Sector: A New Approach', *Oxford Economic Papers*, November 1970.

22 A. Armengaud, 'Population in Europe 1700–1914' in Cipolla (ed.), *The Fontana Economic History*, vol. 3, pp. 32–8.

23 For shares in output see Deane and Cole, *British Economic Growth* (1962), p. 291; Marczewski, 'The Take-off Hypothesis', p. 136. For labour force, see sources for Table 4.1.

24 Lévy-Leboyer, 'La croissance économique'.

25 D. H. Aldcroft and P. Fearon (eds), *British Economic Fluctuations 1790–1939* (London: Macmillan, 1972), p. 9.

26 W. Beckerman, *International Comparisons of Real Incomes* (Paris: OECD, 1966), p. 8; A. Maddison, *Economic Progress and Policy in Developing Countries* (London: Allen & Unwin, 1970), appendix A.

27 M. Gilbert and I. Kravis, *An International Comparison of National Products and the Purchasing Power of Currencies* (Paris: Organisation for European Economic Cooperation, 1954), and M. Gilbert and Associates, *Comparative National Products and Price Levels* (Paris: OEEC, 1958); I. Kravis, 'A Survey of International Productivity Comparisons', *Economic Journal*, March 1976.

28 Usher, *The Price Mechanism*, ch. 6.

29 J. Marczewski, 'Le produit physique', pp. XXI–XLV.

30 ibid., p. XX.

31 Markovitch, 'L'industrie française', table 4.

32 Toutain, 'Le produit de l'agriculture', AF 2, p. 171.

33 Markovitch, 'L'industrie française', table 6.

34 Toutain, 'Le produit de l'agriculture', AF 2, pp. 191–2.

35 Deane and Cole, *British Economic Growth* (1962); C. H. Feinstein, *National Income, Expenditure, and Output in the United Kingdom* (Cambridge: CUP, 1972); R. C. O. Matthews, unpublished manuscript on the growth of the British economy from 1856, ch. 2; Census of Production, *Final Report of the First Census of Production of the United Kingdom (1907)* (London, 1907).

36 ibid.

37 Board of Agriculture and Fisheries, *The Agricultural Output of Great Britain* (London, 1912).

38 P. Deane, 'The Industrial Revolution and Economic Growth: The Evidence of Early British National Income Estimates', *Economic Development and Cultural Change*, April 1957; and Deane and Cole, *British Economic Growth* (1962), ch. 6.
39 P. Deane, 'Contemporary Estimates of National Income in the Nineteenth Century' *Economic History Review*, 1956 and 1957; also Deane, 'The Industrial Revolution'.
40 Deane and Cole, *British Economic Growth* (1962), ch. 6.
41 A. Young, *Political Arithmetic* (London: 1779), as quoted and reconstructed in Deane, 'The Industrial Revolution'.
42 Deane and Cole, *British Economic Growth* (1962), p. 5.
43 Board of Trade, *Report on Wholesale and Retail Prices* (London, 1903).
44 Mitchell and Deane, *Abstract*.
45 A. Sauerbeck, 'Prices of Commodities, 1907', *Journal of the Royal Statistical Society* vol. 71 (1908).
46 T. S. Ashton, 'Some Statistics of the Industrial Revolution in Britain', *The Manchester School*, May 1948.
47 *The Economist*, London (various issues).
48 Board of Trade, *Report on Prices*.
49 Ashton, 'Some Statistics', pp. 230–1.
50 Mitchell and Deane, *Abstract*, pp. 480–9; Board of Trade, *Report, passim*.
51 Sauerbeck, 'Prices of Commodities'; Board of Trade, *Report*.

Part Two
WELFARE

Chapter 3

Per Capita Incomes and Real Wages

3.1 DOMESTIC COMMODITY OUTPUT

At the end of a century marked by crises, including foreign wars, civil strife, plague and inflation, the total population of France in 1715 stood below levels attained in 1640 and 1690.[1] Yet in terms of cultivable area, mineral resources, capital stock, labour force and national product, France could still be ranked as the leading economic power in Europe.[2] Its population was nearly three times that of Britain (19·3 million compared to 6·8 million) and its commodity output might have been as much as two-and-a-half times the comparable British aggregate.[3]

Crouzet's famous article found that domestic output in the two economies probably grew at comparable rates for several decades over the eighteenth century.[4] Indices of industrial and agricultural growth published by Deane and Cole for Britain and Marczewski for France suggest the growth rates shown in Table 3.1; but it should be pointed out that Toutain's figures for agricultural output in the eighteenth century are regarded with scepticism by Le Roy Ladurie and other French historians.

Table 3.1   *Annual Average Rates of Growth in Britain and France 1701–10 to 1781–90*

	Agricultural production	*Industrial production*	*Total commodity output*
Britain	0·4%	1·1%	0·7%
France	0·6%	1·9%	1·0%

Sources: For Britain, the annual rates of growth were calculated from P. Deane and W. A. Cole, *British Economic Growth, 1688–1959* (Cambridge: CUP, 1962), p. 78. Their 'Total industry and commerce' (column 3) is taken to represent our 'industrial production'. Their weighting was used to obtain a total commodity output growth rate. For France, Marczewski's physical output figures for 1701–10 were deflated with his price index (J. Marczewski, 'Some Aspects of the Economic Growth of France, 1660–1958', *Economic Development and Cultural Change*, April 1961, pp. 371 and 378). This gave us figures for 1701–10 and 1781–90 (both at 1781–90 prices). Annual rates of growth were calculated from these figures.

Up to the French Revolution, in relative terms, the scale and productive capacity of the French economy continued to exceed that of

Table 3.2 *Population and Commodity Output in Great Britain and France, Decennial Averages, 1781–90 to 1905–13*

Periods	Population of GB ('000s)	Population of France ('000s)	Commodity output for GB in £m	Commodity output for France in francs m.	French commodity output	
					Converted to £ (conversion rate (a))	Converted to £ (conversion rate (b))
(1)	(2)	(3)	(4)	(5)	(6)	(7)
1781–90	9,369	26,500	65·0	5,097	252·6	210·4
1803–12	11,607	28,425	155·3	7,012	489·0	270·3
1815–24	13,900	30,450	170·5	7,674	344·4	280·7
1825–34	16,039	32,570	193·4	9,301	398·7	323·5
1835–44	18,210	34,230	242·5	10,879	454·6	362·4
1845–54	20,539	35,800	283·2	12,586	511·0	402·2
1855–64	22,875	37,390	350·2	16,453	646·7	505·2
1865–74	25,718	36,190	453·6	18,466	699·5	648·6
1875–84	29,196	37,590	504·6	18,230	663·6	642·4
1885–94	32,625	38,350	590·2	17,767	621·9	627·6
1895–1904	36,456	38,980	722·6	19,299	650·7	683·2
1905–13	40,062	39,623	862·6	25,814	888·9	867·4

Notes:
(a) Francs converted to pounds using the exchange rate based on French output. See Appendix A, p. 47 above.
(b) Francs converted to pounds using the exchange rate based on British output. See Appendix A, p. 47 above.

Sources:
Column 2: British population: Decennial averages for years after 1801 were calculated from the annual estimates contained in B. R. Mitchell and P. Deane, *Abstract of British Historical Statistics* (Cambridge: CUP, 1962), pp. 8–10.

For the pre-1801 period we used estimates in Deane and Cole, *British Economic Growth*, p. 6. There are figures for 1781 and 1791 for England and Wales but there is no estimate for Scotland for 1781. We assumed that the Scottish population increased at the same annual rate between 1781 and 1791 as it did between 1751 and 1791 and estimated a figure for Scotland for 1781. In order to estimate the population of Great Britain for 1781–90, we took a simple average of the figures for 1781 and 1791 related to England and Wales, and Scotland.

Column 3: French population: based on Toutain's reconstruction of census data: table 31, J. Marczewski, 'Le produit physique de l'économie française de 1789 à 1913 (comparisons avec la Grande Bretagne)', *Cahiers de l'ISEA*, AF 4, July 1965, pp. LXXX–LXXXI.

Column 4: British commodity output, 1801–1901, based on Deane and Cole, *British Economic Growth*, p. 166, tabulation of the industrial distribution of national income for Great Britain. The figures relate to census years from 1801. Commodity output includes the sum of totals for 'Agriculture, forestry, fishing' plus 'Manufacture, mining, building'. For both agriculture and industry, we calculated annual rates of growth from census year to census year and reconstructed an annual series for output. From these annual values in current prices we obtained figures for agriculture and industry and commodity output as averages for the decades, set out above.

For years after 1901, we used Feinstein's annual estimates (in Mitchell and Deane, *Abstract*, pp. 367–8) which refer, however, to the UK. We assumed that the national income of Great Britain remained at (a constant) 95 per cent of UK national income for the period 1901–13. This ratio we derived from Feinstein's estimates of national income for UK and Deane and Cole's for Britain (Deane and Cole, *British Economic Growth*, pp. 166–7). See also M. C. Kaser, 'The Share of England and Wales in the National Income of the United Kingdom', *Bulletin of the Oxford University Institute of Economics and Statistics*, 1968. Feinstein did not estimate sectoral shares in national output, so in order to find output estimates for industry and agriculture we assumed a linear rate of change in the shares of industry and agriculture in national income between 1901 and 1924. The 1901 and 1924 estimates for the sectoral composition of national income is from Deane and Cole, *British Economic Growth*, p. 291. We then reconstructed an annual series for commodity output at current prices and calculated decennial averages from these figures.

For the initial decade 1781–90, we employed index numbers for real output for eighteenth century; see Deane and Cole, *British Economic Growth*, p. 78. From these indicators and from the actual figures for agricultural and industrial output in 1801 by backward extrapolation, we obtained output figures for 1780 and 1790, in 1801 prices. Then we reflated these figures in order to estimate figures for 1780 and 1790 in current prices. For agriculture we reflated by using the Schumpeter index for consumers' goods (Mitchell and Deane, *Abstract*, pp. 468–9). For industry we used the same index for 'consumers' goods other than cereals'. Thus we obtained rough estimates for agricultural and industrial output in current prices, and their sum, as total commodity output. The average of the estimate for 1780 and 1790 was used as proxy for the decade average, 1781–90.

Column 5: French commodity output: Marczewski's figures from Table 3, Marczewski, 'Le produit physique', p. XX. These figures are based on Toutain's estimates for agricultural output (J. C. Toutain, 'Le produit de l'agriculture française de 1700 à 1958', *Cahiers de l'ISEA*, AF 1, July 1961, and AF 2, July 1961), and on Markovitch's series of industrial output (T. J. Markovitch, 'L'industrie française de 1789 à 1964', *Cahiers de l'ISEA*, AF 4, July 1965, 'Analyse des faits', AF 5, May 1966, 'Analyse des faits (suite)', AF 6, June 1966, 'Conclusions générales', AF 7, November 1966) which results in an overestimate. Marczewski, in order to correct for the upward bias in manufacturing output estimates (see 'Data') estimated the 'industrial' production of peasants destined for their own consumption. This item he subtracted from the Markovitch industry estimates and added it to agricultural output. His correction changed the structure of output without altering the total value of commodity production.

Britain, perhaps by a growing proportion. On the eve of its great Revolution the population and domestic output of France surpassed British aggregates by an even greater amount than they did at the death of Louis XIV. Looking at the two countries in crude mercantilist terms, appropriate for the eighteenth century, it is not difficult to see France as a far greater economic power than Britain.

Just before the First World War this situation had changed drastically. The population of France ranked below Britain, Russia and Germany while levels of national output for Britain, Germany, Russia and the United States had surpassed the French total.[5] At that crucial turning-point in history, Britain and France, after two centuries of political and economic rivalry, had reached levels of parity in population and output.

Table 3.2 offers figures relevant to an appreciation of changes in the scale (and indirectly the potential military power) of the two economies, namely population and material product. French output data, published in francs at current prices, have been converted into sterling, again at current prices. Although some French figures will be tabulated in francs, comment and interpretation will refer throughout this essay to their equivalent value in pounds sterling.

3.2   DOMESTIC COMMODITY OUTPUT PER CAPITA

Next, we move forward from a mercantilist approach towards a more contemporary one and present figures relevant to some conception of 'welfare levels' in the two countries. Thus Table 3.3 is our first rough proxy for per capita consumption, namely commodity or physical output produced within the borders of the two nations divided by their resident populations, or domestic commodity output per capita.

Estimates for the eighteenth century are no more than guesswork based upon backward extrapolation, but again using that crude method it is possible to agree with Gregory King that in 1700 British per capita output was perhaps 10–30 per cent higher than the French figure.[6] On the eve of the Revolution output per head in France seems to be above British levels, but it falls seriously behind during the Revolutionary and Napoleonic Wars from 1793 to 1815. That particular period witnessed the lowest per capita commodity output (relative to Britain) for the whole century.

France recovered in the first half of the nineteenth century and the figures suggest that it caught up after the mid-forties. During Britain's long Victorian boom French per capita commodity output surpassed that of her rival. There then followed another period of 'relative retardation' which corresponded to the climacteric or the Great Depression in both countries. In the decade before the First World

Table 3.3   *Per Capita Commodity Output in Great Britain and France in Pounds Sterling 1781–90 to 1905–13*

Periods (1)	Great Britain (2)	France (conversion (a)) (3)	France (conversion (b)) (4)
1781–90	6·94	9·53	7·94
1803–12	13·38	17·20	9·51
1815–24	12·27	11·31	9·22
1825–34	11·86	12·24	9·93
1835–44	13·32	13·28	10·59
1845–54	13·80	14·27	11·24
1855–64	15·31	17·30	13·51
1865–74	17·64	19·33	17·92
1875–84	17·28	17·65	17·09
1885–94	18·09	16·22	16·37
1895–1904	19·82	16·69	17·53
1905–13	21·53	22·43	21·89

Sources: See Table 3.2.

War, when its rate of growth accelerated remarkably, per capita commodity output in France again caught up with British levels.

In broad terms these observations accord satisfactorily with recent historiography. French historians generally concede that the Revolutionary and Napoleonic Wars had adverse effects on the growth of the economy.[7] They would also agree that the Great Depression was more serious in France than in England.[8] But in the light of the long discussion on French backwardness it is at first sight surprising to find levels of per capita commodity output in France that, for most of the nineteenth century, are on a par with the British achievement.

Variations in per capita output obviously reflect changes over time in the growth rates of British and French domestic commodity outputs and in British and French populations. It would, however, be misleading to infer anything about rates of change of output from the figures presented in Table 3.3 because the figures are expressed in current, not constant, prices. Thus a relative decline in per capita output could result from a decrease in the rate of growth of real output or from falling prices, as it did, for example, in France between 1875–84 and 1885–94; while the apparent doubling of per capita output in Britain between the first and second sub-periods reflects both rising prices and rising output.

But the table can be used to analyse the very different demographic history of the two countries. To some, perhaps to a considerable, degree the French success in maintaining real per capita product at levels comparable to Britain is a reflection of demographic not economic behaviour. Real commodity output certainly grew at very different rates in the two countries over the nineteenth century. Thus in France the real annual average rate of growth of physical output over eighty years from 1825–34 to 1905–13 is 1·4 per cent and the comparable British percentage (for 1821–1901) is 2·5, nearly double the French rate.[9] Even small differences in growth rates cumulate and make a considerable difference to the absolute size of aggregates like national product over the long run. Thus over eight decades a growth rate of 2·5 per cent a year will multiply initial output by 7·2, and a rate of 1·4 per cent implies a multiplier of 3·2.

With a long-run annual rate of growth of physical output for the nineteenth century which is just above half the British rate, the differential in per capita output did not widen because French families imposed restraints upon fertility, which not only kept the natural rate of increase of the French population well below the British rate but maintained it at a level below the rate attained in France for several decades before the Revolution.[10] On the simplistic and false assumption that rates of change in commodity output were independent of the rate of growth of population, if the population of France had grown at the British rate, it is possible to calculate that by the end of the century French commodity output per capita would have fallen to one-third of the British level. On that same assumption, throughout the period the ratio of French per capita output to the British level would have fallen steadily and there would have been a real decline in the French standard of living over the nineteenth century.

3.3 PER CAPITA COMMODITY FLOW AND FOREIGN TRADE

Such counterfactual arguments help to bring out the significance of the demographic variable, which should not be underestimated. But the impression created by Table 3.3 should not be allowed to evaporate with a brief reference to the slower growth of population in France. After all, it still appears that British domestic per capita output exceeded French levels by a margin likely to be regarded as significant for only four decades between 1780 and 1913. For three decades French per capita output is higher and for the remaining five decades the ranking depends entirely on the rate of exchange selected to convert francs into sterling. Yet from Arthur Young onwards it is almost a commonplace of visitors to both countries to observe that real wages were higher in Britain and that British families at all social levels enjoyed a higher standard of material welfare than families across the Channel. How can contemporary observation be reconciled with these statistics?

So far the comparisons have been conducted in terms of *domestic* production and the answer probably lies in the contribution made by foreign trade and foreign investment to the consumption levels attained by British families. Throughout the nineteenth century, Britain consistently imported more commodities than she exported and paid for the import surplus from payments received from the sale of services to other countries and from earnings upon assets invested abroad. In certain periods the gap between imports and exports added as much as 25 per cent to total domestic commodity production available to consumers in Britain. In other words, through the sale of shipping, banking and other commercial services and, to a more limited extent, from returns repatriated on capital invested overseas, the residents of Britain consumed far more commodities than their economic system made available in the form of domestic product.

Of course the deficit on commodity trade is not a free transfer from the rest of the world to Britain. Factors of production (largely labour), specialised in the organisation and provision of shipping and in the sale of banking, insurance and mercantile services to foreigners, definitely possessed real opportunity costs. Payments to the labour force employed in the international service sector of the British economy included income which represented returns to investment in human capital and to a long tradition of emulation and of learning the skills required to organise and finance international trade. But historians might still legitimately speculate about the real opportunity cost of allocating labour and capital to this profitable sub-sector of the economy and wonder about the political and military conditions which, by the late eighteenth century, had assisted the British mercantile community to capture such a large share of the world supply of international services.

Rather surprisingly, it has been that portion of the trade deficit financed through interest and dividends on British capital invested overseas that has attracted most controversy over gains from 'imperialism'.[11] Imlah's data (see Table 3.4) suggest that the net addition to domestic consumption and investment that *emanated directly* from repatriated earnings on foreign assets was small, and at its highest (over the decade 1896–1905) amounted to only 37 per cent of the import surplus.

While the *direct* contribution of foreign investment to domestic welfare remained slight, we are not asserting that the entire contribution of investment overseas to welfare at home can be comprehended simply by reference to the sources of finance for the British import surplus. British investment overseas undoubtedly played a more important role in widening the boundaries of the world economy, in increasing the volume of international trade and thus in creating

Table 3.4   *British Balance of Payments on Income Account Annual Averages 1816–25 to 1906–13*

Period (1)	Balance of commodity trade (M–X) £m. (2)	Income from services (3)	Other Income (4)	Net repatriation from investment abroad (5)
1816–25	8·5	17·6	− 3·3	− 5·8
1826–35	13·0	16·2	− 3·7	0·5
1836–45	20·5	22·0	− 5·0	3·5
1846–55	27·2	31·8	− 8·9	4·3
1856–65	45·3	59·0	− 8·7	− 5·0
1866–75	60·3	92·1	−14·7	−17·1
1876–85	114·4	104·2	− 7·1	17·3
1885–95	110·7	102·7	−11·3	19·3
1896–1905	167·6	117·8	−12·1	61·9
1906–13	139·2	164·9	−22·4	− 3·3

Notes:

The periodisation in this table follows A. H. Imlah, *Economic Elements in the Pax Britannica* (Cambridge, Mass.: Harvard University Press, 1958). Therefore the import surplus figures which will be used below are not identical with column 2.

Column 2: calculated from the 'Merchandise' balance in Imlah, *Economic Elements*, pp. 70–5. It is the import surplus.

Column 3: calculated from 'Balance on business services', ibid.

Column 4: is the sum of 'Gold and silver bullion and specie', 'Ship sales', 'Emigrant funds', 'Tourists, smuggling and unrecorded imports' accounts, ibid.

Column 5 is calculated as a residual of columns 2, 3 and 4. A minus sign means that net income from services was more than sufficient to finance the deficit on merchandise account (col. 2) and other income (col. 4). It represents the addition to foreign assets from earnings on current account. A positive number means that part of the deficit on merchandise account plus other income was financed by net inflow of dividends and interest repatriated from overseas. The word 'net' here represents the difference between repatriated earnings on foreign debt and capital exports during the period.

markets for British exports and in making it possible for Britain and Europe to obtain cheaper imports overseas.

There can be little doubt, however, that by the close of the eighteenth century the relationship of the French economy to the rest of the world differed markedly from the position attained by the more mature and successful trading and creditor nation across the Channel. Unfortunately the balance of payments accounts for France do not provide the kind of detail supplied by Imlah's estimates for Britain. But it is clear that France did not receive anything like the same volume of earnings from the sale of international services or from repatriated returns from the country's assets abroad.[12] In fact until the middle of the nineteenth century its lending overseas probably exceeded the inflow of dividends and interest from accumulated foreign assets. Furthermore, in terms of a potential for repatriable income from capital invested abroad the British advantage remained clear. Just before the First World War, in per capita terms Britain possessed around £100 of foreign assets for each citizen, whereas France possessed only £40.[13] Assuming full repatriation of dividends and interest at an annual return of 5 per cent, this implies that foreign investment *could have* increased per capita consumption in Britain by something like 23 per cent, but the potential boost to French consumption amounted to only 9 per cent.

In the context of our welfare comparison the significance of the very different positions attained by Britain and France *vis-a-vis* the rest of the world economy can be appreciated from Tables 3.5 and 3.6.

Table 3.5   *Trade Deficits and Total Commodity Flows
1781–90 to 1905–13*

Periods	British trade deficit £m.	French trade deficit francs m.	British commodity flow £m.	French commodity flow francs m.
(1)	(2)	(3)	(4)	(5)
1781–90	6·4	40·8	71·4	5,138
1803–12	10·5	43·9	165·8	7,056
1815–24	6·5	−32·1	177·0	7,642
1825–34	14·5	−37·0	207·9	9,264
1835–44	19·7	−87·3	262·2	10,792
1845–54	26·4	−159·1	309·6	12,427
1855–64	48·2	−133·0	398·4	16,320
1865–74	56·3	10·2	509·9	18,456
1875–84	113·7	885·9	618·3	19,116
1885–94	107·6	821·1	697·8	18,588
1895–1904	164·9	411·6	887·5	19,713
1905–13	141·2	889·6	1003·8	26,704

Sources:
    Column 2: British trade deficit: For the period 1815–1913, the imports minus exports column has been calculated from annual figures for the balance on visible merchandise trade in Imlah, *Economic Elements*, pp. 70–75. A deficit in the merchandise trade balance means a positive M − X. The figures refer to UK.
    For the 1803–12 period, we used Mitchell's computed values (Mitchell and Deane, *Abstract*, p. 282). Here, M − X equals Imports minus Exports and Re-exports. Since Mitchell's table for the UK stops in 1796, for 1781–90 we used his figures for Great Britain and Ireland (ibid., p. 281). We subtracted exports and re-exports from imports for GB and found M − X for GB. We calculated the same value for Ireland. Assuming most of Irish trade to be with Britain, we subtracted the Irish commodity trade deficit from GB commodity trade deficit, and arrived at the M − X figure for

the UK. However, this figure is the 'official' value of trade. We then used the procedure outlined in Deane and Cole, *British Economic Growth*, p. 44, to convert official values to actual values. This procedure provided an estimate in 1796–8 prices. To convert to actual current values for 1781–90 we reflated by using the simple average of the two Schumpeter price indices: consumers' goods except cereals, and producers' goods, on the plausible assumption that at this time very little trade in cereals took place. The price indices are in Mitchell and Deane, *Abstract*, p. 469.

We thus obtained a consistent series of the commodity trade deficit for *the United Kingdom*. Ideally we required the deficit for Great Britain to accord with all other data but we could not separate the Irish account from Imlah's calculations for the UK. But the use of UK estimates biases the $M-X$ figure downward. Since British residents regularly provided services and obtained capital returns from Ireland, and since Irish residents probably contributed little to the invisible exports of the UK, or to investment abroad, the consolidation of the two accounts results in a lower figure than the actual figure for Great Britain alone. Our figures therefore *underestimate* the contribution made by the trade deficit to the material welfare of British residents.

Column 3: French trade deficit: figures for 1827–1913 period are from official statistics. These are figures for 'specific' trade, i.e. excluding transit trade and re-exports. Thus we merely subtracted 'specific' exports from 'specific' imports (these are figures for flows of commodities and exclude gold movements) in order to find annual $M-X$, and averaged over the relevant periods. For our period 1825–34, we had to use the average of 1827 through 1834 (*Annuaire Statistique*, 1966, Partie Retrospective, p. 366).

For the 1803–24 period, we used Chabert's figures for specific trade. Again $M-X$ equals the difference between specific imports and specific exports. Chabert's figures stop in 1820, so our 1815–24 figure is actually an average of 1815 through 1820 (A. Chabert, *Essai sur les mouvements des Revenus et de l'Activité Economique en France de 1789 à 1820*, Paris, 1949, p. 321.)

The remaining figure for the 1781–90 period has been calculated from Levasseur. It is an average of the annual figures from 1777 through 1788. Again the figures given by Levasseur are estimates for the specific trade account for commodities, excluding gold (E. Levasseur, *Histoire du Commerce de la France*, vol. I, Paris, 1911, p. 512).

Column 4 is the sum of column 2 and domestic commodity output from column 4 of Table 3.2.

Column 5 is the sum of column 3 and French domestic commodity output from column 5 of Table 3.2.

Briefly put, Tables 3.5 and 3.6 show that throughout the nineteenth century Britain ran a significant and growing import surplus on its balance of commodity trade; while for France the excess of imports over exports made either a negative or comparatively small contribution to total and per capita flows of commodities available for domestic consumption and investment. Its largest net inflow added just 5 per cent to French domestic commodity production. In contrast, throughout the years 1781 to 1913 a surplus of imports provided on average some 12 per cent of the total flow of commodities available for use in Britain.

Thus some reconciliation of statistics with historiography and contemporary observation can be achieved through a comparison of British and French commodity flows, rather than domestic products. But even on this basis (which is undoubtedly more appropriate for welfare comparisons) the measured gap appears narrower than is often

Table 3.6   *Per Capita Commodity Flows and the Contribution
of the Import Surplus to Per Capita Output 1781–90 to 1905–13*

Periods (1)	Per capita commodity flow G.B. £ (2)	Per capita commodity flow France £ (conversion a) (3a)	Per capita commodity flow France £ (conversion b) (3b)	Import surplus as a ratio of domestic commodity output for G.B. (4)	Import surplus as a ratio of domestic commodity output for France (5)
				%	%
1781–90	7·62	9·61	8·01	9·8	0·8
1803–12	14·28	17·29	9·56	6·7	0·5
1815–24	12·73	11·27	9·18	3·8	−0·3
1825–34	12·96	12·17	9·88	9·3	−0·6
1835–44	14·40	13·16	10·49	8·1	−0·6
1845–54	15·08	14·09	11·09	9·3	−1·2
1855–64	17·42	17·18	13·42	13·8	−0·7
1865–74	19·83	19·34	17·93	12·4	0
1875–84	21·18	18·53	17·94	22·6	5·0
1885–94	21·39	16·98	17·13	18·2	4·7
1895–1904	24·34	17·06	17·91	22·8	2·2
1905–13	25·06	23·21	22·65	16·4	3·5

Note: Commodity flow = Domestic production + imports − exports of commodities.

Sources:
   Column 2 obtained by dividing commodity flow (column 4, Table 3.5 by population (Table 3.2). Columns 3a and 3b calculated by dividing French commodity flow from Table 3.5 by population (Table 3.2) and converting into pounds.
   Columns 4 and 5 = commodity flow − domestic commodity output, as a ratio of commodity output in each country.

suggested. Before the Revolution France may possibly have enjoyed a higher per capita commodity availability, although for this period the estimates for French agricultural production are probably inflated. Thereafter, Britain never relinquished her superior position. On average from 1781 to 1913 British commodity flows per capita are some 11 per cent above French levels if the current values of comparable French aggregates are converted in terms of French weights and 22 per cent higher if British weights are employed to convert francs into sterling. Changes over time in the relative positions of welfare per capita in the two countries can best be visualised on a graph (see Figure 3.1).

With either method of conversion these statistics serve to qualify the impression left by the writings of travellers and historians that in welfare terms France remained significantly backward, retarded or underdeveloped compared with Britain over the nineteenth century. To us the real gap and many of the adjectives used to describe it seem too far apart.

Figure 3.1   *Per Capita Commodity Flow in France as a Percentage of Per Capita Commodity Flow in Britain*

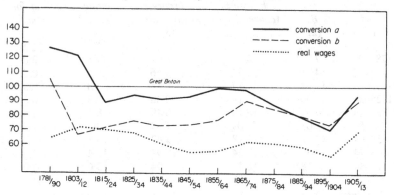

3.4   REAL WAGES AND THE STRUCTURE OF EMPLOYMENT

This rather small differential in material welfare suggested by estimates of per capita commodity flow seemed to be out of line with comments and impressions based upon levels of real wages in the two countries. Thus some investigation into the dichotomy between real wages and real per capita commodity flows seemed necessary.

The statistics required to measure and compare money wage levels in Britain and France should ideally contain estimates of annual wage bills divided by the total number of wage earners in both countries, coupled with measures for dispersion about the national mean. Unfortunately the wage and labour force estimates available are far from ideal, but estimates for 1905 have recently been processed into representative averages by Phelps-Brown.

His study also contains indices which measure rates of change in money wages for Britain and France over the period 1860–1913.[14] Kuczynski's *Short History of Labour Conditions* contains similar indices for the period 1780–1860.[15] Kuczynski's indices were adjusted and spliced on to the Phelps-Brown indices to provide indicators for the long-run movement in money wages from 1780 through to 1913. Estimates of money wage *levels* in Britain and France for 1905 calculated by

Phelps-Brown were then extrapolated backwards to 1780 and averaged into a series of decennial average wage levels in sterling and francs for the period 1780–1913.

Our next task was to convert francs into sterling in order to compare wage levels in the two countries. This conversion required the construction of a basket of goods to represent the consumption patterns of British and French wage earners over the period 1780 to 1913. For British workers we relied upon the methods and sources adopted by Phelps-Brown and Hopkins and designed a simplified modal budget (which consisted of 40 per cent wheat, 40 per cent meat, 10 per cent coal and 10 per cent textiles) or 'composite unit of consumables' to represent the consumption patterns of British wage earners across the entire period.[16] These weights enabled us to construct an exchange rate to convert francs into sterling, based roughly upon the consumption patterns of a British working-class family. Thus the exchange rate utilised in Table 3.7 refers to the number of francs required by wage earners in France to purchase 8s. worth of flour, 8s. worth of beef, 2s. worth of coal and 2s. worth of textiles in Britain, decade by decade from 1780 to 1913. Since British workers spent their wages on commodities that are relatively cheap in Britain compared to France, and French workers would distribute their incomes on commodities that were relatively cheap in France, the employment of an exchange rate even loosely based upon British consumption patterns will tend to make the real wage or purchasing power of French workers appear smaller in comparisons with British workers. Strictly speaking, we should construct an alternative conversion rate based upon the consumption patterns of French workers, but for the purpose of this exercise (which is included here merely as a check on our estimates of real per capita incomes in the two countries) it should be sufficient to point out that the relative wages of French workers could be understated by the conversion procedure adopted here.[17]

Compared to commodity consumption per capita, if the gap in welfare between the two countries is measured in terms of real wages, then welfare levels in France appear markedly lower than the standards attained by wage labour in Britain. In some decades of the nineteenth century real wages in France may have been as much as 45 per cent below British standards. Here, it seems, is far stronger evidence of backwardness (see Figure 3.1 above).

But these estimates of real wages must be interpreted carefully if they are to be used as indicators of relative welfare. There are definite biases against France in the conversion procedure adopted above. For example, the employment of a British basket of goods to represent consumption patterns in both countries has already been mentioned. More important, the same method compares real wages in terms of their capacity to

Table 3.7   *Relative Wage Levels in Britain and France
1781–90 to 1905–13*

Period	GB: Average wage level (in current £s) (1)	France: Average wage level (converted to £s) (2)	Exchange rate (francs per £) (3)	France as % of GB (4)
1781–90	26·4	16·8	18·3	64
1803–12	36·4	25·9	15·8	71
1815–24	33·2	23·3	19·0*	70
1825–34	29·5	20·0	22·2	68
1835–44	30·0	18·1	23·6*	60
1845–54	33·7	18·4	25·0	55
1855–64	37·4	20·8	26·3	56
1865–74	44·3	27·6	22·9	62
1875–84	48·0	29·4	25·3*	61
1885–94	50·5	29·7	27·7*	59
1895–1904	55·3	29·2	30·2	53
1905–13	60·0	41·3	23·5	69

*Interpolated.
Notes and Sources: see text and notes.

purchase commodities alone; the exercise assumes that wage earners spent no income on services. But in so far as a higher percentage of the wage-earning population in Britain resided in towns and probably paid higher rents and consumed services as an unavoidable consequence of their urban way of life, the real wage comparison as set out in Table 3.7 is again biased against France.

But even if real wage levels could be measured more accurately, the comparison would still provide an unrepresentative indicator of relative levels of welfare for the majority of British and French families, because the share of the population who depended on wages for their livelihood varied significantly between the two societies. For most of the nineteenth century the modal or typical member of the British labour force was a wage earner. Between 1860 and 1913 87 per cent of the working population consisted of employees earning wages and salaries.[18] Earlier in the nineteenth century when employers and self-employed workers formed a higher proportion of the occupied population, wage and salary earners still accounted for around 80 per cent of the British work force.[19]

In France, where there is a marked contrast to Britain, a far higher proportion of the work force participated in production as unpaid family labour, proprietors of small enterprises in agriculture, services and industry or as self-employed workers.[20] Between 1850 and 1914 employers amounted to about 2 per cent of the British work force and self-employed workers to around 11 per cent;[21] whereas in France as late as 1906, 24 per cent of the work force were self-employed and another 30 per cent were classified as employers of labour, and there is a strong presumption that the degree of wage dependency among the occupied populations of Britain and France would have been even more different for earlier decades in the nineteenth century.[22] Thus in 1866 when employers of labour amounted to only 2 per cent of the British work force, the comparable proportion in France was 42 per cent.[23]

Even a cursory examination of the labour force statistics for Britain and France reveals significant differences in the ways in which workers engaged in production in the two economies. There seems to be no doubt that throughout the nineteenth century a far higher proportion of the British work force depended upon wage labour for its livelihood; while across the Channel a far greater, if declining, share of the occupied population worked as employers of labour, as part of family enterprises and above all with their own equipment, tools, land and commodity stocks. In Marxist terms the separation of labour from the means of production had already in 1800 proceeded much further in Britain than in France, where (as Kuznets recognised in a more general context) it was rational for peasants, artisans, craftsmen and small proprietors to hold on to capital 'despite low or zero returns because possession of land or of a few tools, or of a small commodity inventory meant a larger income than could be secured by reliance on employment alone.'[24] In fact the average annual earnings of this sector of the French labour force, who derived income not only from labour but also from entrepreneurship and from the ownership and control of capital utilised in agriculture, industry and services, amounted to a multiple of average earnings from wages and salaries; a multiple which declined from about three around the beginning of the century to about 1·5 by 1911.[25]

When, and only when, a comparable majority of the occupied population are wage earners is it permissible to employ average wages as indicators of relative standards of living across countries. For Britain and France in the nineteenth century the marked differences in the structure of their occupied populations, which in turn reflect the relative importance of agriculture and rural industry in the two economies, make any comparison based upon wages alone highly ambiguous.[26]

Even if comparison is restricted to that part of the work force whose earnings consisted only of wages, the available data are still an ambiguous proxy for relative levels of real consumption in the two societies. For example, average wage levels without reference to possible variations in family size and the numbers of wage earners per family are clearly a misleading index of welfare. Unfortunately it is not possible to measure the dependency burden for wage earners *per se* in Britain and France because information on relative family size and the participation of wives and children in paid employment is not available for wage-earning families. Comparisons are only possible if we are prepared to make the assumption that the average dependency burden for wage earners was identical to the average dependency burden for the labour force as a whole. On this assumption the ratio of the work force to total population (the standard participation rate) provides some indication of the average dependency burden on wage earners in Britain and France.

The relevant figures are presented in Table 3.8. British and French dependency rates change over time, mainly in response to differences in fertility in the two populations, so that by the end of the nineteenth century the modal French wage earner seems to have supported a smaller number of dependents than his British counterpart.

Given the problems involved in defining a labour force, the figures in columns 1 and 3 may be a more accurate indicator of the dependency burden on wage earners. These ratios refer to the numbers of adults in the total population ('adult' means men and women from 10 to 65 years of age). These figures also suggest that by the end of the century a smaller proportion of the potential labour supply was actually at work in Britain.

Table 3.8   *Dependency Ratios 1801–1911*

	France		Great Britain	
	Potential participation rate	*Actual participation rate*	*Potential participation rate*	*Actual participation rate*
	(1)	(2)	(3)	(4)
	%	%	%	%
1801	68	—	—	45
1821	69	—	69	44
1851	68	—	68	47
1861	67	39	68	47
1871	66	41	68	46
1881	66	44	68	44
1891	65	43	69	44
1901	65	51	71	45
1911	65	53	72	45

Sources: The ratio of labour force to population for France is from J. C. Toutain, 'La population de 1700 à 1959', *Cahiers de l'ISEA*, AF 3, January 1963, p. 122. For Great Britain, population figures from Deane and Cole, *British Economic Growth*, p. 8 and labour force, p. 143. Potential participation rate means the ratio of persons aged 10–65 to total population. For France the figures are from M. Lévy-Leboyer, 'La décélération de l'économie française dans la seconde moitié du XIXᵉ siècle', *Revue d'Histoire Economique et Sociale* (1971), 4, p. 487. For Great Britain we used Mitchell and Deane, *Abstract*, pp. 11–12.

Furthermore, the estimates of average wage levels in Britain and France, calculated with care by Phelps-Brown, are *not* the same as the annual average earnings or income of employees who depended on wages and salaries for a living. This discrepancy between wages and earnings is not an oversight or a problem of sources. Phelps-Brown derived his estimates from familiar collations of data related to wage rates. Moreover, the coverage is similar for both countries and included approximately the same groups and categories of workers – that is, skilled and unskilled males, females and juvenile labour employed for the most part in industry, building and public utilities. (Agriculture seems to have been excluded for both Britain and France.) Phelps-Brown did, however, attempt to convert a weighted average *wage rate* into an estimate of *average annual earnings.* 'We decided,' he writes, 'to take as our measure of wages the average earnings in a year of employment that is normally continuous but subject to departures from standard hours through short time, overtime and absence for personal reasons.'[27]

Phelps-Brown is not really interested in comparing levels of real income in Britain and France. If there is a systematic bias in his figures it cannot be perceived in the data and methods used to obtain an average or representative 'money wage rate' for the two societies. But average earnings does refer to workers in *continuous* employment in the industrial sector and that particular assumption appears to bias the comparison in favour of Britain, a country where urbanisation had proceeded further and faster than in France.[28] In a more urban economy the proportion of the wage-earning population who are engaged in services, transport, and construction and who appear on the labour market as casual or temporary labour of one kind and another is likely to be high. In France underemployed or low-productivity labour tended to remain in peasant households in the countryside. In Britain, by contrast, the teneurial institutions of agriculture could not hold much 'excess' population which crowded into towns as a 'lumpen proletariat' or reserve army of labour.

French visitors to Britain, such as Tocqueville, Faucher, Doré and Taine, appreciated the different social realities in the two economies, and their comments on the prevalence of poverty and casual labour in Victorian cities find statistical support in the works of Mayhew and Booth.[29] If their impressions are correct and the urban labour force in Britain included a higher proportion of workers in irregular employment, then a comparison of average annual earnings, constructed on the assumption of full and continuous employment at the going wage rate, could lead to a systematic overstatement of real earnings in Britain compared to the situation in France.

National income estimates for the years 1905–13 certainly suggest that this contrast between the structure of the two economies may have been important. Just before the First World War per capita incomes (as conventionally defined) stood at £38·4 in France and around £50 per head in Britain.[30] At that time the share of wages and salaries in the national income of Britain came to 47·2 per cent, while the comparable ratio for France was 44 per cent. But the proportions of wage and salary earners in their respective labour forces varied from 87 per cent in Britain to only 46 per cent in France.[31] Thus the average annual earnings (or expenditure) of employees and their families in France was close to per capita income ($\frac{44}{46}$ per cent of £38·4 or £36·7). In Britain where wage earners and the salariat formed 87 per cent of the occupied population, the incomes of the majority fell below per capita income: $\frac{47}{87}$ per cent of £50 comes to an average expenditure of £27 per annum.

These calculations, which assume that wage earners in both countries received no income from the ownership of productive assets, suggest that the earnings of workers in France were far closer to average incomes for the population as a whole than they were in Britain, where income from the ownership of property accrued to a far smaller proportion of the population. They also support our previous contention that very little about relative standards of living for the majority of Englishmen and Frenchmen can be deduced from simple comparisons of real wage estimates. National income figures, which become more reliable by 1905–13, indicate that on average the real earnings of wage and salary earners in France may have been 30 per cent above British levels.

This discrepancy between real wage estimates (calculated by Phelps-Brown and assembled in Table 3.7) and estimates of real earnings calculated from national income and labour force data is no doubt partly a matter of statistical error, but the gap also reflects real differences. First it suggests that the salariat in France either formed a larger share of total employees or received incomes well above those enjoyed by wage earners.[32] More important, the figures support our earlier contention that a larger share of the wage-earning population in the more urbanised British economy suffered the effects of casual labour and unemployment on their earnings. In France, where the share of the work force permanently committed to intermittent employment in construction, services and transport and to casual and seasonal occupations in industry was smaller, the 'lumpen proletariat' did not drag average earnings downwards to the same extent as it did across the Channel.

To sum up: real wage rates in France were consistently and appreciably lower than real wage rates in Britain throughout the period 1780–1914, but for several reasons this fact tells us very little about average levels of earnings and therefore welfare in the two countries.

Our calculations biased the comparison against France. Secondly, the assumption of full and continuous employment also biases the estimates in favour of Britain where a higher share of the labour force did not enjoy full and continuous employment. Above all, the very different ways in which labour participated in production in the two societies mean that the average earnings of wage labour in France are not a representative estimate for the average incomes of the occupied population as a whole.

All these calculations reflect the long survival of agriculture in France; the persistence there of a rural and artisanal economy in which the ownership and control of the means of production were more widely distributed than in Britain, a country where the separation of workers from land and capital occurred earlier. Up until the First World War the two economies and their attendant social structures continued to grow and operate in very different ways. But in welfare terms this did not mean that the French system of production offered the majority of people in France a significantly lower standard of living than the so-called advanced system of capitalism in England.

3.5 CONCLUSIONS

Further and potentially more interesting inferences might be drawn from the calculations of per capita commodity flow and from the relative levels of real earnings enjoyed by employees in the two societies. First of all, it seems that the measured difference in material welfare between the inhabitants of Britain and France cannot be properly explained in terms of the superior efficiency of the British economy but emanated instead from a trade deficit or import surplus that increased from £0·66 per head of the population in 1781–90 to £4·52 per capita in 1895–1904.

Through French eyes Britain's more rapid structural change, technological leadership and earlier diffusion of a factory system might be regarded as developments that, objectively speaking, maintained domestic output per head on a par with France, where population increased at a far more modest rate. From that same French viewpoint it seems logical to single out international trade, foreign investment, shipping, banking, insurance and other mercantile services as the area of economic activity that provided British families with their higher levels of consumption and welfare, illustrated in Figure 3.1. Successful mercantilism, not the factory system, might seem to Frenchmen to be at the centre of British superiority for a century after Waterloo, while British industrialisation simply helped to offset the advantages French families derived from restraints on fertility.

Of course, Britain's capacity to finance an import surplus is connected with the relative efficiency of its domestic economy, but such connections are complex and by no means flow in one direction. British banking, shipping and commercial services developed over the eighteenth century to serve both domestic and foreign producers and it might be argued that the competitive position achieved by British shipping and mercantile services in the international economy originated ultimately from linkages or a learning process related to the development of domestic commodity production.

But in the present state of knowledge it is perhaps as orthodox to stress the feedbacks and spinoffs from the foreign trade sector to the long-run growth of the domestic economy. Britain's industrial revolution has to some extent been explained by its historians as the outcome of a commercial revolution, a revolution that preceded it in time and which contributed to its momentum in the late eighteenth century.[33] If any separation is feasible, the impetus to economic growth seems to flow from the international sector to the domestic economy. There are, of course, obvious links between shipbuilding and shipping and no doubt many merchants who engaged in international trade served their apprenticeship in internal distribution. But it is difficult to account for the importance of the City of London in the organisation and finance of international commerce and shipping as the outcome of the development of a relatively efficient system of internal trade and distribution. It is perhaps easier to see Britain's paramount position in international services as being more closely linked to stable government, to a well-ordered system of public finance and above all to superior naval power directed by statesmen with a sharp perception for the nation's long-run economic interests.[34] Trafalgar was not, as Napoleon supposed, victory for a nation of shopkeepers. On the contrary, it represents the culmination of successful mercantilism which condemned commercial enterprise in France to 'domestic shopkeeping' and left world commerce to British merchants. As Thiers recognised, 'Nous n'avons pas gagné la bataille de Trafalgar. Nous ne sommes pas restés maitres des mers et nous n'avons pas 200 millions de consommateurs, comme l'Angleterre les possède. Voilà tout le secret de notre inferiorité.'[35]

NOTES TO CHAPTER 3

1 F. Crouzet, 'England and France in the Eighteenth Century: A Comparative Analysis of Two Economic Growths' in R. M. Hartwell (ed.), *The Causes of the Industrial Revolution in England* (London: Methuen, 1967), P. Goubert, 'Recent Theories and Research on French Population between 1500 and 1700' in D. V. Glass and D. E. C. Eversley (eds), *Population in History* (London: Arnold, 1965).

2 Crouzet, 'England and France'.

3 J. C. Toutain, 'La population de 1700 à 1959', *Cahiers de l'ISEA*, AF 3, January 1963, p. 16, and P. Deane and W. A. Cole, *British Economic Growth, 1688–1959* (Cambridge: CUP, 1962), p. 6, for population figures.

British commodity output was calculated by backward extrapolation of total commodity output for 1781–90 (for derivation see sources for Table 3.2) using the Deane and Cole index of real output in the eighteenth century (Deane and Cole, *British Economic Growth*, p. 78, table 19. 'Total industry and commerce' plus 'Agriculture' were the indices used for commodity production.) This method gave us £37 million as the commodity output c. 1700 in 1781–90 prices. French commodity output was calculated from J. Marczewski, 'Some Aspects of the Economic Growth of France, 1660–1958', *Economic Development and Cultural Change*, April 1961. His figures for physical product in current prices (p. 371) in 1701–10 were deflated by his price index (p. 378) and the 1701–10 physical product was obtained in 1781–90 prices. This was 1,955 million francs, which at our 1781–90 exchange rates is equal to £97 million or £81 million.

4 F. Crouzet, 'England and France', p. 154. But on Toutain's controversial figures for agriculture see Chapter 2, note 9 above, and M. Morineau, *Les faux-semblants d'un démarrage économique . . .* (Paris: Armand-Colin, 1970), pp. 1–95.

5 V. Parett and G. Bloch, 'Industrial Production in Western Europe and the United States', *Banca Nazionale del Lavona Quarterly Review*, no. 39 (1956), p. 294.

6 The physical output figures obtained above (see Chapter 2, n. 31) were divided into population figures for c. 1700. The result is a per capita commodity output of £5·44 for Britain, and of £5·00 or £4·17 for France, depending on whether the French basket or the British basket exchange rate is used.

7 F. Crouzet, 'Wars, Blockade and Economic Change in Europe, 1792–1815', *Journal of Economic History*, December 1964.

8 M. Lévy-Leboyer, 'La décélération de l'économie française dans la seconde moitié du XIXᵉ siècle', *Revue d'Histoire Economique et Sociale* (1971), 4, pp. 485–507.

9 British growth rate calculated from Deane and Cole, *British Economic Growth*, pp. 282 and 291; French growth rate from J. Marczewski, 'Le produit physique de l'économie française de 1789 à 1913 (comparaison avec la Grande Bretagne)', *Cahiers de l'ISEA*, AF 4, July 1965, p. XCIII.

10 D. V. Glass and E. Grebenik, 'World Population, 1800–1950' in M. M. Postan and H. J. Habakkuk (eds), *The Cambridge Economic History of Europe* Cambridge: CUP, 1966), vol. VI, part I, p. 102.

11 D. K. Fieldhouse, *Economics and Empire 1830–1914* (New York: Cornell University Press, 1973).

78   *Economic Growth in Britain and France 1780–1914*

12 See R. E. Cameron, *France and the Economic Development of Europe, 1800–1914* (Princeton: Princeton University Press, 1961), pp. 526–95, for estimates of French invisible exports.
13 A. Emmanuel, 'White-settler Colonialism and the Myth of Investment Imperialism', *New Left Review*, May–June 1972, p. 50, and W. Woodruff, *Impact of Western Man* (London: St Martin's, 1966).
14 H. Phelps-Brown, *A Century of Pay* (London: Macmillan, 1968), appendix 3, pp. 41–8. 432–3 and 444–6.
15 J. Kuczynski. *A Short History of Labour Conditions Under Industrial Capitalism in Great Britain and the Empire* (London: Muller), vol. I, 2nd edn, 1972, appendix to ch. 1, pp. 55–9, and appendix to ch. 2, pp. 88–9. For a review of this and other British wage data see M. Flinn, 'Trends in Real Wages, 1750–1850, *Economic History Review*, August 1974, pp. 395–411. For France: J. Kuczynski, *A Short History of Labour Conditions Under Industrial Capitalism*, vol. IV, *France 1700 to the Present Day* (London: Muller, 1946), pp. 64, 70, 75 and 79. For a review of French wage data see J. Lhomme, 'Le pouvoir d'achat de l'ouvrier français au cours d'un siècle, 1840–1940', *Le Mouvement Social*, April–June 1968, pp. 41–69.
16 H. Phelps-Brown and S. Hopkins, 'Seven Centuries of the Prices of Consumables, compared with Builders' Wage Rates' in E. Carus-Wilson (ed.), *Essays in Economic History* (London: Arnold, 1962), vol. 2, pp. 179–82. We employed weights modified from the article cited above and used representative prices (e.g. flour to represent bread, beef to represent meat and dairy produce, coal to represent fuel and cotton yarn to represent clothing). In other words, the methods and data employed in this exercise were the same as those utilised for the construction of the overall exchange rate between francs and sterling described in Appendix A above. Again we excluded services from the comparison of real wage levels expressed in sterling.
17 See sections 2.4 and 2.5 above, where we discuss the exchange rate problem. The price data employed are cited in Appendix A above.
18 S. Kuznets, 'Quantitative Aspects of the Economic Growth of Nations: IV. Distribution of National Income by Factor Shares', *Economic Development and Cultural Change*, April 1959, pp. 86–7.
19 Deane and Cole, *British Economic Growth*, pp. 149–51.
20 For a good analysis of the structure of the labour force in France see M. Lévy-Leboyer, 'La décélération de l'économie française', pp. 489, 492 and 502.
21 Kuznets, 'Quantitative Aspects IV', p. 87, and Deane and Cole, *British Economic Growth*, p. 150. *The Final Report on the First Census of Production of the UK (1907)* (London, 1912), p. 8, which refers to 'trades other than agriculture or fisheries', listed 9,250,000 employed persons of whom 260,000 were employers, 600,000 worked on their own account and 8,390,000 worked for employers.
22 P. Bairoch et al., 'The Working Population and its Structure' in *International Historical Statistics*, vol. 1, p. 178, published by Institut de Sociologie de l'Université Libre de Bruxelles, 1968. For somewhat different ratios see Kuznets, 'Quantitative Aspects IV', p. 89.
23 Bairoch, 'The Working Population', p. 178.
24 Kuznets, 'Quantitative Aspects IV', p. 27.
25 ibid., p. 89.
26 Bairoch's figures for France 1906 show that employees (wage and salary earners) formed a minority of the work force in agriculture (30·4 per cent), transport (48·3 per cent) and commerce (45·2 per cent): Bairoch, 'The Working Population', p. 178.
27 Phelps-Brown, *A Century of Pay*, p. 42, and the discussion of data and methods on on pp. 41–4, 349–50 and 351–2.

28 In 1851, 10·6 per cent of the French population resided in cities of more than 10,000 inhabitants. The British ratio was 39·5 per cent: C. P. Kindleberger, *Economic Growth in France and Britain, 1851–1950* (Cambridge, Mass.: Harvard University Press, 1964), p. 249.

29 These conditions are described and referenced in S. Pollard and D. W. Crossley, *The Wealth of Britain* (London: Batsford, 1968), pp. 240–7, and see pp. 289–92.

30 The relevant estimates are in Deane and Cole, *British Economic Growth*, pp. 282 and 330, and we adjusted the 1911 estimate, which refers to the UK on to a Great Britain basis – on the assumption that the percentage gap between the Great Britain and United Kingdom estimates for 1911 was the same as the ratio for 1901. The population for Great Britain is from B. R. Mitchell in C. M. Cipolla (ed.), *The Fontana Economic History of Europe* (London: Fontana, 1973), vol. 4, p. 747. French per capita income in francs was calculated from the above source, pp. 747 and 803. We converted francs into sterling at 25 francs to the pound.

31 These ratios come from Kuznets, 'Quantitative Aspects IV', pp. 86–8, and Deane and Cole, *British Economic Growth*, pp. 247–8.

32 Bairoch's statistics for France in 1906 suggest that the salariat formed 12 per cent of the occupied population: Bairoch, *Historical Statistics*, p. 178. The UK *Census of Production* for 1907, p. 8, suggests that the comparable UK proportion may have been 6 per cent, but this census excludes agricultural employment which would probably lower the ratio.

33 See P. K. O'Brien, 'Government Revenue 1793–1815, A Study in Fiscal and Financial Policy in Wars Against France', unpublished D. Phil. thesis (Oxford: 1967), ch. 8, on the factors affecting the growth of international services. For a summary of the argument on commercial origins of the Industrial Revolution, see M. W. Flinn, *Origins of the Industrial Revolution* (London: Longmans, 1966), ch. 4. Also W. E. Minchinton, *The Growth of English Overseas Trade* (London: Methuen, 1969), Introduction.

34 C. Wilson, *England's Apprenticeship 1603–1763* (New York: St Martin's, 1965), ch. 13.

35 The quotation cited in J. Lacour-Gayet (ed.), *Histoire du Commerce* (Paris: Spid, 1952), vol. V, p. 76.

Part Three
PRODUCTIVITY

Chapter 4

The Productivity of Labour and Structural Change

4.1 CONCEPTS AND DATA

Our comparison of 'welfare' levels in Britain and France proceeded from domestic production to total commodity flows and emphasised the importance of the import surplus in Britain's economic lead over France. In the next three chapters we return to domestic production and to the problem of labour productivity in the two economies.

The central issue can be posed first in British and then in French perspective. For Britain, with a population growing far more rapidly than that of France, historians ask: how did the economy successfully maintain domestic output per head at French levels? For France the issue can be expressed in a counterfactual form: why didn't the productivity of labour employed in the production of commodities increase at a rate fast enough to compensate for advantages possessed by Britain in servicing the international economy? Questions of this kind cover the whole economic history of the two countries from 1780 to 1914. In this and subsequent chapters we again offer some statistical anatomy. As always, these statistics are merely a prelude to historical investigation.

The productivity of labour employed by an economy, by a sector of an economy or by an enterprise within that sector is a ratio of labour input to output. For an entire country, like Britain or France, labour productivity is an index of productive capacity which measures the potential of its economic system to supply the population with goods and services. Although productivity can be defined with respect to any bundle of inputs or related to any single input, we propose to concentrate upon labour productivity, partly because accessible data are available only for labour but mainly because that ratio reflects what Marshall once called the dual nature of man as the end and the means of production. Marshall did not mean that labour was a unique factor of production or that the productivity of labour is a good proxy for total factor productivity. But he recognised that, over the long run, the relationship between output and labour input is correlated to the standard of living attained by a population. In other words, given the quantity and quality of resources available, the productivity of labour

84 *Economic Growth in Britain and France 1780–1914*

is closely linked to per capita income and per capita consumption.

Thus domestic output per person resident in Britain and France is simply the average productivity of labour employed in the production of commodities multiplied by the share of the population employed in agriculture and industry. Symbolically

$$O/P = a(O/L)$$

where O/P is commodity output divided by population, a is the participation ratio, and O/L is labour productivity (i.e. commodity output divided by labour).

Global measures of labour productivity are coefficients that reflect the full range of factors operating upon the efficiency and utilisation of labour in production. Such factors include the quantity and quality of all complementary inputs such as capital, technology, intermediate goods, natural resources, raw materials, organisation and management as well as the quality, skill, motivation and effort of labour itself.[1]

Higher levels of productivity attained by one economy compared to another reflect either a more efficient utilisation of labour within existing activities or a better allocation of labour among activities. Thus the productivity of labour employed to supply farm produce and manufactured goods in Britain and France from 1780 to 1914 is the weighted sum of the productivity of labour employed in agriculture and industry. Differences in labour productivity between the two states reflect differences in labour productivities within agriculture and industry as well as variations in the share of the labour force allocated between those two sectors. Symbolically

$$O/P = a(O/L) = xL(O/L)_a + yL(O/L)_i$$

where O/L is the average productivity of the labour force employed in commodity production, x is the share of the labour force employed in agriculture, and y is the share employed in industry. $(O/L)_a$ is the productivity of labour utilised in agriculture, and $(O/L)_i$ is the productivity of labour employed in industry.

For comparisons of labour productivity across countries over the nineteenth century, the major problem is to find suitable data. Our output statistics relate to commodity output and have already been described and evaluated (Section 2.1). Output is gross domestic or sectoral output, valued at factor cost. Gross means that neither British nor French estimates exclude an allowance for the depreciation of capital used up in production.

Measurement of the labour input presented greater difficulties. Ideally, the figures required for Britain and France should be comparable and should include total *hours* of labour utilised in the production of agricultural and industrial commodities year by year from 1780 to 1914. But our figures are estimates for the total work force employed in commodity production which were derived from censuses of population. They consist of unweighted totals of employees (man, woman and child years), with each individual counted as one unit of labour input regardless of age, sex, skill, education, health, motivation and other characteristics that affect the efficiency of labour (see Table 4.1).

Obviously there are differences in the quality of labour employed in production from country to country, and for exercises designed to separate out and to measure the distinct contribution made to the growth of output by labour, capital, and technical progress it is necessary to correct or to standardise census figures for variations in the age, sex and skill composition of the work force.[2] But our concern is to relate the productivity of labour to per capita output, and for that purpose labour input can be properly defined as the total number of people employed in agriculture and industry, regardless of age, sex, skill and other attributes of British and French workers (i.e. $O/P = a(O/L)$).

But differences in the average number of hours of work performed by the labour force in Britain and France could still seriously distort comparisons of labour productivities across countries. The concept required is the total number of hours worked year by year in the two economies including normal working hours, overtime and time spent waiting or in preparation for work. The figures should exclude holidays, sick leave, meal breaks and time spent on travel to and from the work place.[3]

Although the measure required can be clearly defined it proved impossible to find accurate information about the actual number of hours of work performed by the British and French work forces year by year from 1780 to 1914. For France the Conseil de Prud'hommes published figures for 1896 and 1901 which suggest that workmen in Paris worked about $9\frac{1}{2}$ hours a day, while in the provinces they worked just over 10 hours.[4] Their claims are supported by a Board of Trade inquiry of 1905 into the cost of living of the working classes in France which shows that industrial workers in Paris, Lille, Lyons, Marseilles and Rouen tended to work a 60-hour week.[5]

A further and far more comprehensive survey by the Board of Trade of British industrial workers for 1906 indicates that they worked 54 hours a week, excluding overtime.[6] Thus at the end of our period it looks as if French industrial workers may have worked an extra hour per day compared to their British counterparts. But they probably enjoyed more holidays. Maddison's evidence for the twentieth century gives 28 days vacation for French workers compared to 18 in Britain.

Taking these two figures as datum and ignoring all other factors germane to a calculation of average hours worked per annum (including such factors as part-time workers, sickness, unemployment, overtime, meal breaks, etc.), it is possible to assume that the number of hours worked over the year by French industrial workers exceeded the time worked by British workers by 7 per cent.[7] British agricultural labourers worked 60 hours a week in 1906.[8]

Unfortunately the information for earlier periods cannot be processed into representative averages. For Britain, Matthews worked with a figure of 65 hours a week for 1856 and the figure printed in the

Table 4.1　*Labour Force Engaged in Commodity Production 1803–12 to 1905–13*

Period	British labour force engaged in commodity production ('000,000s)	French labour force engaged in commodity production ('000,000s)
(1)	(2)	(3)
1803–12	3·4	8·0
1815–24	4·1	8·8
1825–34	4·7	9·8
1835–44	5·2	10·5
1845–54	6·0	11·1
1855–64	6·6	11·5
1865–74	6·9	11·0
1875–84	7·4	12·3
1885–94	8·0	11·8
1895–1904	9·0	14·1
1905–13	10·0	14·9

Sources:

Column 2: British labour force: For 1801–1913 we used Deane and Cole's figures (P. Deane and W. A. Cole, *British Economic Growth, 1688–1959*, Cambridge: CUP, 1962, p. 143). They provide estimates of the labour force for every census year after 1801. For each of these dates we found the proportion of the industrial and agricultural labour force to total population, and assumed that this proportion persisted over the decade tabulated above. From these participation rates and our population figures, we calculated decennial figures for the labour force engaged in agriculture and industry. Since figures are rounded to one decimal point, we did *not* calculate annual figures based on growth rates.

Column 3: French labour force: J. Marczewski, 'Le produit physique de l'économie française de 1789 à 1913 (comparaison avec la Grande Bretagne)', *Cahiers de l'ISEA*, AF 4, July 1965, table 31 includes figures for labour force employed in material production for the decade 1781–90, then 1835–44, and 1855–64 and from then on through to 1905–13. For four sub-periods we had no figures and assumed that the proportion of the labour force employed in material production to total population exhibited a linear development. Thus total labour force figures for 1815–24, 1825–34 and 1845–54 are interpolated.

standard *Histoire du Travail en France* suggests that the French workers again worked about an hour a day above the British figure.[9]

Our figures for labour input (presented in Table 4.1) are an improvisation and consist of unweighted estimates of the total numbers employed in commodity production. These estimates are *not* corrected for variations in hours worked over the year, and from the evidence cited above we expect this to bias the comparisons of productivity against Britain. But we do not expect a rather small bias (estimates for the early 1900s suggest 7 per cent as an order of magnitude) to seriously qualify the conclusions we reach in Table 4.1.

4.2 GLOBAL PRODUCTIVITY AND THE QUALITY OF LABOUR

Keeping potential biases in the estimates for labour inputs in mind, we are now in a position to investigate the relationship between labour productivity and per capita domestic commodity output in Britain and France. The relationship can be expressed in the form of an identity $(O/P = a(O/L))$, and the relevant facts are a comparison of the labour output ratios (O/L) set out in Table 4.2.

Table 4.2 *Productivity of Labour Engaged in Commodity Production in Pounds Sterling 1803–12 to 1905–13*

Periods	Great Britain		France	
(1)	(2)	(3a)	(3b)	
1803–12	45·7	61·4	34·0	
1815–24	41·6	39·0	31·8	
1825–34	41·2	40·8	33·1	
1835–44	46·6	43·3	34·5	
1845–54	47·2	46·0	36·2	
1855–64	53·1	56·0	43·8	
1865–74	65·7	63·4	58·8	
1875–84	68·2	54·0	52·2	
1885–94	73·8	52·8	53·3	
1895–1904	80·3	46·3	48·6	
1905–13	86·3	59·9	58·4	

Note: For conversions of francs into sterling with rates (a) and (b) see Section 2.4 and Appendix A, p. 47.

Sources: See Tables 3.2 and 4.1. Figures represent average labour productivities obtained by dividing commodity output by labour force figures.

By backward extrapolation to 1781–90 we constructed crude estimates that suggest that the productivity of labour employed in French commodity production (agricultural plus industrial output) was above

British levels before the Revolution. We do not place much reliance on 'guesses' for the late eighteenth century, but by the early nineteenth century Britain had jumped into the lead and maintained a position of superiority throughout the classic period of industrialisation and the long Victorian boom. But the productivity of the British labour force only moved decisively ahead during the Great Depression, and the century concludes with a French recovery just before the First World War. This chronology is surprising, because it does not accord either with traditional history or with more recent work on the history of technology which tends to be periodised in terms of a very definite and widening British lead up to mid-century followed by a period when France slowly caught up as its economy diffused techniques and modes of organisation found to be efficient in Britain. The remarkable French upswing just before 1913 is, however, already well documented.[10] Finally, there is no doubt that had French productivity increased at the British rate and thus maintained the differential in output per worker that probably existed before the Revolution, then per capita incomes in France in 1913 would have been well above British levels. Whenever underdeveloped or backward is defined as a failure to realise a potential for economic growth equivalent to a British *rate* of advance in labour productivity, then the performance of the French economy from 1780 to 1914 will be seen as unsatisfactory.

Of course, this kind of judgement begs the question of whether the potential for growth was similar in the two economies, a question that will engage our attention in the analysis of agriculture and industry in Chapters 5 and 6. Meanwhile Table 4.2 does underline the point that estimates of labour productivity in commodity production are a less ambiguous guide to the relative backwardness of the French economy than figures of per capita income – specifically, because the French economy offset the advantage that Britain derived from higher levels of labour productivity by allocating a larger share of its potential labour supply to the production of agricultural and industrial commodities. Thus the proportion of the population aged 10 to 65 years engaged in commodity production seems to have ranged from 42 to 58 per cent in France, compared to 35 to 44 per cent in Britain. This difference in the allocation of labour operated to narrow the gap between output per head and labour productivity. For example, in 1895–04 the gap in the productivity of labour engaged in commodity production came to about 38 per cent in favour of Britain, whereas the British advantage in *domestic output per head* came to only 10 per cent.[11]

There are, moreover, differences in the quality of labour employed from country to country and it would certainly be relevant to estimate the degree to which the productivity of the French labour force fell below British levels because of differences in the age and sex structure, the health, experience, motivation, skill and education of French workers compared to their British counterparts. Data upon these and other attributes which bear upon the quality and intensity of effort made by British and French workers are unfortunately impossible to collate into the kind of indicators that might make systematic comparisons viable.[12] At an impressionistic level there seems to be little in the figures for 1821 and 1911 to suggest that there might have been significant variations in the age and sex composition of the two work forces. For example, in 1911 the French work force contained a higher proportion of manpower in what is normally defined as the most productive age group of 20–64 years – 76 per cent compared to 73 per cent for Great Britain. But this potential advantage was to some extent counterbalanced by the employment of a higher share of female labour in French industry and agriculture – 37 per cent compared to 30 per cent.[13] In 1821 the sex structure of the two *populations* seems to have been almost the same and in so far as the labour force reflects the age and sex characteristics of the population at large, there should have been no significant variations in the quality of British and French workers on that score.[14]

Nor is there any evidence in the proxies for educational attainments of workers in the two societies to indicate any marked differences in the quality of labour available to the two economies. Cipolla's figures suggest that illiteracy among young adult males in 1855 was 32 per cent for France and 28 per cent for Britain. By the end of the century the ratios had fallen to 6 per cent for France and 4 per cent for Britain.[15]

At higher levels of education, descriptive studies of technical, secondary and university education in the two countries do not suggest that formal institutions of learning in Britain were more extensive than, or superior in quality to, comparable intitutions in France. Skills and experience acquired on the job may have raised the relative efficiency of labour available to British industry, particularly in the earlier decades of the nineteenth century. But French industry seems to have compensated for that short-lived disadvantage by importing skilled labour from Britain and Switzerland.[16]

Finally, differences in the actuarial calculations for life expectancy at birth in the two societies are so similar for both earlier and latter decades of the nineteenth century that it would be difficult to maintain that either the British or the French working class enjoyed higher standards of health over the nineteenth century.[17]

To sum up: although our treatment of human capital is too cursory to be conclusive, we are not disposed to expect that variations in the quality of labour available to the two economies constitute anything but a small part of the explanation for the differential in labour productivity set out above.

4.3   LABOUR PRODUCTIVITIES IN AGRICULTURE AND INDUSTRY

The productivity of labour engaged in commodity production also depends upon the weighted sum of labour productivities for agriculture and industry. Differences in productivity across countries are therefore a function of differences in labour productivities within industry and agriculture and of variations in the shares of the labour force allocated between these two sectors (i.e. $O/L = xL(O/L)_a = yL(O/L)_i$).

Thus as we now go on to disaggregate the figures set out in Table 4.2 it is convenient first to compare British and French labour productivities *within* agriculture and industry before turning attention to structural change or the allocation of labour between the two sectors.

First, some reconsideration had to be given to the method adopted to convert francs into sterling. For comparisons of total and per capita commodity output an exchange rate calculated on the basis of overall purchasing power parities for francs and pounds was appropriate. But in order to compare productivities in agriculture and industry the exchange rates should be based upon prices and output weights relevant to those sectors. For example, a comparison of value added per worker in textiles across countries requires a 'textile exchange rate' and an exchange rate based upon a weighted average of all commodity prices would clearly not be suitable.

To solve this problem we calculated pairs of exchange rates for agricultural and industrial commodities based first upon British and then upon French output weights. We had recourse to the data and the methods already described in Sections 2.4 and 2.5 to derive overall commodity exchange rates. Thus in Table 4.3 the conversion of francs into sterling is based upon two separate exchange rates for agricultural and industrial products, weighted first by the composition of French output in the two sectors and secondly by the composition of British output.

Table 4.3 is interesting in many ways, not least because the data appear at several points to run counter to established interpretations of British and French economic development over the nineteenth century. It is certainly surprising to find labour productivity in French industry above British levels until the 1890s. But perhaps the only uncontroversial conclusion that might be accepted on the basis of these estimates is that labour productivity in British farming was consistently and appreciably higher than in French, so that, except for an upswing after 1895, the productivity gap between the two agricultures widened over the entire period. In any case these facts will be discussed in Chapters 5 and 6.

4.4   STRUCTURAL CHANGE

The gap in overall levels of labour productivity between the two

Table 4.3 Labour Productivities in Agriculture and Industry in Pounds Sterling 1781–90 to 1905–13

Periods	Productivity in agriculture Great Britain	Productivity in agriculture France*		Productivity in industry Great Britain	Productivity in industry France*	
(1)	(2)	(3a)	(3b)	(4)	(5a)	(5b)
1781–90	24·7	25·6	25·2	22·3	77·3	53·2
1803–12	52·2	44·8	39·4	38·4	111·2	48·3
1815–24	45·6	32·9	31·3	38·4	56·8	41·2
1825–34	44·3	34·2	32·4	39·2	54·6	42·8
1835–44	50·3	29·9	28·8	44·5	61·6	49·7
1845–54	53·0	29·7	28·9	44·3	64·8	53·5
1855–64	58·4	36·7	36·0	50·7	71·2	60·1
1865–74	67·0	41·9	43·2	62·3	96·5	86·7
1875–84	67·0	33·4	33·8	68·5	85·1	76·4
1885–94	68·8	31·5	31·2	75,0	82·6	74·3
1895–1904	64·6	27·3	26·6	83·7	70·0	73·1
1905–13	64·3	41·6	44·1	90·4	85·2	88·3

*For conversions of francs into sterling at rates (a) and (b) see Sections 2.4 and 2.5.

Sources:

See Tables 3.2, 4.1, 4.4 and 4.5. Figures are average productivities obtained by dividing output of one sector by labour force employed in that sector. The division of the labour force in France between those employed in industry and those employed in agriculture was a problem. J. C. Toutain 'Le Produit de l'agriculture française de 1700 à 1958', *Cahiers de l'ISEA*, AF 2, July 1961, p. 201 has figures for the period after 1855–64 for agriculture and we could estimate the industrial labour force as a residual. For years before 1855 Toutain published figures for males active in agriculture. We calculated the proportion of male labourers in agriculture to total labour force in agriculture for the 1855–1913 period. The figures show a consistent decline, but undoubtedly at a faster rate than would have been the case during the first half of the century. The decline from 1855–64 to 1875–84 is 1·1 per cent, 70·7 per cent to 69·6 per cent. We assumed that this rate of decline also pertained to the first half of the century. Thus for 1781–90 we found male labour force as 73 per cent of total labour in agriculture, and in 1845–54, 71 per cent; the period in between calculated linearly. From these ratios and Toutain's figures on the male labour force in agriculture, we calculated the total agricultural labour force. The industrial labour force was found as the difference between the labour force engaged in commodity production and the agricultural labour force.

Table 4.4   The Structure of Commodity Production (at current prices) 1781–90 to 1905–13

Periods	Great Britain agricultural output £m.	Great Britain industrial output £m.	Great Britain % of commodity output industrial	France agricultural output francs m.	France industrial output francs m.	France % of commodity output industrial
(1)	(2)	(3)	(4)	(5)	(6)	(7)
1781–90	38·3	26·7	41	2,927	2,170	43
1803–12	93·9	61·4	40	3,752	3,260	47
1815–24	82·1	88·4	52	4,206	3,468	45
1825–34	79·8	113·6	59	4,761	4,540	49
1835–44	95·7	146·8	61	4,891	5,984	55
1845–54	105·9	177·3	63	5,654	6,932	55
1855–64	116·9	233·3	67	7,697	8,756	53
1865–74	127·3	326·3	72	8,653	9,787	53
1875–84	113·9	390·7	77	7,992	10,238	56
1885–94	110·1	480·1	81	7,302	10,465	59
1895–1904	103·4	619·2	86	7,560	11,739	61
1905–13	102·9	759·7	88	10,266	15,548	60

Sources: See Table 3.2.

economies also reflects differences in the allocation of labour between industry and agriculture. Almost every version of the retardation hypothesis argues that domestic output per capita in France could have increased more rapidly and that the differential between British and French productivity could have narrowed substantially if the French economy had undertaken more industrialisation. The composition of commodity output and the allocation of resources (labour) between agriculture and industry certainly remained very different in the two countries, right up to 1913.

Table 4.4 simply illustrates the well-known and striking difference in the pace at which the two economies altered the composition of their commodity production over time. At the beginning of the eighteenth century contemporary guesswork suggests that the British economy may have been more industrialised with perhaps between 30 and 34 per cent of its commodity output industrial in form; whereas the comparable French ratio (again a guess) comes to only 26 per cent.[18] Just before the French Revolution the structure of commodity output (in current prices) seems to have been roughly similar in the two countries. Thereafter the composition of physical output changed rapidly in Britain and more gradually in France so that by 1905–13 some 40 per cent of French commodity output consisted of agricultural produce compared to only 12 per cent of British output.

Structural change can also be traced through the allocation of labour between the two sectors. But there are very real difficulties involved in the classification of labour into agricultural or industrial workers in the early stages of industrialisation, particularly for France where the specialisation of labour in agricultural or industrial production alone proceeded more slowly than it did in Britain. Not only are the census categories themselves somewhat arbitrary, but both Toutain and Deane and Cole found it necessary to make questionable assumptions in their attempts to derive separate estimates for agricultural and industrial labour forces. We have already noticed that their estimates cannot be corrected for differences in age, sex and the quality of labour employed in the two sectors. In the end the data in Table 4.5 offer estimates which *suggest* that throughout the period from 1780 to 1914 the share of the labour force engaged in the production of industrial commodities in Britain was around double the comparable ratio for the French economy.

Over the nineteenth century structural change, defined as the reallocation of resources from primary to industrial production, proceeded much further in Britain than it did in France. Yet a comparison of average levels of labour productivity in industry and agriculture (see Table 4.6) suggests that France, not Britain, had far more to gain from the reallocation of labour from agriculture to industry. In fact, until the

Table 4.5   *The Allocation of the Labour Force Employed in Commodity Production 1781–90 to 1905–13. Labour force figures in millions of individuals*

Periods	Great Britain agricultural labour force	Great Britain industrial labour force	Great Britain % of labour force in industry	France agricultural labour force	France industrial labour force	France % of labour force in industry
(1)	(2)	(3)	(4)	(5)	(6)	(7)
1781–90	1·6	1·2	43	5·75	1·35	19
1803–12	1·8	1·6	47	6·03	1·93	24
1815–24	1·8	2·3	56	6·39	2·44	28
1825–34	1·8	2·9	62	6·67	3·10	32
1835–44	1·9	3·3	63	7·04	3·46	33
1845–54	2·0	4·0	67	7·46	3·64	33
1855–64	2·0	4·6	70	7·55	3·99	35
1865–74	1·9	5·0	73	7·20	3·83	35
1875–84	1·7	5·7	77	7·86	4·44	36
1885–94	1·6	6·4	80	7·22	4·56	39
1895–1904	1·6	7·4	82	8·18	5·38	42
1905–13	1·6	8·4	84	8·56	6·29	42

Sources: See tables 4.1 and 4.3.

1870s average output per worker employed in British agriculture (measured in current prices) remained above output per worker in British industry; while in France the average product per worker engaged in industry stood at more than double the product of workers employed in agriculture throughout the nineteenth century. There appears, moreover, to be no tendency for the labour output ratios in the two sectors to converge over the long run – a fact which is in line with Kuznets's expectations based upon long-run trends for a wider sample of countries.[19]

Table 4.6   *Relative Productivities in Industry and Agriculture in Britain and France 1815–24 to 1905–13*

Periods (1)	Great Britain $\frac{(O/L)_i*}{(O/L)_a}$ (2)	France $\frac{(O/L)_i*}{(O/L)_a}$ (3)
1815–24	0·84	2·16
1825–34	0·88	2·05
1835–44	0·88	2·49
1845–54	0·84	2·51
1855–64	0·87	2·15
1865–74	0·93	2·13
1875–84	1·02	2·27
1885–94	1·09	2·27
1895–1904	1·29	2·16
1905–13	1·41	2·06

Sources:
Tables 4.3–4.5. The productivity ratios of industrial compared to agricultural workers have been calculated at current prices in sterling and francs.
*$(O/L)_i/(O/L)_a$ is the ratio of labour productivity in industry to labour productivity in agriculture.

Of course, these estimates are based upon defective statistics. For example, the labour force estimates for agriculture inflate the labour input compared to industry, especially for France where the work force in agriculture was larger in absolute terms and contained a higher proportion of female and child labour. It is also likely that a higher share of industrial output in France was in fact produced by workers classified as agricultural labour in official statistics. Nevertheless, they indicate that with given ratios of labour productivity in industry and agriculture, the French economy obtained relatively large gains from a rather slow process of structural transformation; while the more rapid redeployment of labour in Britain exercised only a marginal impact on the overall increase in labour productivity over the nineteenth century.[20]

French retardation is usually analysed in terms of a failure to industrialise more completely before 1914. Structural change raises the productivity of labour because agriculture (particularly in a nineteenth-century context) was subject to diminishing returns while industry enjoyed a greater potential for technical progress and increasing returns to scale. Furthermore, the rate of growth in the productivity of labour is often correlated with the speed at which labour is absorbed into the industrial sector. Thus structural change is usually favourable because it increases the weight in the economy of sectors with higher productivity levels and with a greater potential for growth in productivity.

All this is obvious enough, but a rise in the share of a country's labour force allocated to industry does not necessarily produce higher levels of development. Nor can the shift of labour from agriculture to industry be equated with the optimal growth path for an economy to take over any period of its history. We have already shown that the slower pace of industrialisation in France did not lead (at least before 1913) to levels of per capita consumption that fell conspicuously below British standards. Only if it can be demonstrated that the more gradual reallocation of labour from agriculture into industry was in some sense economically irrational would it be reasonable to refer to a 'failure' of the French economy to undertake structural transformation.

It is easy to demonstrate that *if* France had reallocated its labour force between agriculture and industry in proportions identical to those observed for Britain from 1780 to 1914 and *if* average product per worker remained at the actual levels already measured for French industry and agriculture, then throughout the nineteenth century both the productivity of its labour force and income per capita would have exceeded British levels by a substantial amount.[21] Counterfactual assumptions of this kind are implicit in many a critique of French retardation. But the idea that structural transformation is an exogenous variable in the growth process, capable of rational manipulation, is certainly unwarranted because the allocation of labour is also a reflection of different patterns of demand for agricultural and industrial commodities. Furthermore, the assumption that the French economy could somehow have undertaken structural transformation more or less along British lines seems unrealistic. A glance at Table 4.5 will show that the proportion of the British work force engaged in industry was double the ratio so employed in France, as early as 1800. *If* the French economy had reallocated labour and duplicated British patterns of structural change, the labour force in French agriculture would have fallen from nearly 6 million in the 1780s to just over 2 million by the First World War and employment in industry would have increased nine times over that same period. In Britain the numbers of workers employed in agriculture actually remained roughly constant for nearly a century and those engaged in industry went up just seven times. Thus the redeployment of labour at the rate implied by some critics was not feasible for the French or any other European economy during the nineteenth century. Emulation of the British model of industrialisation presupposed that something like 45 per cent of workers engaged in commodity production were already employed in industry at the turn of the nineteenth century. The so-called 'failure' of France to catch up with her neighbour had its roots well back in the eighteenth century and possibly earlier.

It is safer to assert that the French economy could have benefited from a more rapid rate of structural transformation between 1780 and 1914, without specifying any feasible rate for the reallocation of labour. Historians of France are, however, willing to entertain the idea that French farms retained reserves of underemployed labour and that if the 'modernisation' of agriculture had occurred over the nineteenth century a large number of farm workers could have been released for employment in industry and urban services. While this may be plausible, it leaves unspecified the magnitude of the gains that might have been derived from the reallocation of labour. The measurement of that magnitude involves assumptions about the numbers of workers who could have been released from agriculture and also assumptions about movements in output per worker in industry and agriculture as labour moved between the two sectors. Many assumptions are possible. In the following exercise we propose to make several which we hope will command acceptance as a more-or-less plausible alternative growth path for France in the nineteenth century.

Perhaps because this is a comparative study we are attracted by the hypothesis that the reorganisation of teneurial institutions, together with the consolidation of French farmland into larger units and some investment, were preconditions for modernisation along British lines. Plans of this type were, moreover, a commonplace conclusion to commentaries on French agriculture at the time. Accepting such plans as a possible choice, we propose to assume that if they had been put into operation then French agriculture could have coped with a labour force which left French farmers to operate with the same number of workers per hectare of cultivated land as British farmers. Table 4.7 is based entirely upon this premise.

All the figures set out in Table 4.7 represent a hypothetical growth path for the French economy from 1815 to 1914. To construct that scenario we assumed that French agriculture retained increasing numbers of redundant workers over the nineteenth century and that with reorganisation the sector possessed sufficient capacity to maintain output at the observed levels while operating with 1 million fewer workers in 1815–24, nearly 2 million fewer workers in 1845–54, and 3·8 million fewer workers in 1905–14. These figures imply that the work force engaged in French agriculture (like British agriculture) would have remained roughly constant over the nineteenth century. Furthermore, we assumed that half the surplus labour released from primary production could have been absorbed into industry without raising or lowering the productivity of labour engaged in that sector. Our model is based upon industry's capacity to absorb surplus labour from agriculture at a constant level of productivity and agriculture's capacity to grow at a constant rate with a smaller labour force.

Thus, having rejected the assumption that a British rate of structural transformation was a feasible target for France over the nineteenth century, we have attempted to *guess* at the difference that a more rapid but more plausible sequence of labour redeployment might have made to levels of productivity and per capita income in France and we have ventured to give the model some arithmetical substance. Comparisons between the hypothetical levels of labour productivity (Table 4.7) and their real levels (Tables 4.2 and 4.3) show that the overall gap in the productivity of labour employed in commodity production in Britain and France would have disappeared, that the superior productivity of British agriculture would have persisted, and that structural transformation (again as posited in the model) would have been almost sufficient to eliminate any gap in per capita income between the two economies. At a rough guess, our hypothetical arithmetic suggests that a plausible reallocation of labour could have boosted French commodity flow by margins that ranged upwards from 4 per cent in 1815–24 to 18 per cent in 1905–14. These ratios might be taken as a very rough measure of the 'loss' sustained by French society for failing to undertake more rapid structural transformation between 1780 and 1914.

That loss was probably not inconsiderable, and French retardation can certainly be conceived in terms of an unrealised potential for economic growth derived from a failure to transfer labour from a low-productivity agricultural sector into industry. Just what that potential was depends entirely on the assumptions made about movements in output per worker in industry and agriculture during the process of structural transformation. Finally, it must be re-emphasised that labour could not be reallocated by fiat. France was not a planned economy. Critics from Britain or America tend to assume that the barriers to structural transformation in nineteenth-century France were largely institutional and cultural in character and had less to do with natural resources, location, climate and other geographical disadvantages. They also tend to ignore demand and the long-term advantages that the British economy enjoyed through trade and commerce with the rest of the world, advantages which originated from

Table 4.7 Hypothetical Labour Productivity in France 1815–24 to 1905–13

Periods	Industrial labour force ('000,000s)	Agricultural labour force ('000,000s)	Labour productivity in industry (£s)	Labour productivity in agriculture (£s)	Labour productivity in commodity production (£s)
(1)	(2)	(3)	(4)	(5)	(6)
1815–24	3·0	5·3	56·8	36·0	43·6
1845–54	4·5	5·6	64·8	53·9	58·7
1875–84	5·8	5·1	85·1	50·1	68·2
1905–13	8·2	4·8	85·2	74·4	81·2

Notes and Sources:

Column 2: Industrial labour force was calculated as equal to the actual labour force hypothetically released from agriculture. The other half is assumed to be employed in services. Throughout the nineteenth century the ratio of workers in services to workers in industry was roughly 1:1 (see Tables 4.1 and 4.5, and Marczewski, 'Le produit physique', table 31).

Column 3: Agricultural labour force is the actual numbers employed in agriculture minus surplus labour employed in agriculture. We calculated 'surplus labour' as equivalent to the residual between actual labour force and 'required labour force' which was in turn defined as the labour force French agriculture *would* have required to farm the same number of hectares per worker as the number of hectares per worker farmed in Great Britain during the same decade. For example, in 1815–24 the agricultural labour force of Great Britain farmed 8·17 hectares per worker; assuming that with modernisation French workers could farm the same number of hectares per worker, the labour force required to farm 43·0 million hectares (the cultivated area of France) was 43·0 ÷ 8·17 = 5·26 million. 5·26 is the 'required' labour force, 6·39 million is the actual labour force and the residual 1·13 million is defined as surplus labour. (Land labour ratios are from Tables 4.5 and 5.1 and the agricultural labour force from Table 4.5).

Column 4: labour productivity in industry is actual productivity copied from Table 4.3.

Column 5: hypothetical labour productivity in agriculture calculated as actual agricultural output (Table 4.4) divided by required labour force, column 3.

Column 6: calculated as agricultural output (Table 4.4) plus hypothetical industrial output = hypothetical labour force in industry (column 2) × actual productivity of labour employed in industry (column 4) divided by hypothetical labour force engaged in commodity production (columns 2 and 3). These hypothetical figures can be compared with actual figures in Table 4.3.

two centuries of successful mercantilism. In any case there is no evidence that the incentives or premiums offered to migrants from agriculture to industry were sufficient to attract far larger numbers of workers into industry. At the same time, the compulsion to move which operated more strongly in the rural economy of Britain seems far weaker in France, where potential migrants preferred to stay in villages and could not be easily forced out. This argument will not conclude that France developed at some warranted rate of growth given by natural resources and political power in the world economy. We have taken the point that French agriculture could have been reorganised in order to release labour while maintaining constant levels of production. We propose to discuss the whole issue of structural transformation in our final chapter. Meanwhile we do plead for recognition of the real constraints that operated upon the rate at which the French economy could redeploy labour between 1780 and 1914.

NOTES TO CHAPTER 4

1 L. Rostas, 'Alternative Productivity Concepts' in *Productivity Measurement*, vol. 1 (Paris: OECD, 1955), and I. Kravis, 'A Survey of International Productivity Comparisons', *Economic Journal*, March 1976.

2 E. F. Denison, *Why Growth Rates Differ* (Washington: Brookings Institution, 1967), and 'Classification of Sources of Growth', *Review of Income and Wealth*, April 1972; S. Kuznets, *Economic Growth of Nations* (Cambridge, Mass.: Harvard University Press, 1971), ch. 2.

3 UN Statistical Commission, *Methodological Problems of International Comparison of Labour Productivity* (New York: 1971), annex III.

4 J. Kuczynski, *A Short History of Labour Conditions Under Industrial Capitalism in Great Britain and the Empire*, vol. IV, *France 1700 to the Present Day* (London: Muller, 1946), p. 133; P. Sorlin, *La société française, 1840–1914* (Paris: Arthaud, 1969), p. 182.

5 A. D. Webb, *New Dictionary of Statistics* (London: Routledge, 1911), p. 624.

6 UK Board of Trade, *Hours and Earnings Inquiry*, 1906–7 (vols 1–8).

7 A. Maddison, *Economic Progress and Policy in Developing Countries* (London: Allen & Unwin, 1970), p. 229. The British worked 295 days at nine hours a day and the French worked 285 days at ten hours a day.

8 Board of Trade, *Hours and Earnings*, vol. 5.

9 R. C. O. Matthews, unpublished manuscript on the growth of the British economy from 1856, ch. 3, appendix 3B; A. Bowley, *Wages and Income in the UK* (Cambridge: CUP, 1937), p. 10; and E. Dolleans and D. Dehove, *Histoire du travail en France* (Paris: Domat, 1953), vol. 1, pp. 286–8.

10 M. Lévy-Leboyer, 'La croissance économique en France au XIXᵉ siècle. Résultats préliminaires', *Annales ESC*, July–August 1968, and F. Crouzet, 'Essai de construction d'un indice annuel de la production industrielle française au XIXᵉ siècle', *Annales ESC*, January–February 1970.

11 Population aged 10–65 are from B. R. Mitchell and P. Deane, *Abstract of British Historical Statistics* (Cambridge: CUP, 1962), pp. 11–12, and M. Lévy-Leboyer, 'La décélération de l'économie française dans la seconde moitié du XIXe siècle', *Revue d'Histoire Economique et Sociale* (1971), 4, p. 481. Figures for labour actually engaged in commodity production are from Table 4.1.

12 See H. Correa, *Economics of Human Resources* (Amsterdam: North Holland Publishing Company, 1963).

13 These ratios were calculated from figures in P. Bairoch, 'The Working Population and its Structure', in *International Historical Statistics*, vol. 1, p. 178, published by Institut de Sociologie de l'Université Libre de Bruxelles, 1968; Mitchell and Deane, *Abstract*, section 1; and J. C. Toutain, 'La population de 1700 à 1959', *Cahiers de l'ISEA*, AF 3, January 1963, ch. 3.

14 For 1821 we used Mitchell and Deane, *Abstract*, p. 11, to show that 52 per cent of the British population were between 20 and 64 years of age and 49 per cent of that group were males. For France the comparable ratios are 53 per cent and 48 per cent. J. Bourgeois-Pichat, 'The General Development of the Population of France since the 18th Century' in D. V. Glass and D. E. C. Eversley (eds), *Population in History*, (Woking: Arnold, 1965), pp. 500–2.

15 C. M. Cipolla, *Literacy and Development in the West* (London: Penguin, 1969), table 28(a). The ratio is calculated as the proportion of bridegrooms who could not sign marriage certificates.

16 W. O. Henderson, *Britain and Industrial Europe, 1750–1870* (Liverpool: University Press, 1954), p. 30.

17 The figures are in A. E. Wrigley, *Industrial Growth and Population Change* (Cambridge: CUP, 1961), table 23, and A. Armengaud, 'Population in Europe' in C. M. Cipolla (ed.), *The Fontana Economic History of Europe*, (London: Fontana, 1973), vol. 3, p. 48.

18 The French figure of 26 per cent is calculated from J. Marczewski, 'Some Aspects of the Economic Growth of France, 1660–1958', *Economic Development and Cultural Change*, April 1961, p. 371 The British figure of 34 per cent is Gregory King's estimate for 1688 in P. Deane and W. A. Cole, *British Economic Growth, 1688–1959* (Cambridge: CUP, 1962), p. 156. The ratio of 30 per cent is based upon backward extrapolation from 1781–90 levels, using eighteenth century real growth rates. We used Deane and Cole's real output indices (*British Economic Growth*, p. 78) to find output in 1700, in prices of 1781–90. We then reflated these values, using the Consumers' Goods price index compiled by Schumpeter and Gilboy for agriculture, and their Producers' Goods index for industry (in Mitchell and Deane, *Abstract*, pp. 468–9). Thus in current prices of 1701, we had an output value of £24 million for agriculture, and £10 million for industry, or 30 per cent of commodity output originating in industry.

19 Kuznets, *Economic Growth of Nations*, pp. 289–95.

20 We owe this point to Professor W. P. Parker of Yale.

21 We did undertake such an exercise and assumed: (a) that France reallocated its labour force between agriculture and industry in proportions to those observed for Great Britain; (b) that average product per worker remained at the observed or measured levels. On these assumptions, agricultural output in 1905–13 fell to 28 per cent of the factual level. Per capita output in France exceeded the level of per capita output in Great Britain by amounts that ranged from 15 per cent in 1815–24 to 36 per cent in 1905–13.

Chapter 5

Agriculture

5.1 LABOUR PRODUCTIVITY

We have already shown that between the late eighteenth century and the First World War labour productivity in British agriculture remained appreciably and consistently higher than productivity per worker employed in French agriculture (see Table 4.3). In a taxonomic sense French retardation might be attributed or imputed entirely to the relative inefficiency of French agriculture, because if French farms had produced an output per worker similar in value to that produced on British farms then, *ceteris paribus*, the gap in total productivity would have disappeared; commodity flow per capita in France would have been between 21 and 41 per cent higher (that is, above British levels throughout the nineteenth century) and historians would be engaged in a discussion of British, not French, retardation, despite the technological superiority of British industry.[1]

Of course statements of this kind, based upon imputed changes in agricultural productivities, ignore the fact (already discussed in Chapter 4) that France retained a relatively high share of its work force in a sector of low productivity. Such statements also beg the question whether French agriculture possessed the capacity to employ the extra 2·8 million workers it did absorb between the 1780s and 1913 (see Table 4.5) and at the same time sustain the kind of increases in marginal and average product per worker that characterised agricultural development in Britain.

Over the nineteenth century (1815–24 to 1905–13) productivity per worker employed in French agriculture grew at 0·25 per cent per annum, compared to a British rate over the same period of around 1 per cent per annum. This marked difference in rates of change in labour productivity occurred partly (but only in small part) because total output grew more slowly. (The rates are close to 1·3 per cent per annum for France and 1·8 per cent for Britain.[2]) The main reason was that the French economy retained a far higher share of its labour supply in the countryside despite the potential advantage that could have been derived from the reallocation of labour to industry. In Britain the work force engaged in agriculture seems to have remained roughly stable for over a century while real output just about doubled.

But the wide and widening gap in the productivity of labour employed in the two agricultural systems does not imply that French peasants simply ignored or failed to take advantage of the new crops and new rotations which raised yields on British farmland.[3] Nor does it mean that British agriculture was more efficient in all its branches or that the institutional framework adhered to in France after the Revolution can be blamed out of hand for the backwardness of agriculture. Simplistic diffusion models are particularly inappropriate devices for understanding the relative efficiency of agricultural systems. Furthermore, and as usual, a comparison of rates of change fails to take account of the 'potential' for development in France. It could be the case that by the end of the eighteenth century productivity in French arable and animal farming was, as Arthur Young thought, well below not only British but potential levels and that the rate of growth in total output achieved by French farmers over the nineteenth century might be criticised for being suboptimal.[4] But that case still needs to be substantiated.

This chapter will analyse the major factors affecting the productivity of labour employed in French agriculture in order to explain and evaluate the relative backwardness of that sector compared to Britain. The gap in value added per worker is related, first, to the area of land cultivated per worker (the land–labour ratio), and secondly, to the yields per hectare of land used to grow crops and to rear animals. Such yields, expressed in value terms, are a compound of physical productivity (measured as bushels per acre, hectolitres per hectare and the weight of animal produce per unit of land devoted to animal feedstuffs) and the product mix. Variations in the latter are relevant because if British farmers and labourers produced a more valuable range of crops and animal produce than agricultural workers in France, then differences in the allocation of land between animal and arable farming and in the mix of crops grown on the arable might be sufficient to account for the gap in labour productivity.

Physical yields per hectare depend upon the quantity and quality of capital available per worker and per hectare, techniques of cultivation, teneurial institutions (organisation) and human capital. Human capital includes the education, skill, knowledge and capacity for work embodied in the agricultural work forces of Britain and France. Techniques of production refer to the organisation and methods employed by farmers for the cultivation of crops and the rearing of livestock. Since so much contemporary writing on British and French agriculture tends to assign primary responsibility to institutional obstacles for the slow diffusion of more efficient techniques of production among French farmers, it seemed appropriate to approach the problem through an analysis of the quantity and quality of land and capital available per worker employed in British and French agriculture from 1780 to 1914. Institutions can then be discussed in their proper place as affecting the rates of capital accumulation in the two agricultural systems.

In formal terms this chapter is organised as a discussion of factors affecting value added per worker employed in British and French agriculture from 1780 to 1914 where:

1   O/L (labour productivity) depends upon H/L (the land–labour ratio, or hectares per worker) and O/H (yields per hectare in value terms).
2   O/H depends upon C (crop mix) and K/H (capital per hectare) and R (a residual that includes the institutions affecting the stock and productivity of capital and labour employed per hectare as well as the quality of labour engaged in agriculture.)[5]

5.2   THE QUANTITY AND QUALITY OF LAND

Among factors affecting the productivity of agricultural labour, traditional emphasis was placed upon the quantity and quality of land cultivated per worker. But the preoccupations of physiocrats and classical economists with land and diminishing returns have almost disappeared from modern literature on agrarian development, largely because relatively cheap substitutes for land have been developed in this century including chemical fertilisers, improved seeds and mechanical power for farm operations and transport. Chemicals restore and can radically improve the nutrient qualities of soil. They allow farmers to cultivate land continuously without recourse to the traditional practice of fallow and also to produce a given output from a smaller area of cropped land. Selected seeds have similar effects. Mechanised forms of power provide substitutes for draught animals and thus 'save' on land, devoted in the past to the production of animal feedstuffs or used as pastures for cattle, oxen and horses.

Between 1780 and 1914 alternatives for land also developed, but cheap substitutes such as chemical fertilisers, electric power and the internal combustion engine only became widely available after the end of the nineteenth century. For most of that century, agricultural production continued to be constrained by the quantity, quality and accessibility of cultivable land. In these technological conditions the preoccupations of classical economists seem well conceived. Even if some of their gloomy prognostications about the effects of the agricultural bottleneck on the overall rate of growth failed to take sufficient account of technical progress and possibilities for international trade in farm produce, they 'knew one big thing', namely that agriculture was strongly conditioned by soil, climate and topography (included here under the generic term of land). Thus any investigation into the gap in labour productivity in British and French agriculture needs to give primary emphasis to supplies of cultivable land in the two countries.

There are, however, serious problems involved in the definition and measurement of the total area of land utilised for agricultural production. Our definition relies upon Toutain's broad or gross definition of *territoire agricole cultivé* for France.[6] This concept was formulated by government officials employed to conduct the agricultural census for France, taken almost every decade from 1840 onwards.[7] It includes land under crops, grass and trees and excludes land left fallow, uncultivable land and land used for non-agricultural purposes. Since possibilities for adjusting the French estimates were limited we decided to use the French definition of *land input* for comparative purposes and to adjust British data to bring them into line with the French concept of cultivated land.

Table 5.1   *Estimates of Land Cultivated in Britain and France 1815–1913*

(1)	France Cultivated area (m. hectares) (2)	Great Britain Cultivated area (m. hectares) (3)	Hectares per worker employed in agriculture France (4)	GB (5)
1815–24	43·0	14·7	6·7	8·2
1825–34	—	14·6	—	8·1
1835–44	42·8	—	6·1	—
1845–54	43·7	15·7	5·9	7·9
1855–64	44·8	—	5·9	—
1865–74	—	14·4	—	7·6
1875–84	44·6	14·9	5·7	8·8
1885–94	44·5	15·4	6·2	9·6
1895–1904	—	15·5	—	9·7
1905–13	46·6	15·6	5·4	9·8

Notes and Sources:
Column 2: the figures are from J. C. Toutain, 'Le produit de l'agriculture française de 1700 à 1958', *Cahiers de l'ISEA*, AF 2, July 1961, p. 214. His definition of '*territoire agricole cultivé*' is set out in AF 1, July 1961, pp. 26–7.
Column 3: British data have been adjusted to bring them into line with Toutain's definition of *territoire agricole cultivé*. The figures for 1865–74 to 1905–13 (inclusive) are official estimates published in Ministry of Agriculture, *A Century of Agricultural Statistics* (London: 1968, table 41) which gives the area under crops and grass in Great Britain from 1866 to 1966. We added an estimate for 'rough grazing land' based upon official figures for 1892–1913 in table 39 of the same publication. We also added official estimates for woodland in Britain (woods, coppices and plantations) published for various years in UK *Statistical Abstract*. We deducted estimates for 'bare fallow' from B. R. Mitchell and P. Deane, *Abstract of British Historical Statistics* (Cambridge: CUP, 1962), pp. 78–9. The British data for cultivated land thus include crops, grassland, woodland and rough grazing. They exclude fallow and land not used for agricultural purposes and are comparable with Toutain's estimates for France. For years before 1867 we used the following contemporary estimates – again adjusted to bring them into line with French definition.

1815–24: This estimate relates to 1812 and comes from J. R. McCulloch, *Statistical Account of the British Empire* (London: Longman, Brown, Green & Longman, 1837), p. 528. McCulloch based his figures on estimates by Middleton, Comber and Stevenson and the *General Report of Scotland*, vol. 1, pp. 37 and 58. We checked his references and adjusted his figures to bring them into line with French concepts and used: J. Middleton, *General View of the Agriculture of Middlesex* (London: Macmillan, 1804), p. 641; W. T. Comber, *An Inquiry into the State of National Subsistence* (London: Cadele & Davies, 1808), p. 52; R. Stevenson, *A General View of the Agriculture of Surrey* (London: Thomas Wilson, 1812), p. 64; H. Beeke, *Observations of the Produce of the Income Tax* (London: Wright, 1800), p. 30, for area of pasture in England and Wales (which is an adjustment of Middleton's estimates). Middleton, Stevenson and Comber are frequently cited by most statisticians who tried to estimate the cultivated area of Britain before 1867. The first two wrote reports for the Board of Agriculture.

We added an estimate for woodland of 2,175,000 acres for 1871–2 based on official returns (cited above). Middleton, *General View of the Agriculture of Middlesex*, p. 641, estimated woodland in 1804 at 2 million acres. Comber, *An Inquiry into the State of National Subsistence*, p. 52, estimated woodland at 1.6 million acres. Our estimate (the official figure for 1871–2) is in line with contemporary estimates. Bare fallow land is excluded from the estimate.

1825–34: Our estimates are based on Couling's figures for 1827 which he compiled for the Select Committee on Emigration, *British Parliamentary Papers* 1826–7 (V), p. 358. Couling was an engineer and surveyor and according to Porter based his estimate on the 'best authorities and a personal inspection during which he travelled over 50,000 miles': G. R. Porter, *Progress of the Nation* (London: Knight, 1836), p. 171. Couling's figures seem to be regarded as the best available by nineteenth-century statisticians such as Porter, McQueen, Poole, Caird and Spackman and are in McCulloch, *Statistical Account of the British Empire* (1837), pp. 528 and 537. Our estimate for woodland is described under 1815–24. Bare fallow land is excluded.

1845–54: The estimate relates to 1846 and is from J. R. McCulloch, *Statistical Account of the British Empire* (London: Heath 1854), pp. 548 and 563. McCulloch surveys all available contemporary estimates but bases his own estimates on Couling's figures for arable adjusted to include additional wasteland brought into cultivation since 1827. We added the official estimate for woodland of just over 2 million acres for 1871–2. Rough grazing land seems to be included in these contemporary estimates. Bare fallow land is excluded from our figures.

Columns 4 and 5 are columns 2 and 3 divided by estimates for agricultural labour force set out in Table 4.5.

Unfortunately, figures for the area cultivated in Britain do not exist before 1866 and we fell back upon contemporary estimates for the first half of the nineteenth century. There is no need to remark on the crudeness of some of the estimates for cultivated area in the two countries. Nevertheless, British farmers and their labourers had significantly more land available to them than farm workers in France. Our table indicates that the addition per worker ranges from 21 per cent in 1815–24 to 79 per cent in 1905–13.

But the British not only farmed a larger area of land per worker, they also obtained higher yields per hectare cultivated than agricultural workers in France (see Table 5.2). It is unrealistic to be precise about the share of the differential in labour productivity that might be imputed to differences in crude land endowment per worker simply because the two factors are interconnected. For example, a more favourable land endowment allowed British farmers to retain more animals per hectare of arable land which raised crop yields via the application of organic fertiliser. Nevertheless, a *lower bound* estimate for the effects of variations in land endowment might be defined as equivalent to the gap that remained in labour productivity after British superiority in yields per hectare has been eliminated. What is involved here is an arithmetical exercise designed to separate out the relative importance of land endowment from crop mix and efficient use of land as causes of the gap in output per worker employed in British and French agriculture. The calculations shown in Table 5.2 rest upon the simple assumption that French farmers obtained the same yield (again measured in value terms per hectare) as British farmers throughout the nineteenth century.

Table 5.2   *Yields Per Hectare and Hypothetical Labour Productivities in British and French Agriculture over the Nineteenth Century*

Years	Actual yields per hectare		Output per worker	
	Great Britain in £s	France in £s	Great Britain (actual output) in £s	France (hypothetical output) in £s
(1)	(2)	(3)	(4)	(5)
1815–24	5·6	4·0	45·6	37·6
1845–54	6·7	5·1	53·0	39·5
1875–84	7·6	6·0	67·0	43·3
1885–94	7·1	5·1	68·8	43·8

Notes and Sources:
Columns 2 and 3 were calculated by dividing estimates for the value of agricultural output in Table 4.4 by estimates of the hectares of cultivated land set out in Table 5.1. Yields per hectare in francs at current prices were converted into sterling at an 'agricultural' exchange rate based on the prices of two commodities (wheat and beef) weighted by the contribution of the arable and animal sectors to total agricultural production in Britain and France. This exchange rate is based upon the methods fully described in Section 2.4. To simplify the data we presented column 3 as an average of output per hectare based upon two exchange rates, one which employed British weights and the other French weights. The conversion rates in francs per £ were: 24·81 for 1815–24; 25·14 for 1845–54; 28·3 for 1875–84; and 34·3 for 1885–94.
Column 4: Labour productivity for Great Britain is copied from Table 4.3.
Column 5: Hypothetical output per worker in France was calculated as follows. The cultivated area for France (see Table 5·1) was multiplied by yield per hectare (in £s) cultivated in Britain. This is the hypothetical output for France *if* yields per hectare had been at British levels. The hypothetical output was then divided by the French agricultural work force to obtain hypothetical output per worker.

This table exposes different facets of efficiency in British and French agriculture. It shows that differences in value added per hectare were not nearly as wide as the gap in labour productivities. Yields per hectare cultivated in France were around 75 per cent of the British level for most of the nineteenth century while the differential in labour productivity ranged downwards from that level at the beginning of the period to 42 per cent in 1895–1904 (compare Tables 4.3 and 5.2). On the basis of admittedly imperfect data, the superiority of British agriculture appears far less pronounced when yields per hectare are taken as the index for comparison.

Furthermore, our exercise suggests that even *if* the efficiency of French agriculture had been pushed to a level where yields per unit of cultivated land were the same in Britain and France, most of the gap in labour productivity would still remain. From the four observations (in column 5 of Table 5.2) and the figures on labour productivity it is possible to calculate that the superior land endowment enjoyed by British farm workers explains somewhere between 58 and 71 per cent of the differential in value added per worker in British and French agriculture. Perhaps not more than 40 per cent of the gap is left to be accounted for by variations in physical yields and in the crop mix.[8]

Another, and perhaps more satisfactory, way of measuring the share of the gap in labour productivity that emanated from a superior endowment of land per worker would be to define that share as equivalent to the decrease in total output per worker that would follow from a hypothetical reduction of the area cultivated in Britain to the point which equalised land–labour ratios in the two agricultural sectors, while leaving the total amount of other inputs (capital and labour) employed by British and French farmers unchanged.

Empirically this exercise presupposes that historians could estimate the yield of land at the extensive margin – a margin equivalent to about one-third of the cultivated area of Britain (one-third is roughly the fraction required to equalise land–labour ratios in Britain and France). The exercise also presupposes that returns (marginal products) from the capital and labour used on such lands, and hypothetically reallocated on to intra-marginal land, could be calculated. There is, however, no way of specifying the shape of the production function for British agriculture over the nineteenth century and we cannot calculate the elasticities of farm output with respect to changes in inputs of land, labour or capital, either over time or across countries.

All these estimates are possibly an overelaborate way of making the point that the relative backwardness of French agriculture cannot be properly understood with reference to the lower productivity of labour employed in that sector, which is much more a reflection of lower rates of structural change and internal migration than inefficient farming *per se*. Nevertheless, the gap in yields (value added) per hectare is still wide enough to support the view that French farmers failed to fully exploit techniques available to them for raising agricultural output (Table 5.2). But before that gap is taken as an indicator of French backwardness, it is necessary to look at the quality of land endowment in the two countries.

Our figures of land input are crude and refer to hectares of cultivable land that differed widely in potential for agricultural production. All too often comparisons of yields per hectare between Britain and France assume that the land in both countries offered a roughly similar potential for agricultural production and that national averages of physical yields per hectare are a valid index for comparisons.[9] That assumption is more acceptable in the second half of the twentieth century because science has steadily diminished the importance of differences in soil, climate and topography. (Bananas can now be grown at the North Pole.) But for most of the period 1780–1914 even slight differences in natural endowment could be significant simply because the technology available to compensate for such variations had not emerged or remained too expensive.

But the problem is how to give proper weight to variations in natural endowment across countries because the injunction presupposes that land can be classified in terms of its natural or inherent capacity for primary production. That capacity is a compound of soil type, precipitation, temperature, relief and elevation, etc.[10] We propose to use modern scientific evidence in an attempt to classify and measure possible variations in the quality of land available to British and French farmers over the previous century.

Physically Britain and France are alike. Both countries have a similar geological base, natural vegetation and climate. Since these interdependent factors determine the quality of soils, Britain and France share a comparable range of soils. But small differences in geology and location have generated differences in their endowments of cultivable land. Furthermore, France is a larger country and thus exhibits wider variations in geological formation and climate than Britain.

Our preliminary classification of land in Britain and France begins with soil. Soil fertility is often discussed in the context of crop production because varieties of plant life require differing types of soil. Nevertheless, all soils possess an inherent fertility as well as a potential for induced fertility. The productive capacities of soils are generally analysed with reference to seven qualities: root room and root hold, aeration and drainage, oxygen and moisture, percolation and temperature, a thermal profile of sixteen essential elements (pH), stable site and erosion.[11] In its recently published soil map of Europe, the Food and Agricultural Organization distinguished the land areas of Britain and

France into twenty-two soil types, overwhelmingly of the gray-podzolic variety which are usually very good for agricultural purposes.[12] France possesses a greater diversity of soils with nineteen different varieties while Britain has thirteen.

Our first task was to convert the Soil Map of Europe into arithmetical shares of the total area occupied by different soils. The areas were measured with a plenimeter and calculated as percentages of each country's total area.[13]

Our initial classification, based on soil alone, showed that compared to Britain the ground surface of France contained 4 per cent more unproductive soil (located in large part on upland and mountainous regions), 4 per cent less soil of a secondary potential and roughly the same share of prime soil. Thus estimates based upon the FAO Soil Map did not lend much support to the traditional view that French agriculture had the advantage of better-quality soils.[14]

However, the quality of a country's natural endowment cannot be appreciated on the basis of soil alone. Climate relief and topography had also to be taken into account. In general terms, the climates of Britain and France are similar. France is somewhat wetter, in that a larger area of the country receives 750–1,000 millimetres of rain per annum and a smaller area receives 500–750 millimetres per annum. The farming areas of both countries are, however, fed with water at an average rate of 24–30 inches a year and heavier rain tends to fall at higher elevations on soil with a low capacity for agriculture, such as Wales and the Scottish Highlands or the Morvan, Vosges and Alps in France.

Again in general, temperatures are somewhat more extreme in France where summers are warmer and winters colder. Southwards from Paris the July temperature averages 68–70° whereas around London the average is only 64°; while the eastern and mountain regions of France remain under snow for months every winter.[15]

Topography not only conditions the process and costs of cultivation but modifies the climate. Thus height alters the length of the growing season; while the slope and aspect of land are important both for ease of ploughing and other operations and also for the incidence of frost. Land may also lie at a level that renders it too wet for the plough or susceptible to flooding. Thus there are upper and lower limits to cultivation, but farming takes place at a variety of elevations above and below sea level and upon slopes that differ enormously in steepness and aspect.[16]

There is no need to belabour points described in standard geographical texts. We used maps and other geographical evidence on climate and topography to amend the preliminary distribution of land in the two countries based on soil alone. Essentially we divided land into seven sub-groups, classified in terms of capacity (soil, climate and relief) to support different types of primary production.

Thus land is used as a technical term defined by its constituent properties of soil, relief, aspect, drainage, and climate. Land quality was determined by juxtaposing the soil profiles of Britain and France against other relevant profiles related to climate, relief, etc. There are numerous systems for the classification of land but we tried to make the system presented here (Table 5.3) 'as objective and uncomplicated as possible'.[17] We preferred a seven-category system cross-cut by reference to elevation in order to produce information on the agricultural potential of land located in Britain and France. The categories used depend heavily on Dudley Stamp's land classification system for Britain.[18]

At the end of a lengthy investigation it remains difficult to arrive at a precise classification of the quality of land available to British and French farmers. Our percentages suggest that the French farmed within a physical environment that (hectare for hectare) was inferior to the natural endowment available to British agricultural workers.

For example, it seems that only 42 per cent of the land surface of France could be classified as land of prime quality, compared with 47 per cent of Great Britain. Nearly 19 per cent of the land of France seems to have been unfit for agriculture or fit only for rough grazing but only 7 per cent of Britain falls into that group (RG and U). Turning to the large residual category (land of secondary potential S^{1-3}) a larger proportion of land of that type in France (29 per cent for S^3) appears to be best suited to forest and low-grade polyculture. In Britain a larger share of such land (some 30 per cent in all for S^{1-2}) seems to possess adequate capacity for arable, mixed farming and good pasture.

In terms of elevation, the sub-totals indicate that France has more of its land at higher levels than Britain. Thus 91 per cent of Britain is located on low plateaux, hills and plains but only 83 per cent of France. Roughly 7 per cent of France is mountainous compared to just under 2 per cent of Britain. There is no necessary relationship between elevation and soil quality, but France does contain less lowland and less productive soils and more mountainous and more unproductive soils.

Our investigation into land–labour ratios in Britain and France cannot offer 'measured' conclusions, but the data do indicate that the land endowment available to British farmers and their labourers exceeded the endowment available to French agricultural workers by a large margin. Furthermore, the 'quality of land' available to British farmers was hectare for hectare definitely superior to the quality of French farmland.

Table 5.3   *The Quality of Land in Britain and France (percentages of total area)*

Soil type	Britain P	S¹	S²	S³	RG	U	France P	S¹	S²	S³	RG	U
Low plateaux, hills, plains												
Acid brown forest	2·0	1·0	6·4	8·5				1·0		4·4		0·3
Podzolised		1·0	6·96	3·0	3·7					1·4		1·4
Podzolised/organic			3·0	2·0	2·0							
Organic	3·42		3·43									
Organic/podzolised		1·0	1·6									
Gray brown podzolic	23·86						22·2					
Gray brown podzolic/podzolised	0·6								3·0	3·1	1·2	
Gray brown podzolic/pseudogley										2·0		
Gray brown podzolic/brown forest	12·39						17·5			0·16		
Regosols								0·5		6·0		
Regosol/rendzinas								1·0		9·0		1·5
Brown forest/regosol												
Alluvial	4·5					0·17	2·5	0·4		1·5	0·4	0·5
Red mediterranean												
	46·77	3·0	19·79	15·1	5·7	0·17	42·20	1·90	3·0	21·76	1·6	2·0
Subdued mountains, high plateaux												
Brown forest/rendzinas								0·4			4·2	
Acid brown forest/rankers		6·87							0·9	1·8		
Brown mediterranean/lithosols								0·2			1·0	0·8
Red mediterranean/lithosols								0·15			0·63	0·62
		6·87						0·75	0·9	1·8	5·83	1·42
Mountains												
Lithosols											0·1	0·5
Lithosols/podzolic					1·1						0·3	
Lithosols/rendzinas								0·2			1·7	
Lithosol/ranker/podzolic				0·8				0·3			1·8	1·8
				0·8	1·1			0·5			3·9	2·3
	46·77	9·87	19·79	15·9	6·8	0·17	42·2	3·15	3·9	29·36	11·33	7·42

Notes and Sources:

P = Prime land suitable for intensive farming, horticulture

S = Land of secondary quality, best suited for:

S¹ = Arable
S² = Mixed farming
S³ = Forest and low-grade polyculture
RG = Rough grazing
U = Unproductive land.

The sources and methods have been given in the text.
The percentages are subject to rounding.

5.3 PRODUCT MIX AND VALUE ADDED PER HECTARE

While differences in the quantity and quality of land account for most of
the gap in the productivity of labour employed in British and French
agriculture, something like 40 per cent was still due to the superior
yields per hectare achieved by British farmers and their labourers. Some
part of that advantage came from contrasts in the product mix, especially from the higher British share of net value added in agriculture
derived from animal husbandry. Our estimates suggest that animal
produce (meat, milk, eggs, poultry, fibres, skins, etc.) provided 42 per
cent of net output in 1815–24 and that this share rose to 68 per cent by
1905–13.[19] In France that share rose from about 30 per cent at the
beginning of the century to around 43 per cent just before the First
World War.[20]

Unfortunately, we cannot present a detailed breakdown of the
commodity composition of agricultural output in Britain and France.
For Britain relevant data are not available before 1867 and the estimates
after that date, for both countries, relate to gross output – that is, to
the gross value of sales plus farm consumption for ten sub-sectors of
agriculture (Table 5.4).

Table 5.4 *The Composition of Agricultural Output/Sales*
in Britain and France 1865–74 and 1905–14

	Commodity	1865–74		1905–14	
		GB	*France*	*GB*	*France*
		%	%	%	%
1	Cereals	24	26	11	20
2	Potatoes	6	3	5	5
3	Fruit and vegetables	5	4	5	8
4	Industrial crops	2	3	1	2
5	Hay, straw, animal feed	4	25	3	28
6	Vines and cider	—	14	—	8
7	Meat	37	12	44	14
8	Milk	15	8	23	10
9	Wool and silk	4	1	2	—
10	Eggs and poultry	3	4	6	6

Notes and Sources: The percentages refer to the gross value of output (*produit global*)
in each sub-sector of agriculture in current prices. The French data are from Toutain,
'Le produit de l'agriculture' (AF 1), pp. 7–9. The British estimates are from E. M.
Ojala, *Agriculture and Economic Progress* (London: OUP, 1952), table XXII.
Ojala's figures refer to the UK and to 1867–76 and 1904–13. The figures are not
strictly comparable. Ojala's figures refer to gross output but Toutain seems to be
working with a concept of gross sales.

Ideally, we required estimates for net value added in various branches
of agriculture, but some contrasts are obvious enough. Looking first at
the mix of crops produced within the arable sector, we observe that

there is no British equivalent to the cultivation of vines and that French farmers continued to grow more wheat and other cereals at a time when Britain became steadily more dependent upon imported grains. If we complement the information contained in Table 5.4 with some estimates related to the allocation of arable land for 1892, we observe that British farmers allocated higher percentages of their land to root crops and oats than French farmers, who favoured the cultivation of wheat.[21] This does not imply that the latter could have increased the value added per hectare by reallocating arable land along British lines. On the contrary, if French farmers had adopted a British crop mix, output per hectare of arable land in France would have declined.[22]

British superiority was not due to a more efficient allocation of arable land among different crops, and the really significant difference is found in the different proportions of output derived from animal farming. Britain was far more orientated towards animal husbandry than France and higher returns per hectare could usually be obtained from the allocation of land to stock rearing. In the 1860s and 1870s value added per hectare in British agriculture may have been 15 per cent higher in animal than arable husbandry. With the influx of American wheat and the depression of grain prices after 1870 the return may have been as much as 65 per cent higher by 1905–13.[23] Although we hestitate to cite figures, returns in animal husbandry seem to have been even higher in France.[24] Thus if French farmers had found it possible to devote something like the British proportion of their farmland to animal husbandry, the observed differential in value added per hectare would have been smaller.

We knew this would have been the case but unfortunately cannot measure the effects that flowed from the different allocation of land because no estimates for the *total* area of land devoted to the production of grass, hay, straw, artificial grasses and other fodder crops (including grains) are available. The missing figures are the acres and hectares of land used to grow fodder crops, such as oats fed to animals, clover, lucerne, sainfoin, root crops, etc.[25] All we have on the input side are estimates for the area of land given over to grass, pasture and rough grazing in the two countries, but striking contrasts again emerge. Thus between 1815 and 1914 about 54 per cent of the cultivable land of Britain was used as pasture for cattle, sheep, pigs, horses and goats, compared to only 23 per cent of France.[26] Already at mid-century from a far smaller area of farmland British farmers used some 8 million hectares for pasture while French farmers used only 9 million hectares of land for pasture.

Farmers in Britain and France used meadows along waterways and better pasture to raise cattle while poorer grazing land tended to support sheep. The capacity of land used as grass pasture and rough grazing to support animals seems to have been roughly similar in Britain and France. In 1852 the number of sheep per 100 hectares of pasture was 350 in France and 320 in Britain and the ratios for cattle come to 120 for France and 70 for Britain.[27] Furthermore, the animal stock of France contained a far higher proportion of cattle and pigs than Britain where sheep accounted for roughly three-quarters of the stock. During the period 1862–1914 cattled formed 18 per cent of the British animal stock and 29 per cent of the French stock, pigs 7 per cent and 15 per cent respectively, and sheep 75 per cent and 56 per cent respectively.[28] In 1862 French cattle cost ten times as much as sheep and a mature pig sold at twice the price of a sheep.[29]

From these figures it looks as though French agriculture sustained more animals and more valuable animals per unit of grass and pasture than animal husbandry in Britain. We do not know the proportions of arable land farmers allocated to grow fodder crops for their animals either in Britain or in France. But unless British farmers obtained significantly higher physical yields per hectare in animal husbandry (physical yields measured as meat per live animal, litres of milk per cow, eggs per hen, kilogrammes of wool per sheep, etc.), these figures lead to the conclusion that the yield or value added per hectare of *all* land allocated to animal farming in Britain was probably not greater than land similarly deployed in France.

Of course the information available did not permit us to conduct an adequate investigation into the efficiency of animal husbandry in Britain and France. Nevertheless, that information does not dispose us to expect that much if anything of the differential in value added per hectare stemmed from more efficient stock rearing in Britain. It was not the higher yields or greater efficiency of the animal sector of British agriculture that stands in marked contrast to France. Nor can it be maintained that French farmers allocated arable land inefficiently among different crops. It was rather the allocation of a far greater share of farmland and other resources to the rearing of stock, especially sheep, that distinguished British farming in the nineteenth century. This contrast between an animal-intensive agriculture in England and a far greater emphasis on arable farming in France is, however, central to the explanation of differences achieved in value added per hectare in the two countries: not only are animal products more valuable, but the density of animals per hectare of arable land was a critical determinant of the level physical yields achieved in the cultivation of grains, vegetables and other crops.

5.4 FARM ANIMALS AS CAPITAL GOODS

Differences in labour productivity should be related to differences in the ratios of land to labour (hectares per worker employed in British and French agriculture) and to ratios of capital to labour in the two agricultural systems. Capital refers to reproducible capital such as buildings, machinery and equipment, implements, hedges, trees, drains, roads, tracks and animals used in the production of farm output.

During the nineteenth century capital in agriculture was, to a considerable extent, formed with inputs produced within the sector. Capital purchased from industry, such as machinery, implements and chemicals, formed a small, if growing, proportion of the capital stock. Capital formation in both British and French agriculture might be described as a labour-intensive process, designed to make each hectare of cultivable land into a hectare of comparable quality and accessibility. Gestation periods were long and the productivity of investment at the margin depended on the size and quality of the stock of capital already in place. There could be jumps in the capital output ratio as capital per unit of labour and land approached some critical minimum level. Although the process of capital formation can be described usable estimates of the quantity of capital available per worker in British and French agriculture have not been compiled.[30] We intend to concentrate upon a single but critical component of the capital stock, namely farm animals.

Over the nineteenth century the employment of steam engines in European agriculture increased but remained on a fairly limited scale. Power in agriculture continued to be provided by people, the elements (wind and water) and above all by animals, particularly horses and draught cattle which supplied most of the energy required for cartage, transport, ploughing, harvesting and other operations on the farm. Obviously some index of the availability of animal power to British and French farmers is relevant if we are to understand variations in output per worker employed in the two agricultures. That index is provided in Table 5.5.

Our estimates suggest that the animal power available to the agricultural work force for the cultivation of arable land in Britain exceeded the amount used by French workers by a considerable margin. This margin is, moreover, understated by the figures cited in Table 5.5 because the horse was considered to be a more efficient animal than the ox and other *boeufs travail* which constituted the majority of animals used on French farms.[31]

For the kind of pre-chemical agriculture that operated over most of Western Europe during the period 1780–1914, animals also supplied most of the organic fertiliser utilised in arable farming. Historically, farm animals functioned as capital goods for transport and the production of organic fertiliser vital for higher yields per hectare deployed in the cultivation of grain, vegetables and other crops.

Table 5.5   *Animal Power in British and French Agriculture in 1892*

	Draught horses 000s (1)	Draught cattle 000s (2)	Ratio of animal power per hectare of 'arable' land (3)	Animal power per worker employed in agriculture (4)
Great Britain	1,027	—	1 : 6·4	1 : 1·6
France	1,322	1,387	1 : 11·4	1 : 2·6

Notes and Sources: Draught animal totals for Great Britain are from Ministry of Agriculture, *Agricultural Statistics* (London, 1893), p. 64. For France they are from Statistique de la France, *Résultats généraux de l'enquête décennale de 1892* (Paris, 1897), pp. 120 and 124. Our figures are horses and *boeufs travail*. The sources for hectares of arable land and workers employed in the two agricultural systems are cited under Tables 4.5 and 5.1.

There are figures available for the stocks of live animals (cows, sheep, pigs, horses) in Britain and France and it is possible to produce rough estimates of the annual *flows* of manure produced by these animals. Such flows can, in turn, serve as a proxy for the volume of organic fertiliser potentially available for application on to the arable land of Britain and France.

An exercise along these lines generated estimates for the volume (measured in chemical equivalents) of domestically produced organic fertiliser *available* per hectare of arable farmland in the two countries for the 1830s, 1850s and 1890s (Table 5.6). The sources and methods used to construct these figures have been outlined below the table where the steps involved in converting figures related to the animal populations of Britain and France into flows of manure and finally into nitrogen, phosphorus and potassium equivalents have been fully specified. We have *not* measured the actual amount of organic fertiliser *applied* to the arable land of Britain and France. Manure was not all gathered. Its properties were vulnerable to leaching and imperfect storage. Dung could be improved by the addition of straw and its quality varied with the food intake of the animals excreting it. Furthermore, our figures take no account of imports of organic or chemical fertilisers, but the British advantage over France could only appear more marked if import figures were taken into the comparison. Between 1871 and 1880 Britain imported about 365,000 metric tons of fertiliser a year compared to a French import of around 116,000 metric tons.[32]

Inevitably the estimates are no more than guesses at orders of magnitude but they help to bring out one very significant difference between the two farming systems, namely that supplies of domestically produced fertiliser *available* for application on to the arable land of France

Table 5.6   *Production of Domestic Organic Fertiliser*
in Great Britain and France 1837–92

Year	Total availability in millions of metric tons		Arable land (millions of hectares)		Volume of fertilisers available in kilogrammes per hectare of arable land	
	Great Britain	France	Great Britain	France	Great Britain	France
1830s	1·034	1·787	5·5	25·4	188	70
1850s	1·148	1·964	6·6	26·1	174	75
1890s	1·644	2·070	6·6	23·7	249	87

Notes and Sources:
The methods and sources used to calculate the volume of organic fertiliser per hectare for Great Britain and France were as follows.
1. Figures for the animal population of France are from: l'Archive Nationale F20/724, *Tableau des recensements des animaux*, 1839 – for 1839; Statistique de la France, *Statistique Agricole* (Paris, 1858), vols 1 and 2 – for 1852; *Enquête décennale de 1892* – for 1892.
2. Figures for the animal population of Great Britain are from: McCulloch, *Statistical Account of the British Empire*, p. 530, and *Edinburgh Encyclopaedia* (Edinburgh: Longmans, 1830), pp. 730–2, and P. Deane and W. A. Cole, *British Economic Growth, 1688–1959* (Cambridge: CUP, 1962), p. 195 – for 1837; McCulloch, *Statistical Account of the British Empire* (1854), pp. 489, 495 and 500, and B. Poole, *Statistics of Commerce* (London: 1852), p. 69, and M. Block, *Statistique de la France* (Paris: Amyot, 1860), p. 93 – for 1854; Ministry of Agriculture, *Agricultural Statistics* (London, 1892) – for 1892.
We next attempted to group the animal populations by age and weight.
The age distribution for the British animal population for 1892 was derived from age profiles for the animal population of 1916–20 (Ministry of Agriculture, *A Century of Agricultural Statistics*, p. 123) and from the French data for 1892 from the source cited above. For 1854 and 1837 the age profile was based on French data for 1862, Statistique de la France, *Résultats généraux de l'enquête décennale de 1862* (Strasbourg: 1870).
For France the age profiles are given in the *enquête décennale* for 1862 and 1892. For 1839 we used the source cited above for animal population.
For the *live* weights of cattle, pigs, sheep and horses we used the figures from the Statistique de la France, *Statistique Agricole*, vols 1 and 2. In other words, we used a constant average weight for each animal at each age throughout the century.
To estimate the weight of manure produced per animal per year we deployed coefficients for the average volume of dung produced by modern animals of the same weight and age per year. Finally the estimates for manure produced were converted into nitrogen, phosphorus pentoxide and potassium-oxide equivalents – again using modern conversion coefficients. Both sets of coefficients came from: S. L. Tisdale and W. L. Nelson, *Soil Fertility and Fertilizers* (New York: Collier-Macmillan, 1956), p. 231, and K. Paisley, *Fertilizers and Manures* (London: Collingridge, 1960), p. 116.
Sources for the estimates of hectares of arable land are cited under Table 5.1.

was around 45 per cent of the amount available per hectare in Britain. Organic fertilisers are produced mainly by farm animals, and the stock of such animals depends on the allocation of land between arable and pasture. Thus the relatively high availability of fertiliser in Britain reflects the fact that a far greater proportion of the land utilised consisted of pasture and rough grazing.

To reiterate, it is the allocation of so much land to pasture that seems peculiar to Britain. The accumulation of a stock of animals which provided British cultivators with more draught power and far greater quantities of organic fertiliser per hectare of arable land gave them the superiority not only over French farmers but over farmers in other regions of Europe as well. Just how far back in history these advantages can be traced is difficult to ascertain. They seem to have been obvious to some agronomists as early as the seventeenth century and became really significant when European population growth accelerated in the second half of the eighteenth century. But there is no mistaking the benefits that accrued to agriculture and the British economy from the accumulation of farm animals. Value added per worker went up as the product mix shifted in favour of higher value outputs associated with animal farming. At the same time increased supplies of animal power saved labour per unit of arable output. There is no way of measuring the amount of labour time saved through the substitution of animal power in British agriculture, but farm animals must be considered in any discussion of variations in labour productivity and land–labour ratios observed for British and French agriculture. Agricultural capacity to release labour for industrial employment is, of course, related to the availability of substitute forms of draught power for ploughing, cartage and transport of all kinds. More important, animal husbandry in most of its branches is a less labour-intensive and seasonal activity than arable farming. Certainly it would be interesting to know the proportion of the French labour force retained in the countryside in order to cope with the more cyclical work rhythms of cultivating arable land, as compared to a more regular work cycle of labour engaged in rearing livestock.

5.5 OUTPUT PER HECTARE IN PHYSICAL TERMS

We propose to conclude the attempt to explain variations in the productivity of labour engaged in British and French agriculture by comparing physical yields per hectare employed in the cultivation of crops, particularly cereals and potatoes. These ratios have been deliberately considered last because too many commentaries on French retardation assume that Britain's superiority in labour productivity emanated from higher yields in animal and arable husbandry. That was not the case. In agriculture French backwardness stemmed mainly from a lower endowment of farmland per worker and an allocation of land that gave far less emphasis to animals than Britain. Differences in the land–labour ratio probably accounted for well over half of the gap in labour productivity and variations in product mix accounted for a substantial share of the remainder. We are not disposed to think that the gap in physical yields per hectare could account for more than a third of the marked superiority in the productivity of British agricultural workers.

There is, moreover, little evidence that the animal sector of British agriculture was more efficient than its counterpart in France. On the contrary, in terms of animal produce obtained per hectare of land allocated to grass and pasture it appeared that French farmers obtained slightly better yields already by mid-century. Our selection of partial productivity indicators for the 1900s also suggests that French farmers

Table 5.7   *Productivity Ratios for Animal Husbandry, 1892 to 1907/8*

	Great Britain		France	
	Weight	*Years*	*Weight*	*Years*
1 Meat produced per head of cattle slaughtered	306 kg	For 1907–8	421 kg	1909–11
2 Veal produced per calf slaughtered	44 kg	For 1907–8	96 kg	1909–11
3 Meat produced per sheep slaughtered	30 kg	For 1898–1903	26 kg	1909–11
4 Lamb produced per animal slaughtered	18 kg	For 1898–1903	—	—
5 Pork produced per pig slaughtered	71 kg	1907–8	114 kg	1909–11
6 Milk produced per cow and heifer in milk or in calf	1375 l	1907–8	1600 l	1885–94
7 Wool produced per sheep	2·2 kg	1892	2·4 kg	1892
8 Eggs produced per fowl	48	1907–8	46	1892

Notes and Sources: The French figures for 1909–11 relate to the abbatoir for Paris (La Villette) published in Ministère de l'Agriculture, *Statistique agricole annuelle*, 1912. The figures for eggs and wool which refer to 1892 are from *Enquête décennale de 1892*. Milk yields per cow in milk are from J. C. Toutain, *La consommation alimentaire en France de 1789 à 1964* (Paris: Presses Universitaires de France, 1971), p. 1951. The British ratios were calculated from estimates published by Board of Agriculture and Fisheries, *The Agricultural Output of Great Britain* (London, 1912), and *Journal of the Royal Statistical Society*, 1904.

did as well as, and often better than, their British rivals in the production of meat, milk, eggs and wool, and their superiority went back at least to 1852 and possibly earlier (Table 5.7).[33]

No, it was on arable land that British farmers obtained results way ahead of those achieved by farmers in France. By the end of the nineteenth century their superiority was patently obvious to officials of the Ministère de l'Agriculture who regularly published comparisons with British grain yields in *Statistiques agricoles* and *Enquêtes décennales*. Physical yields which are averages for the whole of Britain and France conceal regional disparities, and the figures cited in Table 5.8 refer to only a sample of crops grown on arable land. Nevertheless, such averages are frequently used as the basis for condemning French farmers for their failure to adopt techniques of cultivation, larger units of production and modern systems of tenure, perceived as 'preconditions' for higher yields and held to be at the back of the outstanding performance by British farmers. The differentials are very wide. By 1902

Table 5.8 *Physical Yields on Arable Land in Britain and France in 1862, 1892 and 1902 (in kilogrammes per sown hectare)*

	1862		1892		1902	
Crop	Ireland	France	Great Britain	France	Great Britain	France
Wheat	1,399	1,201	1,840	1,267	2,293	1,359
Barley	1,802	1,207	2,092	1,186	2,105	1,366
Oats	1,487	1,122	1,739	1,084	1,903	1,211
Potatoes	6,783	11,555	14,618	10,500	14,114	7,671

Notes and Sources:

1862 France: *Enquête décennale de 1862*.

1892 France: *Enquête décennale de 1892*.

1902 France: Ministère de l'Agriculture *Statistique agricole de 1902*.

Yields expressed in quintals and hectolitres per hectare were converted into kilogrammes per hectare by using the conversion coefficients published by Ministère de l'Agriculture in *Statistique agricole de 1902*.

1862 Ireland: from Mitchell and Deane, *Abstract*, p. 92. To compensate for the bad harvests of 1861 and 1862 we took average yields 1860–5. The figures are in tons and cwts and converted at 220·46 lb = 100 kg. We know from Craigie's estimates for 1882 that Irish yields were slightly below British yields for wheat, above British yields for barley and below British yields for oats – Craigie, 'On Statistics of Agricultural Production', *Journal of the Royal Statistical Society*, March 1883, p. 19. It is clear, however, that Irish potato yields were well below yields in Britain – compare Mitchell and Deane, *Abstract*, with Ministry of Agriculture, *A Century of Agricultural Statistics*, table 59.

1892 and 1902 Great Britain: from ibid., tables 56–9.

Converted to hectares and kilogrammes at 2·471 acres = 1 hectare and 2·2046 lbs = 1 kg.

average wheat yield in Britain was 69 per cent above the yield obtained in France; for barley the differential amounted to 54 per cent, for oats 57 per cent and for potatoes as much as 84 per cent. There seems, moreover, to be no tendency for the gap in output per hectare to diminish over time. Whether we take comparisons back to 1862 or forward to 1913 British superiority seems to rise steadily in almost all grains and potatoes.[34]

Before such 'facts' are taken as proof of gross inefficiency and placed high on the list of factors retarding the development of France the analysis must be taken further. Within the wider context of French backwardness, we have already argued that even *if* French farmers had raised yields on arable land to British levels, most of the differential in output and income per worker employed in agriculture would have remained. This is mainly because cereals and potatoes formed only a part of French agriculture – 30 per cent of gross output in 1905–13 – and there is no evidence that yields in other sectors fell substantially below British levels. In the cultivation of hay and other fodder crops and in sugar beet French yields seem to have been up to and above British yields.[35] We know that French farmers were not 'backward' in animal husbandry – that is, in the production of meat, milk, eggs, silk, wool, butter and cheese. No data are available for fruit and horticulture. Industrial crops grown in France (such as vines, olives, tobacco, hemp, flax and linseed) have no British counterpart. But there are no reasons to expect lower French yields for market gardening or in the cultivation of industrial crops.

Thus their presumed incompetence seems to have been based on low yields in the cultivation of grains and potatoes – not an insignificant part of agriculture, but not large enough to have made all that much difference, because it can easily be shown that even if French yields in the cultivation of cereals equalled the levels obtained in Britain, total output and output per worker would have been not more than 20 per cent higher.[36] In other words, an outer bound estimate of the share of the gap in labour productivity that could be attributed to some sort of entrepreneurial failure by French farmers comes to about 30 per cent.

Although this estimate relates to the very end of the period, we are disposed to regard it as a representative average for the whole of the nineteenth century because the gap in output per hectare sown with cereals was definitely wider in 1904–13 than it had been fifty years before (see Table 5.8). It probably narrowed during the Agricultural Revolution in France from the 1820s to the 1870s.[37] Furthermore, we also favour explanations for the gap in physical yields that emphasise two things: firstly, the long-run relocation of cereal crops on to land with natural advantages for the cultivation of wheat, barley, oats and rye; and secondly, the long-term rise in the volume of fertiliser applied to arable land, with chemicals assuming greater importance in the twentieth century. These trends are well documented in the histories of agricultural development in the two countries. Thus although the absolute numbers of hectares sown with cereals seem to have remained about constant between 1800 and 1900, those hectares became steadily more concentrated in Britain, whereas in France most farms and every department continued to produce grain throughout the century.[38] The growing disparity in the application of organic fertiliser to arable land can be seen from the data in Table 5.6 and those facts can be complemented by Dovring's estimates of chemical fertiliser applied per hectare of arable land in the two countries.[39]

While higher yields could certainly have increased labour productivity in France, the potential loss from the failure of French farmers to obtain British levels of output per hectare in cereal cultivation was never very large. Nevertheless, the rather wide differentials in the average quantity of wheat, oats, barley and potatoes harvested per unit of land in Britain and France need to be considered further, basically because the backwardness of French agriculture is usually analysed in terms of physical output per hectare. At the centre of most explanations for the gap in yields are arguments which emphasise differences in farm size, tenure and the quality of farm workers in the two countries. This thesis of 'entrepreneurial failure' finds graphic expression in a book published in 1852, *Claret and Olives*.

The French are undoubtedly at least a century behind us in agricultural science and skill. . . . When I say this I mean that the immense majority of the cultivators are unlettered peasants – hinds – who till the land in the unvarying mechanical routine handed down to them from their forefathers. Of agriculture, in any other sense than the rule of thumb practice of ploughing, sowing, reaping and threshing, they literally know nothing. Of the rational management of land . . . they think no more than honest La Balafre, whose only notion of a final cause was the command of his superior officer. I do not mean to say that here and there, all over France, there may not be found active and intelligent resident landlords, nor that in the north of France, there may not be discovered intelligent and clear headed tenant farmers; but the rule is as I have stated. Utterly ignorant boors are allowed to plod on from generation to generation wrapped in the most dismal mists of agricultural superstition. . . . The infinitesimal patches of land are cultivated in the most rude and uneconomical fashion. Not a franc of capital further than that sunk in the purchase of spades, picks and hoes is expended on them. They are undrained, ill-manured, expensively worked . . .[40]

There is no need to chronicle further a tradition of castigation which comes right up into modern literature. We are, however, extremely sceptical about the weight placed upon human factors in explanations offered for the backwardness of French agriculture before 1914.[41]

Lavergne, a contemporary of Caird's who had studied both French and British agriculture, regarded French peasants as 'the most laborious, intelligent and economical, perhaps that exist'.[42] His views certainly deserve more attention than the random impressions of English travellers. But some reference to the human factor is called for because even if the capacities and skills embodied in the agricultural work forces of Britain and France cannot be measured with any degree of accuracy, it would be myopic to ignore some rather obvious differences in their composition.

For example, French agriculture employed a higher proportion of female labour. Between 1851 and 1911 that percentage proportion amounted on average to about 33 per cent of the labour force, compared to a British ratio of $7\frac{1}{2}$ per cent.[43] Our previous discussion on literacy suggested that differences in the educational levels attained by workers in the two societies could not be regarded as a significant source for overall differences in labour productivity; but for the agricultural sector which employed a relatively high proportion of female labour, education could be more important simply because women were on average less well educated than men.

Such facts should be mentioned but they do not permit us to 'measure' possible differences in the quality of agricultural workers in Britain and France. We could adopt the kind of assumptions now common in the estimation of production functions across countries and assign weights to the number of female workers employed on British and French farms in order to standardise statistics for the labour input in agriculture.[44] Such weights are inputed on the basis of wage differentials between male and female labour. But we see no reason to assume that wage rates paid by French farmers were proportional to the marginal productivities of their male and female workers; particularly as a fairly high proportion of female workers in the agricultural sector of France consisted of relatives and there is no institution quite so efficacious for extracting optimal work loads as the family.

Male agricultural workers probably worked longer hours and were perhaps endowed with a greater skill and physical capacity for farm work than their female partners but, *a priori*, there is still no basis for the argument that variations in the sex composition of the two work forces may have been significant, because even if we define each unit of female labour engaged in agriculture as equivalent to half the input supplied by each male employed, the overall gap in the productivity of labour would still remain very wide. For example, between 1855 and

1913 labour productivity in French agriculture fell 33–58 per cent below British when measured with an unweighted index for labour input (see Table 4.3, p. 91). With labour input figures revised in the way suggested to take account of the higher proportion of women employed in French agriculture, the gap in productivity continued to range from 25 to 56 per cent.[45] Other factors such as education, health and motivation which affect the *relative* quality of agricultural labour are not likely to have exerted any significant influence on yields per hectare in the two countries. We must, however, admit that there is almost no historical writing on British or French farmers that would allow us to evaluate the managerial abilities of the two groups. The same is, of course, true for British and French industrialists, but poverty of evidence does not seem to have inhibited controversy about the supposed entrepreneurial failure in French industry.[46] However, turning again to the hypothesis of entrepreneurial failure, we reiterate that low yields were confined to arable farming. Even within that sub-sector of agriculture, estimates that refer to Britain and France conceal regional and local deviations from national averages. The dispersion about the mean may have been far wider in France than in Britain, where grain production had become concentrated in the 'right' locations, whereas in France cereals and potatoes continued to be grown on soils and at elevations and in climatic conditions long since abandoned in England to animal husbandry or to more suitable crops. We have already shown that the quality of land available to British farmers tended, hectare for hectare, to be superior to French farmland, and a recent text on wheat found that 'taking everything into consideration England is probably the best country in the world from the wheat producer's point of view'.[47] Since a comparable French study on cereals held that variations in the quality of soil had a great deal to do with higher wheat yields obtained in Britain in the late nineteenth century, we decided to compare yields per hectare *on land of prime quality* sown with wheat between 1815 and 1892.[48]

Unfortunately, the data available do not refer to farms, *per se*, but consist of estimates of yields per hectare on land sown with wheat in various departments of France and counties of England and Wales. These figures are still useful because it is possible to select samples of administrative units which are in large part (80 per cent was the proportion used) located on land of the best quality (see Table 5.3). The samples include such counties as Norfolk, Lincolnshire and Worcester and such departments as Nord, Pas de Calais and Seine, long recognised as the best-endowed farming regions in both countries (see Table 5.9).

While these figures are far from ideal (particularly for 1815) they are accurate enough to make one large point, namely that over the

Table 5.9   *Average Wheat Yields (hectolitres per hectare) on Prime Quality Land in Britain and France, 1815 to 1892*

Year	England	France	France/ Great Britain
circa 1815	18·7	14·3	76%
circa 1850	23·0	18·5	80%
1892	23·8	20·5	86%

Notes and Sources:
  The wheat yield for Britain relates to Herts, Beds, Norfolk, Lincs, Essex, Leicester, Warwick, Middlesex, Worcs, Hunts, and Northants. In 1892 the total number of hectares sown was 329,212, producing 7,903,069 hectolitres of wheat. The official data are from Ministry of Agriculture, *Agricultural Produce Statistics of Great Britain for 1892* (London, 1893), vol. C, p. 6904. 1892 for France from: *Statistique agricole de 1892*, pp. 2–4. The departments in our sample are: Aisne, Eure, Eure-et-Loire, Manche, Mayenne, Nord, Oise, Pas de Calais, Seine, Seine-Inférieur, Seine-et-Marne, Seine-et-Oise. The total hectares sown with wheat are 1,282,743 producing 26,266,792 hectolitres. 1892 was a year of below-average harvest in both countries.
  1852 for Great Britain: the same sample of counties has been used. The yield data are from J. Caird, *English Agriculture in 1850–51* (London: Longmans, 1852), p. 480. The land sown with wheat in each county is from Ministry of Agriculture, *Agricultural Statistics for 1866* (London, 1867). The figures are in the *Journal of the Royal Statistical Society*, vol. 30 (1867), pp. 196–9.
  1852 for France: official data from the Agricultural Census contained in Statistique de la France, *Statistique agricole* (Paris, 1858), vol. 1, pp. 4–19, and vol. 2, pp. 4–17.
  1815 for Britain: we began with McCulloch, *Statistical Account of the British Empire* (1837), p. 482. We cross-checked McCulloch's data against original reports of the Board of Agriculture, county by county. The data relate to a span of years 1800–16. Wheat acreage data came from the Board of Agriculture's *General Report on Enclosures* (London, 1808), p. 229.
  1816 for France is from *Les Archives Statistiques de la France* (Paris, 1837). The same data are contained in Ministère de l' Agriculture, *Récolte des céréals et des pommes de terre* (Paris, 1878).

nineteenth century on land of comparable quality French farmers could achieve yields in grain production not very far below British levels. They will also help to place in better perspective the precise degree of inefficiency that might be associated with farm management, small-scale holdings, and teneurial institutions that characterised French agriculture. But that perspective is still questionable unless we can also show that the sample of departments included on the basis of land endowment alone were also characterised by a system of tenure and a scale of production that did not differ significantly from the rest of France. Otherwise the wheat yields obtained in those thirteen departments might be strongly influenced by the very factors we tend to underplay.
  Fortunately the *Enquête* of 1892 reported on the percentage of land in each department farmed under 'Biens Cultivé Par Le Proprietaire',

'Metayage' and 'Fermage'.[49] The profile of land tenure for France and for our sample appears below.

	Owner-occupied	Share-cropped	Tenant-farmed
All France	53%	11%	36%
The sample	48%	2%	50%

Our sample does contain departments with a higher-than-average percentage of land cultivated by tenant farmers, the system of tenure preferred by critics of *metayage* and peasant proprietorship. They are in this respect a bit more like Britain than the rest of France. These departments were also characterised by a size of farm slightly above the national average (9·2 hectares compared to an average for all France of 8·7 hectares). But in scale and tenure the sample does not differ widely from the rest of France. At least the difference is not significant enough to invalidate our basic point that even in the late nineteenth century the quality of land was a more important determinant of physical yields per hectare. On the basis of fairly accurate data for 1892 it is possible to show that in the cultivation of wheat the *average* yield achieved in Britain was 45 per cent above the average for France. But on prime soils French farmers managed to push their yields up to 86 per cent of British levels.

In the 1890s 85 per cent of the land of England and Wales was farmed by tenants on holdings that were on average double the size of holdings in France. Only 6 per cent of the land was cultivated in units below twenty acres in extent, twenty acres being roughly equivalent to the average size of a French farm.[50] Yet despite the handicaps associated with farms far smaller in scale than those that characterised British agriculture and a system of tenure dominated by peasant proprietorship, on land of comparable quality French farmers obtained yields that turn out to be surprisingly close to British levels.

5.6 THE SYSTEMS OF TENURE

Between the Revolution and the First World War French agriculture seemed to most observers to be extremely inefficient. Certainly there can be no doubt that the productivity of labour employed on French farms fell below the average level achieved in neighbouring countries such as Britain, Holland and Belgium. This fact stimulated a widespread condemnation of the agricultural institutions of France and of French farmers, a tradition of criticism which is not misplaced but is sometimes superficial and badly specified. In one sense the trouble with French agriculture was not peasant tenure and peasants slow to innovate. On the contrary, there is every reason to expect owner-occupiers to be as efficient as tenant farmers. Even Young admitted that property in land, is of all others, the most active instigator to severe and incessant labour.[51] Eighty years later that great admirer of English agriculture, Leonce de Lavergne, observed that the best cultivation in France, on the whole, was that of the peasant proprietors.[52] Furthermore, our own preliminary investigation into the relationship between wheat yields and tenure for 1892 found little correlation between the hecto-litres of wheat obtained per hectare and the share of cultivated land under different forms of 'tenure' in our sample of thirteen departments located on prime soils.[53]

We would not pretend that every farm in France operated near optimum levels of efficiency between 1780 and 1914. No doubt the diffusion of best practice from region to region and from farm to farm took too long a time. Agricultural innovation proceeded more slowly than it did in Britain, but we are *not* disposed to accept as self-evident the proposition that French institutions and French farmers were peculiarly and perversely resistant to new techniques of cultivation or that they allocated their resources in an inefficient manner. No, we prefer to argue that those who tilled the soil of France probably achieved a level of production not far short of the optimum, given the supplies of land capital and other inputs available to them.

Thus our analysis of land showed that essential differences between British and French agriculture went back a long way and were geo-graphical as well as institutional in origin. In Britain, where the terrain (acre for acre) was of higher quality and by nature better suited to pastoral than to arable farming, agriculture employed far fewer workers per acre of cultivable land, devoted a greater proportion of land and other resources to animal husbandry and obtained significantly higher levels of labour productivity.

By way of contrast, France retained more of its work force in the countryside, concentrated more on the cultivation of cereals and obtained lower output per worker employed in agriculture. Retardation in French agriculture stemmed far less from incompetent farming and far more from unfavourable land–labour ratios, which reflect the fact that the majority of Frenchmen (for perfectly good reasons) preferred to remain on farms. This in turn led to pressure of population on the land and to the cultivation of soils of declining fertility. Thus British super-iority in grain production can be explained in large part in terms of less pressure to cultivate soils of inferior quality. The gap in yields per hectare achieved on the *best* arable land in Britain and France was far narrower than the differential in average yields over each country con-sidered as a whole.

Through British eyes, there was simply too much agriculture in France. Too many families cultivated land which yielded a low return for all their skill and effort. Only heavier investment in fertilisers, draught power, drainage and traction could really make up for the relative scarcity and low quality of the basic endowment of land. The intensification of labour input (noticed by the more acute observers of the French agricultural scene) or the sheer toil captured so vividly by Millet in his paintings were not enough to make up for British advantages in the form of higher amounts of capital per acre and per worker.

Given the state of agrarian technology that persisted until the twentieth century, a critical component of the capital stock in 'premodern' agriculture consisted of animals. Farm animals saved labour, and provided cultivators with draught power and the bulk of their supplies of organic fertilisers. Animal power for traction rendered heavy soils more friable, and the application of manure on to arable land constituted the main way of raising yields per hectare. Over the nineteenth century the stock of cattle, horses, sheep and pigs was large enough to supply British farms with organic fertiliser at a rate per hectare of arable land that was 2·63 times the French rate (Table 5.6). That alone made a considerable difference to yields of grain, potatoes and other crops. Modern coefficients for chemical fertilisers indicate an elasticity of response falling within a range from 0·1 to 0·3. If the response to the application of organic fertilisers on to the soil in the eighteenth and nineteenth centuries fell within a similar range, the larger stock of farm animals in Britain could have raised average yields on the arable by anything from 16 to 48 per cent above French yields.[54]

Caird spotted this critical difference in the middle of the nineteenth century and wrote:

> In 1855 while travelling in France my attention was drawn to the very low yield of wheat as compared to ours and after publishing my own views on the question I had an opportunity of discussing them with the very eminent French statistician M. Leonce de Lavergne who agreed with me that apart from the difference in soil and climate it is probably to be accounted for by the fact that while our grass and green crops . . . are as 2 to 1 to our corn, France is exactly reversed, her corn or exhaustive crops being as 2 to 1 of her grass and green crops.[55]

Clearly something that might be called the 'grass–corn', or better still the 'land–beast', ratio should be at the centre of explanations of French backwardness in agriculture. But how and why British farmers had accumulated larger stocks of animals per unit of cultivated land demands historical investigation that would take us back centuries before the Industrial Revolution of the late eighteenth century, perhaps back to a comparison of the feudal systems of France and Britain, because while land and climate are important, over the long run contrasts in the system of property rights established in the French and British country-side may have been more significant.

But geography should not be ignored. Even our cursory examination revealed that British agriculture was better endowed with pasture of all kinds. For example, where rain is excessive the soil becomes acid and produces only rough pasture and areas of low rainfall are too dry for grass to grow well. Large areas of southern France suffered in comparison with Britain from inadequate rainfall. Thus while fields in the Vendée and Normandy produced up to thirty quintals of hay per hectare, pastures in the Alps and Pyrenees produced less than ten. The *Atlas Historique de la France* revealed the persistence for more than a century of cattle densities and the share of land used as meadows, pasture and rough grazing department by department.[56] Thus large parts of the British Isles seem naturally suited to pasture while large parts of France do not. As long ago as the fourteenth century Britain's special advantages for rearing sheep were recognised and the sheep population of these islands grew from around 8 million at that time to 26 million by 1800, when perhaps half the cultivable acreage of England was under grass – a proportion never yet reached in modern France.[57]

But geography does not explain enough. In the 1780s Arthur Young in his travels across France observed:

> the management of cattle in France is a blank. On an average of the kingdom, there is not, perhaps, a tenth of what there ought to be: and of this any one must be convinced who reflects, that the courses of crops throughout the kingdom are calculated for corn only; generally bread corn; and that no attention whatever is paid to the equally important object of supporting great herds of cattle, for raising manure, by introducing the culture of plants that make cattle the preparative for corn, instead of those barren fallows which are a disgrace to the kingdom. This system of interweaving the crops which support cattle, amongst those of corn, is the pillar of English husbandry; without which our agriculture would be as miserable and as unproductive as that of France.[58]

Young's *Travels* contain the classic critique of the teneurial institutions of France as well as his astringent disagreement with Mirabeau and other members of the Revolutionary Assembly who sought to maintain and extend peasant proprietorship in France. Young begins the polemic 'by asserting with confidence that I never saw a single instance of good husbandry on a small farm'.[59] The words 'on a small farm' go to the heart of the matter, because Young does not disparage peasant cultivators *per se*. He is, however, vehemently opposed to peasant tenure because it leads to the sub-division and more widespread ownership of land, which in turn lead to units of production (farms) too small to accumulate capital at anything but a slow rate. In his words, 'The profit of a large farm supports the farmer and his family and leaves a surplus which may be laid out in improvements; that of a small tract of land will do no more than support the farmer and leaves nothing for improvements. . . . The farms I should prefer in France would be 250 to 350 acres upon rich soils and 400 to 600 upon poorer ones.'[60] We know from his tour of the north of England that Young preferred larger farms because they employed advanced technology, minimised the input of labour per unit of cultivated land and sustained more livestock per acre than smaller farms.[61]

Young is quoted so often because his trenchant views capture what is essential to a critical comparison of the French and British systems of land tenure as they operated over the long term. In France the prevalence of peasant proprietorship, partible inheritance, the wider diffusion of land ownership and above all smaller-scale farm units are facets of a system of property rights that proved incapable, century after century, of generating an investable surplus and a rate of investment per hectare to match the rate of capital formation achieved by British landowners and their tenants. Location, climate and soil apart, the lower productivity of workers employed in French agriculture over the nineteenth century can be explained in institutional terms, as the product of a system of land tenure that encouraged labour to remain on farms badly endowed with capital per hectare and at the same time depressed the rate of investment required to compensate for the lower endowment of cultivable land per worker, itself a reflection of lower rates of structural change.

As a system of agriculture, peasant proprietorship with family labour is not necessarily inferior to a system managed by a combination of large aristocratic landowners and their tenants. Modern evidence suggests that peasants are normally price-responsive, profit maximisers, open to new crops and techniques for the cultivation of their land. Larger farmers and landlords simply possessed greater capacity to save and invest. In agriculture, where gestation periods are often long and risks high, this placed smaller farmers at a disadvantage. Their investable surplus was too small and their capacity to borrow funds too limited in relation to the lumpy and indivisible investment required to move from one level of production or one mix of crops to another.

Young cogently asked the advocates of small farms, 'where is the little farmer to be found who will cover his whole farm with marl, at the rate of 100 to 150 tons per acre? Who will drain all his land at the expense of two or three pounds an acre? Who will float his meadows at the expense of 51 pounds an acre?'[62] Of course, Young brought a British perspective to bear on the small farms of France, but his critique not only echoes advocacy of larger units by the *Encyclopaedia* but anticipates a tradition of writing within France on the disadvantages of *les petites enterprises agricoles*. Even today, when provided with the far greater infrastructural resources of modern transport, power supplies and credit, 'techniquement et economiquement, la petite enterprise est moins bien placée pour réussir que la grande ou la moyenne'.[63]

How and why France first evolved and persisted with a system of land tenure that appeared to many observers to possess such manifold disadvantages, compared both to Britain and to variants of British tenure (*fermage*), found within well-defined regions of France is a very large question beyond the scope of this study; but there is no derogating the importance of that question. 'Indeed', Lavoisier affirmed in 1787, 'it is in our institutions and laws that agriculture finds its most palpable obstacles.'[64] Contrasts with Britain had probably persisted for centuries. Already in the late seventeenth century perhaps not more than a quarter of the land of England and Wales (some 7 million acres in all) remained in the hands of small peasants. Two centuries later that proportion had fallen to 11 per cent, at a time when the small peasants of France continued to control up to 40 per cent of its *territoire cultivé*.[65]

Marc Bloch offers persuasive explanations of the origins of these differences which run in terms of the weaker juridical and political control over tenure exercised by the seigneurs, compared to the lords of English manors.[66] From the Middle Ages royal power was used in France (not consistently, but certainly more consistently than in Britain) to protect peasant and communal lands from encroachment by powerful landed magnates and to preserve traditional forms of tenure and collective rights of access to land; while in Britain the State and the law steadily transferred land under indeterminate or collective forms of tenure into private ownership. Tudors apart, British kings made few and ineffectual attempts to resist the efforts of large and powerful landowners to extend their properties, often at the expense of smaller men. By and large, monarchs and parliaments alike did everything required to facilitate the enclosure and consolidation of cultivable land into larger units of ownership and production.[67] No doubt royal policy in France was basically concerned to protect the King's fiscal base among the peasantry, whereas the British government had less need to tax land because it found other and more lucrative sources of revenue in trade and industry.[68] We simply remark the difference.

What also seems striking about the rural history of France in contrast to that of Britain is the tenacity and violence displayed by French peasants to maintain rights of access and control over land. Bloch described their long history of agrarian revolt as 'apparaît aussi in-

separable du régime seigneurial que, par example, de la grande enterprise capitaliste, la grève'.[69] Lefebvre also remarked that 'the history of
France abounds in jacqueries', and the struggles of French peasants
appear to have been collective, not atomised, organised rather than
spontaneous.[70] Dare we accept Soboul's description of the rural communities of France as far more cohesive and capable of joint action to
defend their interests than English villages?[71] Their defence of communal land and rights of access to land against seigneurial encroach-
ments during the second half of the eighteenth century (encroachment
backed on this occasion by the State) certainly supports such a hypothesis. Moreover, even when the commons and wastes of France passed
into private ownership, compared to England the powers of owners
seem abridged and the criteria applied for the distribution of land among
the residents of a village appear more egalitarian. Thus paradoxically the
laws and customs of Bourbon France may have been more tender
towards the interests of the landless than Acts of enclosure passed by
English parliaments to define and reassert the rights of ownership over
the commons and wastes of England.

Seigneurs found it more difficult to add to their estates by means
other than purchase. Tenancy also appears more permanent in France,
where the equation of ownership with control was far less secure than in
England. For example, even when a lease to land expired, a French
proprietor was in trouble if he refused to renew it in favour of the
former tenant and on almost the same conditions. Worse trouble was in
store for the new tenant from the peasant community, and leaseholders
also claimed the first refusal when their farms were being sold.[72]

Even a cursory examination of secondary sources will reveal stark
contrasts between the British and French systems of land tenure as they
evolved and operated between the later Middle Ages and the French
Revolution. Nevertheless historians should not lose sight of long-run
trends which in both societies proceeded towards the transformation of
property rights in land into full private ownership and (as far as we can
tell) towards a greater inequality of the distribution of land ownership.
For Britain the second trend was perhaps less obvious because modern
research now suggests that there may have been no fundamental shift
in the distribution of land by estate size between 1500 and 1800; whereas
in France, according to Bloch, 'the three centuries between 1480 and
1789 saw the rehabilitation of the large estate'.[73] That rehabilitation was
certainly checked by the French Revolution, while in Britain the distribution of land ownership almost certainly grew more unequal over the
century after 1789, and the New Domesday Survey of 1873 revealed a
country where 80 per cent of the land was owned by a mere 7,000 individuals.[74]

Nothing like that degree of concentration in land ownership had developed in France over the nineteenth century when 'the overall trend', to quote Labrousse, 'was clearly a slow but substantial advance of peasant property. To be sure the land remained unequally distributed. Large noble and bourgeois property holdings remained and there persisted from the top to the bottom of the scale, great disparities among the different peasant groups. But in the general peasant advance the advantage lay with the small landholders.'[75]

What happened to land ownership in Britain after the sixteenth century is still controversial, but there should be no mistaking the contrast with France at various points in time from 1500 to 1789. Nor can there be doubt that the French Revolution checked a long-term movement towards the concentration of land ownership – a movement that seems to have gathered momentum during the seigneurial reaction of the eighteenth century. We are not concerned here with the origins or character of the French Revolution, but simply wish to agree with observations made by several of its scholars, that in broad terms the agrarian laws of the Revolutionary era operated basically to strengthen and consolidate peasant proprietorship. In other words, the penumbra of measures related to seigneurial dues, to tenancy and land ownership, to the layout of fields, to grazing rights and to commons and waste lands that emerged during the Revolution, and continued in force after the fall of Napoleon, effectively precluded any fundamental or rapid transformation of the traditional system of land tenure in France.

For example, the Revolution led to the redistribution of land expropriated from the King, from emigré nobles, considered to be the enemies of the Revolution, and, most important of all, from the Church. Perhaps not more than 10 per cent of the cultivable land of France changed hands between 1789 and the Consulate of 1799, and the absence of relevant statistics on the distribution of land ownership by estate size makes it impossible to discover which categories of landowner increased their relative shares of *the territoire cultivé*.[76] Controversy surrounds the topic, but the procedures adopted by the Treasury for the sale of expropriated land (*biens nationaux*) seem to rule out the possibility that the landless or very small landowners obtained much of this land. As a group the peasantry gained, and in the Nord their share went up from 30 to 62 per cent.[77] Middling proprietors seem to have enlarged their estates, and according to some historians the urban bourgeoisie gained a 'disproportionate' share of *biens nationaux*. Whatever may have happened to the share of land in the hands of urban or absentee proprietors, it is clear that the very large estates lost land to owners farther down the scale. In a technical sense the overall distribution became more equal.

Roughly the same outcome transpired with respect to the enclosure and partition of common and waste land. Under the *ancien régime* the transposition of communal land into private ownership favoured the seigneurs.[78] In 1790 the Constituent Assembly abolished their right to *triage*, under which a seigneur could take one-third of enclosed commons. The Convention went further and allowed 'communes to recover any property in rights of usage of which they had been despoiled unless the lord were able to show he had acquired them by legal purchase'; while 'bourgeois governments of the last years of the Revolution, the Directory and Consulate put an end to forms of partition which favoured poorer villagers'.[79] Basically what the Revolution did about communal property (a problem that had preoccupied agrarian reformers of the old regime) was to pass laws enabling communes to enclose and distribute such land, but the form and timing of repartition was left to local initiative, freed obviously from the constraints formerly imposed by seigneurs and the King. Communal property survived the Revolution, and as late as 1863, thirty-three departments of France had at least 10 per cent of their surface occupied by communal holdings.[80] Egalitarian criteria for the repartition of common and waste land were explicitly abandoned and the long process of selling common land over the nineteenth century implied that the poor and landless in French villages remained dependent for their subsistence upon farmers (laboreurs) who employed hired hands. In other words, the agrarian policy of the Revolution favoured medium proprietors and larger tenant farmers over seigneurs who lost the power to 'appropriate' a disproportionate share of common land. At the same time *manoeuvriers* and landless families were also prevented from acquiring land except by purchase, and thus the supply of labour available for hire was not reduced as it might have been under Jacobin policies for a more egalitarian repartition of communal land.[81]

Finally, and most important, the Revolution abolished seigneurial dues and thus transferred income back to those who owned and farmed the land of France. Lefèbvre and others have shown how the Constituent Assembly and the Convention were pushed by the actual and incipient power of peasant revolt into the abolition without compensation of a wide range of property rights attached to land and the produce of land.[82] As Cobban puts it: 'The abolition of seigneurial dues was the work of the peasantry unwillingly accepted by the men who drew up the town and bailliage cahiers and forced on the National Assembly through the fear inspired by a peasant revolt.'[83]

Historians still debate the precise amount of agricultural income involved in this transfer of property rights. Overall it must have been substantial. Economically its significance lies in the fact that it gave the peasantry a far greater share of produce from their lands. Their burdens were lightened at a stroke and their capacity to survive and even prosper on relatively small plots was enhanced. Marginal properties became intra-marginal, medium proprietors became more viable and the economic strength of the peasantry improved.

While the Revolution checked the rehabilitation of large estates, we would not wish to argue that all the preconditions for a British system of tenure were developing in France before its outbreak in 1789. For example, seigneurs did not apparently invest anything like the same proportion of their incomes in improving their estates. Most had detached themselves from day-to-day management or from such problems as field layout or farm size. Their preoccupations seem to have been more with the collection of rent and other dues attached to the land and far less with the business of farming. Partnership between landlord and tenant, common in Britain, hardly existed across the Channel, where 'The land was but a means to be sucked dry to provide the cream of society the resources to consume, to buy, to pay dowries and to consume again'.[84] In the literature (which lacks the kind of empirical base available in monographs on Britain's landed estates) the magnates of France appear as an unproductive class of *rentiers* who employed chains of parasitic middlemen to squeeze the maximum amount of revenue from their estates.

Yet over the long run only a consistent agrarian policy designed to strengthen and increase the estates of such magnates and to consolidate fields into larger-scale enclosed farms might have eventually generated the rates of investment in agriculture comparable to those achieved in Britain. By the second half of the eighteenth century the Bourbon State seems to have realised the need for change and it took steps in that direction.[85] But the steps were tentative because the Bourbons and their ministers feared to provoke disorder among those 'inevitable victims of progress', the landless and *manoeuvriers* of rural France, millions of whom already 'tottered on the brink between poverty and indigence'.[86] No doubt the *ancien régime* also cared deeply to preserve its fiscal base long, but by the eighteenth century more precariously, established on the backs of the peasantry.

Opportunities for reform came with the Revolution, but once again the militant actions of the peasantry ensured that no agrarian laws were implemented which adversely affected their interests or interfered in any real way with their control of the land. Only the Jacobin Marat seriously contemplated anything like a radical reform of French agrarian institutions. Symbolically, perhaps, he was assassinated by a peasant girl, Charlotte Corday. By their actions during a decade of revolution French peasants checked attempts at reform from above that had gathered some momentum during the second half of the eighteenth century, and ensured that solutions to the problems of inefficiency associated with proprietorship, field layout and scale of farms would not be political. From the Revolution to the First World War the

State left them alone to till the land and to exchange their property rights in the light of incentives and constraints imposed only by the market.

The whole system proved to be extremely resilient to market forces, and significant changes in the distribution of land ownership and the concentration of holdings did not occur until after the First World War,[87] as Bloch observed, 'the economic position of the small and medium peasant was in many respects unstable . . . All the same, it must be admitted that none of the essential features of small peasant farming have disappeared in the course of the nineteenth and early twentieth centuries. Peasant proprietorship . . . has been conspicuously successful in maintaining its ascendancy over much of the soil, and has even some noticeable conquests to its credit.'[88]

5.7 CONCLUSIONS

In this chapter we first measured and then analysed some of the salient differences between British and French agriculture. We began with the contrast in the productivity of labour employed in the two agricultural systems and observed how British superiority became steadily more pronounced over the nineteenth century. Most of that superiority can, however, be explained by the significantly larger and higher-quality endowment of land cultivated by those who tilled the soil of England. At the outside, no more than 40 per cent of the gap in labour productivity between Britain and France can be accounted for in terms of higher yields per hectare. Moreover, even if average yields had been similar in the two countries, the marked contrast in the productivity of labour would have persisted because it reflected, above all, the slower pace of structural transformation in France. For perfectly good reasons the majority of the French labour force preferred to remain in agriculture.

Nevertheless, the lower yields achieved per unit of land cultivated in France required explanation and we shifted the focus of discussion to differences in value added per hectare. Perhaps most of that gap would have disappeared if French farmers had allocated as much land as farmers in Britain to the rearing of livestock. Not only was value added per acre higher in animal than in arable agriculture, but the availability of organic fertiliser exercised a decisive influence on the level of physical yields achieved in the cultivation of cereals, potatoes and other crops.

Thus British superiority in agriculture can be pinned down to the persistence of higher yields on arable land. In the livestock sector or the cultivation of industrial crops there is no evidence of French backwardness. Furthermore, the overall importance of British superiority or the relative incompetence of French farmers should be kept in mind, because even *if* the latter had obtained British yields in the cultivation of grain, potatoes and other vegetables, about three-quarters of the gap in labour productivity would still have remained.

In our discussion of the determinants of observed differences in physical yields on arable land we attempted to bring geography back into the picture and to allay the superficial impression left by a generation of British travellers to France who saw little in the countryside but a backward and conservative peasantry. On soils of comparable quality and in animal husbandry the yields achieved by French farmers do not seem to have been unimpressive. French retardation had less to do with the national or psychological attributes of those who tilled the soil and stemmed far more from the limited capacity of small units of ownership and cultivation to generate an investable surplus. Over the long run the French agricultural sector had failed to accumulate a stock of productive assets to match the capital–labour and capital–land ratios attained in Britain.

By the late eighteenth century this 'central' and persistent obstacle to progress was at the root of the relative backwardness of agriculture in France. In contrast with Britain, the land was short of capital, particularly animals. On each farm, output remained more diversified because smaller units of production devoted resources to meeting their own demands for food and failed to take full advantage of opportunities for specialisation associated with production for the market. Family farms also retained underemployed labour, while in Britain 'capitalist' agriculture was compelled by market forces (and the new Poor Law of 1834) to release or to expel redundant labour. In France the retention of labour in the countryside implied extensive cultivation of sub-marginal land of a quality that in Britain had long since been abandoned to rough pasture.

With higher densities of people on the land and a plethora of small-holdings the competition to buy and rent land must also have been keener than in Britain, where landed magnates were not faced with the same sort of inelastic demand curve for the larger farms that required more capital to stock and greater expertise to manage. In such conditions economists expect the shares of output extracted as rent on land leased to tenants to be lower in Britain. In any case England's large and aristocratic landowners had less need than the bourgeois proprietors of France to extract every last penny or sou of rent from their properties. Of course, a smaller proportion of land was under the control of tenant farmers (*fermiers*) in France, but the pressure remained. Furthermore, in agricultural systems characterised by high rents, insecure forms of tenure and small owner-occupiers, the overall propensity to deploy investable funds to buy land almost invariably intensifies. Thus we were not surprised to find examples of French farmers and landowners heavily engaged in transactions for the purchase of land. In Britain less of the agricultural surplus was dissipated in such transactions and a greater share ploughed back, by tenants and proprietors, into capital accumulation, particularly animals, which over time raised agricultural output and yields from the land.

Only to a small extent should the backwardness of agriculture in France be conceived as a problem of small peasants slow to innovate or to copy the superior techniques deployed by farmers in Britain. Backwardness should be associated far more with high labour densities generated in large part by a system of property rights for the ownership and management of cultivable land that, compared to Britain, held labour in the countryside and depressed the rate of capital accumulation in agriculture. While we are not Panglossian, our comparison of the British and French agricultural systems leads us to conclude that French farmers probably did as well as can be expected given the demographic pressure to extend the margin of cultivation on to soils of lower quality and the constraints on investment exercised by smaller units of ownership and production.

Marc Bloch found the origins of contrasts between the British and French systems of property rights in developments that occurred basically between the eleventh and thirteenth centuries.[89] Whatever the origins, there is no mistaking the dominance of large estates in England and the tenacious strength of peasant agriculture in France, where even the great political revolution of 1789 did little to upset the established layout of fields, communal techniques of cultivation or the distribution of land ownership. Most of those who farmed and worked the land of France displayed little desire for a fundamental transformation in the established system of property rights which might at one and the same time raise the productivity of labour and carry the often reluctant beneficiaries of progress to new industrial towns. They, it seems, remained blissfully unaware of their relative deprivation or the backwardness of their agriculture, compared to Britain. But then even Tocqueville, who found so much to admire in England, expressed serious reservations about the distribution of land ownership over here. 'In England', he observed in his journey of 1833, 'the number of people who possess land is tending to decrease rather than increase, and the number of proletarians grows ceaselessly with the population. . . . The thought of even a gradual sharing of the land has not in the least occurred to the public imagination. . . . The English are still imbued with that doctrine, which is at least debatable, that great properties are necessary for the improvement of agriculture.'[90] French society showed itself consistently reluctant to bear the economic costs and social dislocation associated with that kind of 'improvement'.

NOTES TO CHAPTER 5

1 To give arithmetical backing to these statements we completed an exercise in counterfactual history which generated estimates for hypothetical commodity output and commodity flow per capita with agricultural productivity in France assumed to be at British levels. In other words we assumed that French labour in agriculture, at each period, had the same average productivity (in current prices) as British labour in agriculture. Agricultural output was calculated by multiplying number of agricultural labourers by British productivity levels. It was then added to actual industrial output in sterling – converted at French weights – and finally divided by French population. The data for the exercise are from Tables 4.1, 4.3, 4.4 and 4.5.

2 In order to calculate *changes* in real productivity for France we deflated average product figures in current prices by Marczewski's agricultural price index (J. Marczewski, 'Le produit physique de l'économie française de 1789 à 1913 (comparaison avec la Grande Bretagne)', *Cahiers de l'ISEA*, AF 4, July 1965, p. XXXV). For Britain we deflated by the Rousseau index in B. R. Mitchell and P. Deane, *Abstract of British Historical Statistics* (Cambridge: CUP, 1962), pp. 471–2.

3 As recent research makes clear – see W. H. Newell, 'The Agricultural Revolution in Nineteenth Century France', *Journal of Economic History*, December 1973, pp. 697–703, and P. Hohenberg, 'Change in Rural France in the Period of Industrialization, 1830–1914', *Journal of Economic History*, March 1972, pp. 219–40.

4 A. Young, *Travels in France, 1787–89*, ed. C. Maxwell (Cambridge: CUP, 1950). Young's views on French agriculture have been analysed and given quantitative expression by B. Sexauer, 'English and French Agriculture in the late 18th Century', *Agricultural History*, July 1976.

5 Z. Griliches, 'Specification and Estimation of Agricultural Production Functions', *Journal of Farm Economics*, May 1963.

6 J. C. Toutain, 'Le produit de l'agriculture française de 1700 à 1958', *Cahiers de l'ISEA*, AF 1, July 1961, pp. 26–9.

7 There is a good description of French agricultural statistics in Institut National de la Statistique et des Etudes Economiques, *Les statistiques agricoles en France* (n.d.).

8 Arithmetically these percentages are based upon estimates set out in Tables 4.3 and 5.2. The calculations express the difference between the real and hypothetical labour output ratios for French agriculture as a percentage of the actual gap between labour productivity in British and French agriculture. We took column 5 of Table 5.2 minus an average of columns 3a and 3b from Table 4.3 over colums 4 of Table 4.3 minus column 4 of Table 4.3. The residual is by imputation derived from differences in the land–labour ratio.

9 Lavergne thought the 'natural fertility' of French soil was greater than that of British soil – a view apparently supported by Sexauer. 'English and French Agriculture', pp. 492–3.

10 N. Hilton, 'An Approach to Agricultural Land Classification in Great Britain' in *Land Uses and Resources*, Studies in Applied Geography (London: 1968), p. 128.

11 E. A. Fitzpatrick, *Introduction to Soil Science* (Edinburgh: University Press, 1974), p. 74.

12 Food and Agricultural Organisation, *The Soil Map of Europe* (Rome: FAO, 1967).

13 The method used was to weigh areas classified on the maps associated with a given soil type and to use the weight of the entire map as the denominator. The FAO have not apparently published this data in statistical form – letter from A. Pecrot of FAO dated 11 September 1975.

14 L. de Lavergne, *Rural Economy of England, Scotland and Ireland* (London: Blackwood, 1885), p. 6.

15 P. Thran and S. Brockhuizen, *Agro-Climatic Atlas of Europe* (Amsterdam: 1965).

16 *Atlas économique et social pour l'amenagement du territoire, II Agriculture* (Paris: Geographique National, 1969).

17 Ministry of Agriculture, *Agricultural Land Classification, Technical Report II* (London: 1966), p. 2.

18 L. Dudley Stamp, *The Land of Britain* (London: Longmans, 1962), pp. 363–81.

19 These proportions are based upon the weights used to calculate the purchasing power parity exchange rates and are fully described in Appendix A, Table A.1, p. 44 above.

20 Toutain, 'Le produit de l'agriculture', p. 171.

21 The percentages of *arable* land allocated to various crops in 1892: wheat 54 per cent in France and 20 per cent in Great Britain; barley 6 per cent and 18 per cent; oats 17 per cent and 26 per cent; potatoes 6 per cent and 5 per cent respectively. In Great Britain 17 per cent of arable land grew turnips and swedes and in France 8 per cent grew vines. The figures for Great Britain are from Mitchell and Deane, *Abstract*, pp. 78–9. For France we calculated these proportions from the *Census of Agricultural Production for 1892* which published estimates for gross output per hectare in francs for several crops. We also used Toutain's figures for *produit global* to measure the area under these crops. The French ratios relate to grains, potatoes and vines.

22 Given the information in the Census for 1892 on gross output per hectare for various crops and the shares of arable land devoted to different crops in Great Britain (Mitchell and Deane, *Abstract*, p. 78), we calculated what French output per hectare of arable land *would have been* if French farmers had allocated land in British proportions. Note that our figures refer to arable land under grain, potatoes, vines and root crops only.

23 We calculated these returns by dividing net value added in the cultivation of cereals by the number of acres devoted to cereals and net value added in animal production by the land under rotation grasses and permanent pasture. Net value added in grain production was assumed to be equal to its gross value. Net value added in animal husbandry was derived from sources cited in note 20 above. Land input for the two sectors are from Mitchell and Deane, *Abstract*, pp. 78–9. Since these figures neglect imported animal feed as well as grains and root crops fed to animals, they are very crude estimates that undoubtedly overstate the relative profitability of animal farming.

24 We do not offer figures because although we have cited estimates of output (value added in animal farming) we do not have figures for the relevant input of land required to calculate yields per hectare. The figures available relate to a large proportion of that input, namely land devoted to grass, pasture and artificial meadows. If we divide value added in animal husbandry by that *partial input* of land and compare it with returns per hectare in arable farming then it certainly looks as if animal husbandry in France was even more profitable than in Britain. The relevant output and input figures are cited under Tables 4.4 and 5.1. But see note 23 above.

25 Given data on the total area of land devoted to the cultivation of animal fodder, of all kinds, the exercise would proceed to multiply the hypothetical hectares of

farmland in France allocated to fodder crops by net value added per hectare of land actually used in animal farming. (These hypothetical hectares would represent the British percentage of the cultivable area devoted to animal husbandry.) The residual arable hectares would then be multiplied by the actual yield achieved in arable farming. The sum of hypothetical animal and hypothetical arable output would be the hypothetical agricultural output for France, *if* French farmers had allocated land along British lines. It is then simple to calculate the difference that this hypothetical allocation of land could have made to yields per hectare and output per worker in French agriculture.

26 See notes and sources to Table 4.7.

27 These ratios were calculated by dividing the sheep and cattle populations of Great Britain and France by the hectares of land devoted to grass, pasture and rough grazing. The relevant estimates can be found under Tables 5.1, 5.5 and 5.6.

28 See notes to Table 5.7.

29 Statistique de la France, *Résultats généraux de l'enquête décennale de 1862* (Strasbourg, 1870).

30 But see C. H. Feinstein's forthcoming paper in the *Cambridge Economic History of Europe* on 'Capital Accumulation and Economic Growth in Great Britain 1760–1860'. Toutain has some estimates for capital in ch. IV of 'Le produit de l'agriculture'.

31 See J. A. Perkins, 'The Ox, the Horse and English Farming, 1750–1850', Department of Economic History Working Paper, University of New South Wales.

32 Ministry of Agriculture, *Agricultural Statistics* (London, 1879 *et seq.*), and *Journal of the Royal Statistical Society*, December 1882, p. 605. For France we used *Annales du commerce extérieurs*, 1884–6, pp. 128–9; Ministère de l'Agriculture, *Statistique agricole annuelle*, 1912, and *Enquête agricole 1868–72, Rapport*. p. 95.

33 We compared British yields for the late nineteenth century with French yields for 1852 and 1862 in Statistique de la France, *Résultats généraux de l'enquête décennale de 1852 et 1862*, and C. Dutens, *Essai comparatif sur les formation et le distribution du revenu de la France* (Paris: 1842).

34 *Statistique agricole de 1912* published yield figures for Great Britain in hectolitres per hectare.

35 In 1925 the British yield in sugar beet was 20,314 kg per hectare, compared to a French yield of 24,501 kg already in 1904–13. But for root crops British yields for turnips and swedes, at 35,789 kg per hectare, were a bit above French yields for *betteraves de fourrage*, at 30,326 kg per hectare. French yields of 3,424 kg per hectare from *prés naturels* and 3,313 kg for *herbage* were above British yields for hay (3,214 kg per hectare). The sources are *Statistique agricole de 1913* and Ministry of Agriculture *A Century of Agricultural Statistics* (London, 1968).

36 We conducted the following arithmetical exercise to arrive at 20 per cent. First, we assumed that French yields per hectare in the cultivation of cereals and potatoes equalled average British yields over the period 1904–13. This involved increasing the number of quintals per hectare by approximately 60 per cent in most cases. These hypothetical physical yields were then multiplied by the value of each quintal produced. This gave us hypothetical gross output in francs for the cultivation of eight cereals and potatoes, which was roughly 60 per cent above the real gross output for these nine crops. In 1904–14 the share of these nine crops in the gross value of agricultural output came to approximately 30 per cent and we assumed that their share to net value added would be the same (see Table 5.4). We then adjusted total net output (Table 4.4) by 60 per cent of 30 per cent in order to estimate hypothetical net value added. Dividing by the agricultural labour force produced net value added per worker just 18 per cent above the real

level for 1905–14. The sources for this exercise were *Statistique agricole de 1913* and *A Century of Agricultural Statistics*.

37 Newell, 'The Agricultural Revolution'.

38 See Toutain, 'Le produit de l'agriculture', p. 56 and *Statistique agricole de 1913* for France. See P. Deane and W. A. Cole, *British Economic Growth, 1688–1959* (Cambridge: CUP, 1962), p. 66 for an estimate of 6 million acres sown with cereals in 1800 compared with 6·8 million acres in 1900 from *A Century of Agricultural Statistics*, pp. 98–100. In France the percentage of land sown with grain in all departments throughout the century remained about constant. R. Rémond, *Atlas historique de la France contemporaire, 1800–1965* (Paris: Cofin, 1965), p. 55, and M. Augé-Laribe, *La politique agricole de la France, 1880–1940* (Paris: Presses Universitaires de France, 1950), pp. 51–2.

39 H. J. Habakkuk and M. Postan (eds), *Cambridge Economic History of Europe*, vol. VI, p. 656.

40 A. B. Reach, *Claret and Olives* (London: 1852). cited by S. Pollard and C. Holmes (eds) *Documents of European Economic History* (London: Arnold, 1968)· pp. 199–201.

41 For example in H. Heaton, *Economic History of Europe* (New York: Harper & Row, 1948), pp. 435–7.

42 Lavergne, *Rural Economy*, p. 12.

43 P. Bairoch, 'The Working Population and its Structure', in *International Historical Statistics*, vol. 1 (Institut de l'Université Libre de Bruxelles, 1968), pp. 96–9.

44 Griliches, 'Specification and Estimation', p. 423, and E. F. Denison, *Why Growth Rates Differ* (Washington: Brookings Institution, 1967), ch. 7.

45 For this exercise we used the ratio of females in the agricultural work forces of France and Great Britain cited by Bairoch, 'The Working Population', pp. 96–9, and recalculated labour productivities in the two agricultures using the data cited in Table 4.3 but weighting each female worker as equivalent to 0·5 per male worker. We compared differences in productivity with weighted and unweighted input figures for the agricultural work forces. The differences amounted to an average of 16 per cent for five observations over the period 1855–64 to 1905–13. The Malinvaud study used 0·8 - see E. Malinvaud *et al.*, *La croissance française*, (Paris: Le Seuil, 1972), p. 81.

46 That controversy is reviewed in A. Gerschenkron, *Economic Backwardness in Historical Perspective* (Cambridge, Mass.: Harvard University Press), pp. 61–6.

47 R. H. Biffen and F. L. Engledon, 'Wheat Breeding Investigations at the Plant Breeding Institute, Cambridge', Ministry of Agriculture Research Monograph no. 4 (London, 1926).

48 E. Sérand, *Etude agronomique, statistique, et commerciale sur les cereals* (Paris: Rozier, 1891), pp. 333–9.

49 Statistique de la France, *Résultats généraux de l'enquête décennale de 1892* (Paris, 1897), pp. 230–7.

50 Ministry of Agriculture, *Agricultural Statistics*, tables 6, 7 and 11.

51 Young, *Travels in France*, p. 299.

52 Pollard and Holmes, *Documents*, p. 205.

53 We correlated wheat yields with the percentage of land cultivated under different forms of tenure for the sample of departments located on prime soils (see Table 5.9) and found $r = 0·31$.

54 Y. Hayami and V. Ruttan, *Agricultural Development* (Baltimore: Johns Hopkins Press, 1971), pp. 94–5 for the coefficients, and Table 5.6 for the fertiliser supplies per hectare.

55 J. Caird, *Our Daily Food* (London: Longmans, 1868), p. 27.

56 H. C. Darby (ed.), *A New Historical Geography of England* (Cambridge: CUP, 1973), pp. 94 and 457. Rémond, *Atlas historique*, p. 63 maps these densities from 1842 to 1962.

57 Darby, *A Historical Geography*, pp. 157, 168 and 421.

58 Young, *Travels in France*, p. 286.

59 Cited in J. Kaplow (ed.), *France on the Eve of Revolution* (New York: Wiley, 1971), p. 126.

60 ibid., p. 129.

61 A. Young, *Six Months Tour of the North of England* (London Strahan & Nicoll, 1771), p. 267.

62 ibid., p. 129.

63 J. Chombart de Lauwe, *Les possibilités de la petite entreprise dans l'agriculture française* (Paris: SADEP, 1954), p. 110.

64 Quoted by A. Soboul, 'The French Rural Community in the 18th and 19th Centuries', *Past and Present* no. 10 (1956), p. 88.

65 The British ratios are derived from F. M. L. Thompson, 'Landownership and Economic Growth in England in the 18th century' in E. L. Jones and S. J. Woolf (eds), *Agrarian Change and Economic Development* (London: Methuen, 1969), p. 44. The total cultivated land relates to 1815–24 and the sources are cited under Table 5.1. The French ratio refers to units of cultivation under 20 hectares and is thus comparable with Thompson's figure of 50 acres farmed by small peasants in England. French statistics are from *Enquête decennale de 1892*, p. 232, and Augé-Laribe, *La politique agricole*, p. 36.

66 Marc Bloch, *Les caractères originaux de l'histoire rurale française* (Paris: Armand-Colin, 1952), pp. 133–40.

67 Marc Bloch, *Seigneurie française et manoir anglais* (Paris: Armand-Colin, 1967), pp. 69–90 and 113–43.

68 P. Mathias and P. K. O'Brien, 'Taxation in Britain and France, 1715–1810,' *European Journal of Economic History*, Winter 1976.

69 Bloch, *Les caractères originaux*, p. 175.

70 Our views have been strongly influenced by Bloch and also by E. Le Roy Ladurie's essay 'La civilization rurale' in his *Le territoire de l'historien* (Paris: Gallimard, 1973), pp. 141–68.

71 Soboul, 'The French Rural Community', and J. Meuvret, *Etudes d'histoire économique* (Paris: Armand-Colin, 1971), pp. 176–8.

72 Bloch, *Les caractères originaux*, pp. 172–94 and 202–16, and P. Goubert's chapters in F. Braudel and E. Labrousse (eds), *Histoire économique et sociale de France* (Paris: Presses Universitaires de France, 1970).

73 Bloch, *Les caractères originaux*, p. 154.

74 Thompson, *English Landed Society* (London: Routledge & Kegan Paul, 1963), p. 27.

75 E. Labrousse, 'The Evolution of Peasant Society in France' in E. M. Acomb and M. L. Brown (eds), *French Society and Culture Since the Old Regime* (New York: Holt, Rinehart & Winston, 1966), p. 51; compare Augé-Laribe, *La politique agricole*, p. 36.

76 Labrousse, 'The Evolution of Peasant Society', p. 46.

77 J. Loutchisky, *Quelques remarques sur la vente des biens nationaux* (Paris: Champion, 1913), and the excellent summary in A. Milward and S. B. Saul, *The Economic Development of Continental Europe, 1780–1870* (London: Allen & Unwin, 1973), p. 264.

78 M. Bloch, 'Le lutte pour l'individuelisme agraire dans la France du XVIIIe siècle', *Mélanges Historiques*, vol. II (Paris, 1960).

79 Bloch, *Les caractères originaux*, p. 247, and S. Herbert, *The Fall of Feudalism in France* (New York, Methuen, n.d.), pp. 191–6.
80 F. O. Sargent, 'The Persistence of Communal Tenure in French Agriculture', *Agricultural History*, July 1958, p. 212.
81 F. O. Sargent, 'From Feudalism to Family Farms in France', *Agricultural History*, July 1961.
82 G. Lefebvre, *Etudes sur la revolution française* (Paris: Presses Universitaires de France, 1954).
83 A. Cobban, *The Social Interpretation of the French Revolution* (Cambridge: CUP, 1964), p. 53.
84 R. Forster, 'Obstacles to Agricultural Growth in 18th Century France', *American Historical Review* (1970), p. 1613.
85 Bloch, *Les caractères originaux*, pp. 233–7, and A. Davies, 'The New Agriculture in Lower Normandy', *Transactions of the Royal Historical Society*, vol. 8 (1958), pp. 129–46.
86 O. Hufton, *The Poor of 18th Century France* (Oxford: Clarendon Press, 1974), p. 23.
87 Labrousse, 'The Evolution of Peasant Society', p. 61.
88 Bloch, *Les caractères originaux*, p. 250.
89 Bloch, *Seigneurie française et manoir anglaise*, part 2.
90 J. P. Mayer (ed.), *A. De Tocqueville, Journeys to England and Ireland* (New Haven: Yale University Press, 1958), p. 72.

Chapter 6

Industry

6.1 ESTIMATES OF LABOUR PRODUCTIVITY

Our comparison of levels of productivity attained by labour employed by British and French industry (see Table 4.3, p. 91 above) seems more difficult to reconcile with standard historiography than any other set of estimates generated by this exercise in quantification. Historians might be willing to accept the superior productivity of labour employed in French industry before the Revolution. But few will readily believe in statistics which indicate that output per worker in French industry as a whole remained above British levels throughout the Industrial Revolution and that the British 'lag' (while diminishing steadily in relative terms) persisted into the 1890s. *Prima facie*, our figures seem to threaten the whole paradigm of a first Industrial Revolution and its diffusion to backward 'follower countries' on the European mainland.

Thus a natural reaction is to question the basic data and we can only refer again to the first part of this study, where we argued that statistics regarded as adequate for the measurement of growth within a country should also be accepted for comparisons across countries. Otherwise all recent work in the quantitative history of Britain and France comes into question. Certainly there are biases in French data (outlined in Chapters 2 and 4) that tend to inflate French estimates relative to comparable British figures, but the size of the productivity gap, particularly for the first half of the nineteenth century, appears to be well beyond normal bounds of error and is too marked to be dismissed as a statistical illusion.

Nevertheless, the results that emerged from the attempt to compare industrial productivity levels seemed sufficiently paradoxical to warrant independent checks upon the estimates. We devised two tests: the second simply compares *changes* in the productivity of labour employed in British and French industry over the nineteenth century, but the first, which is more complex, attempts to ascertain if the capital–labour ratios in British and French industry are in line with the estimates of value added per worker set out in Table 4.3. Such ratios are not available for either country and had to be reconstructed from national income estimates, wage data and proxies for the rate of return on capital invested in British and French industry.

Value added in industry, which can be defined as that part of industrial output which remains after all deductions have been made for raw materials, intermediate goods and capital depreciation, can be divided into two components: returns to labour (wages plus salaries) and returns to capital (rent, interest and profits) for participation in production. Returns to capital embrace all payments made for the deployment of property in industrial production, including reproducible and non-reproducible assets, and fixed as well as circulating capital.

For brevity we will refer to labour income as wages (W) and all returns to property as profits (P). Value added (V) is then written as

$$V = W + P$$

Dividing by the number of workers employed in industry gives the following identity:

$$V/L = W/L + P/L$$

or

$$P/L = V/L - W/L$$

Estimates for V/L and W/L in pounds have been presented and discussed above, but it was necessary to reconvert the average wage in French industry by an exchange rate for industrial commodities in order to transform estimates of property income per worker (P/L) employed in French industry into sterling.

Property income or returns to capital is equal to the quantity of capital (K) utilised directly or indirectly in the two manufacturing sectors, multiplied by the average rate of return (r) on capital invested in industry, i.e. $P = Kr$. Hence

$$P/L = Kr/L$$

Given estimates for value added per worker and the wage rate, and given that $P/L = V/L - W/L$ and that $P/L = Kr/L$, if statistics could be found for r (the average rate of return on industrial capital), then capital–labour ratios for British and French industry could be derived by simple arithmetic. Unfortunately estimates for r were not available, and we therefore assumed that rates of interest on long-term government bonds (consols and *rentes*) provided suitable proxies for average rates of return on capital invested in British and French industry. Apart from the familiar theoretical justification for this procedure, the specific assumption employed here is not exactly the correspondence between rates of interest and rates of return on capital, but rather that the relationship or *ratio* for returns on industrial capital in the two economies is equivalent to the ratio between their long-term rates of interest. In other words, the interest rate in France divided by the interest rate in Britain equals the return on industrial capital in France divided by the return on industrial capital in Britain. Table 6.1 was built up on these assumptions.

Table 6.1 *Comparisons of Capital–Labour Ratios for British and French Industry 1815–24 to 1905–13*

Periods (1)	$\dfrac{P/L \text{ for France}}{P/L \text{ for GB}}$ (2)	$\dfrac{r \text{ for France}}{r \text{ for GB}}$ (3)	$\dfrac{K/L \text{ for France}}{K/L \text{ for GB}}$ (4)
1815–24	5·5	1·65	3·3
1825–34	3·1	1·31	2·4
1835–44	2·6	1·26	2·1
1845–54	3·8	1·41	2·7
1855–64	3·4	1·36	2·5
1865–74	3·6	1·47	2·5
1875–84	2·5	1·26	2·0
1885–94	1·9	1·22	1·6
1895–1904	1·4	1·19	1·2
1905–13	1·8	1·04	1·7

Notes and Sources: Column 2 is a ratio of returns to capital per worker employed in British and French industry. It was calculated as the difference between value added per worker and the average wage. The data are from Tables 4.1, 4.3, 4.4 and 4.5. All data have been averaged over the relevant sub-periods.

Column 3 is the ratio between the long-term rates of interest (*rentes* in France and consols in GB). The figures are from: S. Homer, *A History of Interest Rates* (New Jersey: Rutgers University Press, 1963), pp. 194–5, 222–3, 409 and 426.

Column 4 is a proxy for the relationship between capital labour ratios in British and French industry, expressed in current prices averaged over the sub-periods. It was derived by dividing column 2 by column 3.

Our calculations suggest that capital per worker employed in French industry amounted to a multiple of the comparable British ratio throughout the century from 1815 to 1913. Given the usual presumption that output per unit of labour input is closely correlated with the amount of capital utilised per worker, the capital–labour ratios set out in column 4 in Table 6.1 seem to be in line with our findings that labour productivity in French industry remained above British levels for most of the nineteenth century.

But this exercise should *not* be accepted as definite corroboration until all potential statistical biases and errors have been taken into account. For example, the estimates for 'profits' per worker (column 2), derived as a residual, will reflect errors in both the figures for value added per worker (V/L) and returns to labour (W/L). Potential errors in the former have already been discussed, while the estimates used to represent the average earnings of all industrial employees were, in fact, average wage rates. Information about the salariat and their incomes was unobtainable. But given that salary levels exceeded wage levels, their inclusion in the calculation would reduce the P/L ratios for both countries. By how much is impossible to measure. Our discussion of real wages (Section 3.4) suggested that the salariat probably formed a larger and better-paid segment of the industrial labour force in France. That same discussion also concluded that estimates of average wage levels for British industry overstated the average earnings of British workers. Thus the direction of bias in our calculations goes to understate the overall capital–labour ratio for British industry compared to France.

Another source of statistical bias can be found in the quotations for interest rates (r) in column 3. These figures refer to long-term interest rates on government assets sold in Paris and London. If the degree of imperfection in the French capital market implies that the rate for *rentes* quoted on the Bourse in Paris underestimates the rate of return on capital invested in French industry compared to the relationship between interest and profit rates in Britain, this would again indicate that the capital–labour ratios calculated for French industry exaggerate the facts.

Furthermore, the concept of capital employed above includes the full range of physical and monetary assets employed in industrial production and is measured in *current* prices. This means that the higher capital–labour ratios observed for France reflect higher prices charged for the fixed and circulating capital utilised by French industry. Even where they used similar techniques of production, French industrialists probably paid higher prices than their British counterparts for machinery, fuel and raw materials, particularly in the earlier decades of the nineteenth century. Thus the estimates set out in column 4 do not mean that the 'quantity' of capital available to French workers was necessarily larger than the 'quantity' used by British industrial workers. To some, and probably to a diminishing, extent, these estimates reflect higher charges in France for inventories, for work in progress as well as for plant and equipment.

Until proper capital formation series are compiled for the two economies there is no way of correcting these biases. As they stand, our crude estimates in current prices go some way to corroborate the suggestion that labour productivity in French industry was above British levels until the 1890s, particularly as the movements over time seem to suggest a 'convergence' of the two economies as the century progressed. Thus by 1905–13 profits per worker, capital–labour ratios and long-term rates of interest tended to become more in line across the two countries than they had been in earlier periods.

Changes over the century in capital–labour ratios are also interesting. For example, in relative terms capital per worker increased at a faster rate in Britain until the boom of the 1850s, when French industry succeeded in reversing the trend. But from the 1860s capital deepening proceeded more rapidly in Britain, which supports the current view among French historians that the Great Depression had a serious impact on the growth of French industry. The boom in French industrial production after 1905 is again reflected in movements in the capital–labour ratios from 1895 to 1913. Finally, capital deepening not only occurred in periods of cyclical upswing but corresponded fairly closely to movements in labour productivity in the two industrial sectors.

Our second check was designed to ascertain if changes over time in the productivity of industrial labour moved in line with levels of productivity set out in Table 4.3. The data are tabulated in Table 6.2. These indices help to substantiate the findings on levels of productivity (Table 4.3). In particular they suggest that the productivity of labour increased at a faster rate in British industry until mid-century, while 'the long Victorian boom' witnessed comparable rates of productivity change in both countries. During the so-called Great Depression (corresponding on our data to 1865–74 to 1895–1904) French pro-

Table 6.2 *Indices of Labour Productivity in British and French Industry 1815–24 to 1905–13*

Periods (1)	Britain (2)	France (3)
1815–24	35	41
1825–34	40	43
1835–44	50	51
1845–54	58	57
1855–64	67	66
1865–74	83	81
1875–84	89	83
1885–94	93	94
1895–1904	97	88
1905–13	100	100

Sources: For Britain we used Walter Hoffmann's index of industrial production averaged over the relevant sub-periods: W. G. Hoffmann, *British Industry, 1700–1950*, (London: Blackwell, 1955), with 1905–13 calculated as 100. For France the index of industrial production is from T. J. Markovitch 'Les cycles industrielles en France', *Le Mouvement Social*, April–June 1968, p. 39. The labour force indices are derived from the figures presented and discussed in Tables 4.1 and 4.5. The division of the indices of industrial production by indices of industrial labour force produced a rough measure of rates of change in industrial productivity over the nineteenth century.

ductivity grew at a markedly lower rate than British. But in the final period up to the First World War (1895–1904 to 1905–13) the growth in real output per worker employed in French industry went up by 14 per cent compared to about 3 per cent for British industry.

6.2 PRODUCT MIX

Thus we can accept the figures in Table 4.3 as a rough representation of levels and movements in labour productivity, and the basic problem is to explain the long and surprising persistence of a differential in output per worker employed in French industry compared to the average level of labour productivity in the supposedly more efficient industrial sector of Great Britain. Chronologically this problem could be periodised into three stages: first, 1780–1815 when the productivity of labour engaged in British industry apparently increased far more rapidly than it did in France. These are, of course, years coterminous with major political changes in France while the first two decades of the period (1783–1802) have been defined as the stage of 'take-off' for the British economy.[1] There is no intention to relate our findings to controversies over stages of growth, but both recent quantitative research and an older generation of historians would agree that these years witnessed accelerated rates of growth and structural change in Britain.[2] For France, Crouzet's analysis of the deleterious impact of revolution, war and economic blockade leaves the impression that the economic growth of France suffered a severe setback over these four decades.[3] Thus, although our data on levels of industrial productivity are particularly crude for years before Waterloo, the estimates are congruent with recent scholarship which sees British industry forging decisively ahead and French industry falling behind in the era of democratic revolution.[4]

There then followed a second phase lasting roughly six decades when the differential in output per worker hardly changed. In Britain population growth and structural change are more rapid, but French industry managed to hold its own and in some industries to catch up and even surpass British achievements. Finally, from around 1870 to the turn of the century productivity in French industry increased less rapidly compared to Britain to the point where labour productivity in British industry exceeded the overall French level for the first time in the 1890s. But the sharp upswing in France just prior to the First World War then restored output per worker in French industry nearer to British standards.

An analysis of product mix should provide part of the explanation, because labour output ratios for British and French industry are averages that could conceal considerable dispersion about the mean.

A breakdown of sectoral estimates will reveal industries where value added per worker in France was above and below British levels over the nineteenth century and could pin down the sources of variations in the levels and movements in productivity in the two nations. Unfortunately, a really informative breakdown of this kind is impossible to obtain. Our investigation of printed sources which publish figures for the distribution of the labour force among industries and also for the commodity composition of final output convinced us that reliable estimates of value added per worker in different industries could not be compared before the publication of the British census of industrial production in 1907.

A comparison of labour productivity ratios across twenty-three British and French industries for 1905–13 is, therefore, tabulated in Table 6.3, but these estimates refer to the very end of the period, when productivity levels for most industries in the two countries had moved closer together. Furthermore, the classification systems adopted by the British Census of Industrial Production and the French Census of Industrial Establishments are not cast into the kind of analytical cate-

Table 6.3   *Value Added Per Worker in British and French Industries 1905–13*

	Industry	Britain: Value added per worker in £s	France: Value added per worker (converted at 28 francs to the £)
	(1)	(2)	(3)
I	Electricity	247	321
II	Gas	207	142
III	Petrol	169	544
IV	Coal and other combustibles	138	78
V	Metal mining:		
	Iron	155	132
	Non-ferrous	68	57
VI	Mining of construction materials	77	79
VII	Salt, brine, etc.	67	176
VIII	Iron and steel production	115	90
	Copper	137	69
IX	Metal working and engineering (total)	97	96
	Shipbuilding	98	82
X	Glass	94	28
XI	Porcelain and tiles	68	108
	Bricks	78	40
	Cement	132	62

Industry (1)	Britain: Value added per worker in £s (2)	France: Value added per worker (converted at 28 francs to the £) (3)
XII Chemicals	167	156
XIII Rubber	124	273
XIV Tobacco and matches	148	108
XV Soap	155	210
Oil	184	133
XVI Textiles (total)	75	91
Wool	70	94
Cotton	79	174
Silk	55	43
Linen, hemp, jute	61	157
Hosiery	61	85
Bleaching and finishing	101	155
XVII Leather preparation	118	85
Leather articles	71	120
XVIII Paper and cardboard	86	93
XIX Printing	109	66
XX Building, Contracting and public works	83	130
XXI Food industry (total)	196	158
Milling	178	111
Bread and biscuits	104	170
Sugar and alcohol	367	325
Brewing	395	73
Chocolate, etc.	84	298
Preserved meat, etc.	81	98
XXII Clothing, etc.	63	64
XXIII Wood industry (total)	90	43
Timber	82	93
Furniture	101	58
Boxes, crates, etc.	91	47
Carriages	82	25

Notes:

$$VA/L = \frac{\text{Value added}}{\text{Total Labour Force Employed in Industry}}$$

Conversion: We calculated a conversion rate for industry at 28 francs to the £: it is based on British output patterns. The trading rate was 25 francs to the £.

Sources: GB: *Census of Production for 1907.* France: *Résultats statistiques du recensement des industries et professions,* 1896, vol. 4, and *Recensement de la population* for 1901, vol. 4, and 1906, vol. 1. We used the labour force figures from the 1906 census augmented by a constant 4 per cent in order to produce estimates for the 1905–13 period and to make the figures consistent with Tables 4·1 to 4·3. The value added figures are from T. J. Markovitch, 'L' industrie française de 1789 à 1964', *Cahiers de l'ISEA,* AF 4. July 1965.

gories that historians would ideally use to compare productivity levels throughout industry in the two economies. For Britain there is no information on the scale of enterprise in different sectors of industry, and the definitions of an industry in both documents are altogether too broad for detailed comparisons.

But the figures are useful. First of all they validate the estimates for labour productivity for 1905–13 presented in Table 4.3, constructed from national accounts and population censuses. More significantly, comparisons of labour productivity even across broad sectors of British and French industry do leave some general impressions about indus- trialisation in the two countries. For example, the productivity of labour employed in the extraction of British coal and mineral ores exceeded the productivity of labour engaged in the extractive industries of France by a considerable margin. Now British superiority in the mining of coal and mineral ores is more likely to reflect better located and more tract- able supplies of natural resources than more capital-intensive tech- nology or better business organisation.[5] On investigation it may also turn out to be the case that the higher level of productivity observed for basic metallurgy in Britain was also due in large part to the country's cheaper supplies of coal, coke and metallic ores.[6] French ironmasters used less fuel per ton of pig iron smelted than British ironmasters throughout the second half of the nineteenth century.[7] While these estimates for the early twentieth century are not conclusive, they tend to confirm the views of contemporaries and historians who long argued that in the age of coal, iron and steam power French industry suffered from poor natural resources. Their views can only be strengthened by estimates which suggest that in the fields of metal working and engin- eering, French skill, technology and business organisation seem to have compensated for whatever 'natural advantages' the British possessed in the production of basic metals.

Britain enjoyed no obvious advantages in quarrying slate and stone, but British workers in the glass, brick and cement industries produced far higher net outputs per worker than their counterparts in France. When it came to building and constructing with bricks, stone and other inputs the higher productivity of French workmen stands out. A similar impression emerges from a consideration of the estimates for the leather industry, where the British lead is again located in the preparation of the basic input (leather) and French workers appear far more pro- ductive in the manufacture of finished leather goods.

It may surprise historians to discover that by the early twentieth century French labour produced more per head than British labour throughout most sections of the massive textile and clothing industry; while in processed food, drink and tobacco the overall superiority of the British industry seems to lie with more mechanised processes (such as milling, brewing and the making of tobacco), and traditional French skills in baking and confectionery served to narrow the overall differential.

There seems to be no doubt of a marked British lead in the manufacture of furniture and all other articles made from wood and also in paper, printing and publishing. There should be no surprise in estimates which show higher productivity levels for French labour engaged in the manufacture of soap, porcelain and tiles, and French superiority in new industries such as rubber, petroleum and electricity will lend support to proponents of the thesis of a British failure to undertake sufficiently rapid structural diversification before 1914.

Estimates for the early twentieth century are, however, only of limited help in explaining differences in the productivity of industrial labour in Britain and France over more than a century of technical change from 1780 to 1914. Some backward extrapolation seems warranted. For example, the British advantage in the production of mineral ores and coal probably diminished over the nineteenth century as France opened up and developed her natural resources by investment in transport. Yet that advantage with its externalities to fuel-intensive industries such as basic metallurgy, chemicals, gas and glass remained substantial even in the early twentieth century. Secondly, the estimates do suggest that compared to Britain, French industry tended to excel towards the finishing end of the manufacturing process: in textiles as a whole; in baking rather than milling; in confectionery rather than sugar refining; in soap and perfumes rather than oils; in building rather than in the making of construction materials; in metal working rather than basic metallurgy; in leather goods but not in leather.

Estimates of value added per worker in different sections of French industry can be found for earlier years. Figures are available in the ISEA publications. Toutain's figures for the distribution of labour among industries could be used to derive labour productivity ratios for most French industries going back to 1840.

British data are of an altogether more dubious quality; but rough estimates of value added for a sample of British industries can be reconstructed from the weights employed by Hoffmann for his index of industrial production, although Hoffmann's weighting system is not discussed in detail either in his original study or in the English translation.[8] In addition the distribution of the industrial labour force among industries can be derived from Booth's well-known publication.[9] Booth obtained his estimates from the population censuses published decennially from 1841 to 1881, in which the job classifications employed by enumerators were not based clearly upon industries but refer in large part to the 'occupations' of the work force. Moreover, the censuses exhibit inconsistencies from one publication to another and there are residuals of unclassified and marginal categories of labour. Booth did his best, but the recalcitrant nature of census returns means that his estimates contain indeterminate biases.[10]

Given the low quality of the basic data available in printed and official sources, it did not seem feasible to compare labour productivities industry by industry for the two countries for years before the twentieth century, particularly as the conversion of industrial outputs expressed in francs and sterling into a common unit of value raised another set of statistical problems, which could only be satisfactorily solved by the construction of exchange rates for each industry. Thus it appeared less questionable to present a *ranking* of labour productivities industry by industry for years selected simply to take advantage of accessible and comparable data. Table 6.4 has been designed to reveal in very broad terms which industries in the two countries exhibited labour pro- ductivities above and below average for *manufacturing* industry as a whole over the years 1840–80 and, in column 2, the relative importance of particular industries as employers of industrial labour. It is an unsatisfactory substitute for a detailed breakdown of the *overall* in- dustrial productivity ratios already compared in Table 4.3.

These figures provide limited information which, carefully inter- preted, can be used to supplement impressions already derived from the more reliable data for 1905–13. Thus French inferiority in the extractive industries again stands out and the contrast with Britain is more marked for the earlier decades of the nineteenth century. Unfortunately the available information made it necessary to present 'metals' as a conglomerate which includes basic metallurgy, metal working, engineering and shipbuilding. But in this very broad sector of industry labour productivity in France certainly fell below British levels over the period 1840–80. How far the British lead might be attributed to basic metallurgy (and partly to its better endowment of natural resources) in contrast to engineering and the processing of metals is impossible to determine from these figures.

Textiles is an example of an important industry (it engaged about a quarter of the industrial work force in both countries) where the productivity of labour in both Britain and France remained close enough to the countrywide averages to exert negligible influence on the differential for industry as a whole. At first sight this is surprising because the British textile industry figures so prominently in histories of the first industrial revolution. 'Textiles' is, however, an amalgamation of cotton, linen, wool, silk, bleaching and dyeing. There can be no sug- gestion that productivity in spinning and weaving of cotton in Britain fell below French levels from 1840 to 1880, although that seems to have been the case by 1905–13. On the contrary, our investigations into labour productivity measured in physical units of kilogrammes of

Table 6.4   *A Ranking of Labour Productivities for British and French Industry 1840–80 (average for all industry of each country = 100)*

Industry (1)	Share of industrial labour force employed (average 1840–80) GB (2a)	France (2b)	1840s GB (3)	France (4)	1860s GB (5)	France (6)	1880s GB (7)	France (8)
	%	%						
Mining	10·4	4·4	110	37	108	37	114	65
Metals	12·2	11·1	128	51	112	73	107	63
Textiles	24·5	23·8	92	68	95	64	111	115
Food	3·7	6·9	179	206	207	216	222	286
Chemicals	0·6	0·7	360	732	134	525	77	161
Paper	2·1	2·0	85	67	65	69	47	75
Leather	1·3	6·7	499	52	449	75	444	99
Wood	6·5	12·6	99	33	111	48	124	121

Notes and Sources:

Mining includes all mines and quarries. Metals includes production of metals, pig iron and steel plus the transformation of metals; metal-work, tools machines, metal ships, etc. Textiles include dyeing and finishing of cloth, wool, silk, hemp, linen, artificial fibres, etc. Food includes drink, tobacco. Chemicals include sulphuric acid, dyes and miscellaneous. Paper includes printing, books and cardboard, etc. Leather includes canvas, rubber and leather objects. Wood includes furniture, carriages, carpentry and wooden ships.

The industries *excluded* are clothing, construction materials (bricks, tiles, etc), public works, gas, electricity, petroleum, glass, ceramics and building.

Columns 2a and 2b are averages for three years, one each from the 1840s, 1860s and 1880s. For GB the labour force figures are from C. Booth, 'Occupations of the People of the United Kingdom', *Journal of the Royal Statistical Society*, 1886. For France, these ratios are derived from figures given by J. C. Toutain, 'La population de 1700 à 1959', *Cahiers de l'ISEA*, AF 3, January 1963, tables 71, 91–3 and 115–16. The years relate to 1840–5, 1856–61 and 1886–91.

Columns 3–8: we calculated the number of workers and the value added in each industry. To be consistent with the earlier tabulations, we used proportions averaged in columns 2a and 2b multiplied by total industrial labour force figures from Table 4.1. To find value added in each sector in GB, we used Hoffmann's weights as the ratio of value added in a particular sector to value added in all manufacturing. We then multiplied by our industrial output figures (Table 4.4) to find value added in each sector.

For France, we employed weights published by Markovitch in his table 'Structure industrielle (valeurs ajoutes en %)': Markovitch, 'L'industrie française'. Multiplying by our value added figures for 1835–44, 1855–64 and 1885–94 (Table 4.4) gave us value added in each of the industrial sub-groups.

Finally, to calculate the ratios presented in the table, we calculated each figure as a ratio of average productivity in the entire industrial sector.

woven cotton cloth and spun cotton yarn produced the results shown in Table 6.5. Thus the relative advantages of the French textile industry must have been in other sectors of the industry – perhaps, as the figures for 1905–13 indicate, in linen and in bleaching and dyeing.

There is certainly a suggestion in the ratios set out in the table that output per worker in the French chemicals and food processing industries was above British levels over the nineteenth century and an even stronger suggestion that workers with wood and leather in Britain produced more on average than their counterparts in France; while productivities in the paper industry seem to have been similar for most of the century.

Whatever may have been the case earlier, by the twentieth century British superiority over France seems to have been confined to coal and metal mining, to iron, steel and copper smelting, to shipbuilding, to building materials (bricks, glass and cement), to the printing industry, and to the manufacture of articles from wood. While French industrialists still had good reason to aspire to British productivity levels in several industries, they had no reason (as many of them recognised) to feel inferior to their rivals across the entire spectrum of industrial activity:[11] quite the contrary, because it can easily be demonstrated that if value added per worker had been similar (industry by industry) in the two states, industrial output in France would have fallen by about 9 per cent over the period 1905–13. This occurs because total output and the average productivity of all industrial labour depend not only upon the

Table 6.5　*Productivity Per Worker in Cotton Spinning and Weaving 1829–35 to 1907*

Years circa	Yarn output per worker employed in yarn production (in kg)		Woven cloth per worker employed in weaving (in kg)	
	France	*GB*	*France*	*GB*
1829–35	447	702	135	236
1844–50	825	1,251	208	753
1859–61	—	1,668	—	1,457
1880–82	—	2,509	—	1,835
1895–1904	3,440	—	1,040	—
1907	—	2,840	—	1,800*

*Converted into yards at 4·57 yards = 1 lb.

Sources: Moreau de Jonnès, *Statistique de l'industrie de la France* (Paris: 1856), pp. 65, 88, 92 and 100; R. B. Forrester, *The Cotton Trade in France* (Manchester: 1921), p. 9; J. M. Dutens, *Essai comparatif sur la formation et la distribution de revenu en 1815 et 1835* (Paris: 1842), pp. 130–1; T. Ellison, *The Cotton Trade of Great Britain* (Manchester: 1886), pp. 68–9; *Census of Production for 1907*, pp. 337–40.

productivity of workers employed within each industry but also upon the distribution of the labour force among industries.

At the end of our period when the average level of productivity in France had fallen below the average for British industry, the British advantage would have been far greater if the industrial work force of France had not been concentrated in industries where its productivity was on a par with or, in several sectors, above standards obtained in Britain. For example, during 1905–13 about 75 per cent of the French industrial labour force found work in industries where value added per employee was either equal to or above levels obtained in comparable British industries; while nearly a third of the labour force worked in sectors where productivity exceeded British standards by at least 30 per cent. Nearly two-thirds of the industrial labour force of Britain worked in industries where productivity levels were close to or below French standards.[12]

Britain's overall superiority was, it appears, derived from well-defined sectors of industry, while France had allocated its labour force (and other resources) into activities where its productivity compared favourably with British standards. The workings of the market and comparative advantage had operated to produce two very different but complementary industrial structures in Britain and France. Thus our analysis of the scant and rather poor data on labour productivity has already indicated that differences in commodity mix and specialisation (prompted by differences in resource endowments and international competition), could go a long way to explain the paradox of the high levels of labour productivity achieved by French industry over the nineteenth century.

Further disaggregation of the figures now available is impossible. Our Table 6.3 for 1905–13 provides some of the detail required to explain the overall or industry-wide productivity ratios for Britain and France. But in an age of technical change, backward inference from estimates for early twentieth century is hazardous, while estimates of value added per worker for earlier years are of low quality and confined in scope. Until a more detailed breakdown of labour productivity ratios can be constructed industry by industry, it will not be feasible to offer anything more than 'impressions' as to *where* the productivity of French industry exceeded or fell below British levels over the nineteenth century. Certainly no unorthodox presumption can be derived from these figures that productivity in the staple industries of the first industrial nation (coal, basic metallurgy, cotton textiles) fell below French levels over much of the nineteenth century. It may, on the other hand, turn out to be the case that by concentrating upon manufactures like cotton textiles, coal and basic metallurgy some historians of European economic development generalised from a sample of industries where natural advantages as well as the more rapid diffusion of advanced technology made British industry *as a whole* seem more efficient than industry not only in France, but possibly elsewhere on the continent. Our preliminary look at the product mix suggests that 'different' may be a better adjective to deploy than 'backward' when comparing French to British industry.

6.3   DEMAND AND SPECIALISATION

Sir John Clapham often reminded students of the Industrial Revolution how slowly the factory system and new technology spread across British industry, and repeatedly warned them against generalisations based upon a few sectors that happened to be mechanised rather early in the nineteenth century.[13] His caution has been vindicated by a series of monographs on British manufactures as well as regional studies which trace the persistence of traditional forms of organisation and labour-intensive techniques of production well after factories and power looms (to take an obvious example) had rendered hand looms and the domestic system obsolete in weaving cotton and woollen textiles.[14] Insights of this kind (which Clapham derived essentially from keeping the full range of industrial employment and output in view) are relevant to comparative history because they might persuade us to follow up the impression that emerged from our description of commodity mix and analyse the industrialisation of Britain and France as a process of specialisation and labour absorption. Although the concept of technical diffusion is now fashionable in modern European economic history, specialisation is certainly more central to Adam Smith's and David Ricardo's views of industrial development. The problem of employment also preoccupied classical economists as well as those who lived through the transition to industrial society. We believe that to focus our discussion on specialis-ation and labour supplies might help us explain the surprisingly high level of labour productivity maintained by French industry up to the 1890s.

It is an apparent, if statistically unestablished, generalisation that the commodity structure of industrial output in the two countries differed. French industry emphasised expensive manufactures of higher-quality finish and design. British industry produced more minerals and inter-mediate goods and tended to sell cheaper and more standardised goods on larger markets both at home and abroad. These summary remarks are based upon the writings of historians who have studied the two economies. Unfortunately, when it comes to quantification the census categories are too broad to 'measure' fine differences in the product mix of the two industrial sectors, although figures for 1905–13 do reveal that something like 17 per cent of Britain's industrial output came from minerals, compared to only 4 per cent for France. Adopting a plausible assumption that the lion's share of such commodities as iron and steel, copper, glass, bricks, cement, rubber, leather and paper were delivered as inputs to other industries, it is also possible to estimate that a further 14 per cent of British industrial production consisted of intermediate goods, compared to 8 per cent in France.[15] Standard descriptions of the nature of industrial specialisation in France and Britain were, however, borne out by our investigations into trade patterns between the two countries. In Table 6.6 the commodity composition of domestically produced exports has been broken down into five groups: raw materials; intermediate goods for further processing and which were delivered as inputs to other British and French industries;

Table 6.6 *The Commodity Composition of Trade Between Britain and France 1854–1905*

Category	1854 GB %	1854 France %	1865 GB %	1865 France %	1888 GB %	1888 France %	1905 GB %	1905 France %
1 Raw materials	29	8	12	16	15	7	26	8
2 Intermediate goods	33	10	57	5	55	8	35	8
3 Finished industrial products	22	31	13	36	20	43	28	55
4 Processed food	1	21	4	15	2	17	1	14
5 Unprocessed food	6	12	1	20	2	16	3	13
6 Unclassified items	9	18	13	8	6	9	7	2

Notes:
The percentages relate to a category to the total declared value of exports of *domestically* produced commodities in sterling. The years selected were 'normal years' in terms of levels of production, trade and prices and are assumed to be representative of the decades selected.
Major commodities under each category were as follows:
Category 1: coal and wool for British exports; raw silk, hides, wood and wool for French exports.
Category 2: iron, copper, woollen, cotton and linen goods for Great Britain; thrown silk, tanned hides, woollen yarn and turpentine for France.
Category 3: silk manufactures, machinery, chemicals, hardware and cutlery for Great Britain; silk, woollen goods, leather, lace and apparel for France.
Category 4: wines, brandy, flour and refined sugar for France.
Category 5: butter, eggs, grain and vegetables for France.
Sources: Real values of British exports to and imports from France published in *British Parliamentary Papers*, 1856 (LVI), 1866 (LXVIII), 1889 (LXXV) and 1906 (CXVII).

finished manufactured goods; processed food; and unprocessed food. Several arbitrary but consistent assumptions had to be made in order to classify commodities on the margin between finished manufactures and industrial inputs (categories 2 and 3). The major commodities (in terms of their share in gross value of each sub-category) have been listed under Table 6.6 which helps to elucidate some of the salient features of trade and specialisation in the two countries.

Firstly, it seems that between 60 and 70 per cent of British exports to France consisted of raw materials and intermediate goods, including coal, wool, iron, copper and semi-finished textiles, particularly woollens; while over half of French exports to Britain took the form of finished manufactured goods and processed foodstuffs such as silk, leather and cotton manufactures, wine, spirits and refined sugar and flour. Britain sold very little by way of processed food to France and somewhere between one-third and one-fifth of its exports of finished industrial goods included machinery, chemicals, hardware and cutlery, and, surprisingly, silk.

Apart from the absence of machinery in French exports to Britain, there seems to be little in the patterns of trade to suggest that French industry lagged far behind British industry or that it lacked the capacity to compete in its own specialised spheres of activity even in the British market. Britain traded its abundant natural resources such as coal and wool, while France sold raw silk. British industry sent machinery and intermediate goods to French industry which returned finished manufactured goods to British consumers. Our classification of trade data reveals two developed economies trading on the basis of their relatively abundant natural resources and specialised along lines of comparative advantage.

Generalisations based upon commodity mix and patterns of trade refer to broader differences between modal types of industry in the two countries and admit the full range of exceptions. But, if established, they embody important implications for understanding industrial development in Britain and France. For example, if for over a century between the death of Louis XVI and the First World War the labour force employed in French industry grew more slowly than it did in Britain but its output contained a higher proportion of higher-quality manufactures than British industrial output, value added per worker in French industry would remain above British levels, unless British technology could compensate for these variations in product mix. Thus the superior productivity of French industrial labour (observed in Table 4.3) implies that larger segments of French industry served people with higher incomes, with greater discrimination and concern for quality and style than the typical consumers of British manufactured goods. No doubt Paris 'centralised consumer opinion' because, as Audiganne noticed, 'the characteristics attributable to Parisian work are found not only in the work which Paris itself produces. It exerts a considerable influence on a large number of industries which are practised far from its walls. Indeed when one studies the comparative situation of our manufacturing towns, it is soon evident that there are great differences according to whether their products go to the great market.'[16] On the supply side it also indicates that industrial goods made in France embodied a higher degree of labour skill and expertise than could be found in the bulk of British manufactured goods. Such a contrast would not have surprised Richard Cobden who observed at the Great Exhibition of 1851, 'England was unrivalled in those manufactures which owed their merit to great facilities of production and Americans excelled in every effort where a daring mechanical genius could be rendered subservient to purposes of general utility; but there was one country which in articles requiring the most delicate manipulation, the purest taste, the most skilful application of the laws of chemistry and rules of art to manufacturing was by universal consent allowed to hold the first rank; that country is France.'[17]

There is, therefore, a relationship between demand on one side and composition of industrial output and labour productivity on the other that is relevant to explore. That connection is not the influence of changes in aggregate demand upon the growth of industrial production but rather the ways in which variations in the structure of demand probably conditioned differences in the composition of industrial output in Britain and France.

British factory industry marketed a large share of its output in urban areas at home and abroad. In its early stages it catered for families whose money incomes increased at a modest rate and whose expenditure on manufactured goods fluctuated both cyclically and secularly with the price of food. At the onset of the Industrial Revolution (1750–1820) food prices rose at a rate not experienced in Britain since the inflation of the sixteenth century.[18] Population growth accelerated and the larger burden of dependency assumed by wage earners further eroded their capacity to buy manufactures. There is, furthermore, no evidence that income distribution became less unequal during the Industrial Revolution. On the contrary, the limited data now available point to some widening in the gross inequality that had persisted over several centuries.[19]

Of course, improvements in transport and distribution extended the home market, while imperial conquests and the collapse of the Spanish and Portuguese empires removed or modified political obstacles to the sale of industrial goods abroad. But expansion of markets in the Americas and in Asia and Africa was only secured by higher levels of military expenditure financed in large part by a regressive system of taxation (particularly indirect taxes) which reduced purchasing power among the population at home.[20] Thus, during its formative phases British industry seems to have expanded sales among social groups both at home and abroad who may well have been extremely sensitive to variations in relative prices.

There is no need to exaggerate contrasts with France. Industry there certainly attempted to expand sales among consumers with rather limited capacity to buy manufactured goods. French entrepreneurs also found domestic expenditure on their products restrained by rising food prices and population growth. Nevertheless, there were several factors which conditioned demand for the products of French industry in ways that probably pushed its long-term development along a route that varied from the path taken by British industry.

First of all, rates of increase in both total population and in food prices between 1750 and 1820 were slower in France than in Britain, which might, *ceteris paribus*, blunt the incentive for French firms to maintain sales by lowering quality or reducing prices.[21] Secondly, the French Revolution reformed both the system of taxation (using that term to encompass feudal dues and payments to the Church as well as central and local taxes) and the structure of land ownership in ways that definitely made the distribution of income in France less unequal than it had been under the *ancien régime* and perhaps significantly less unequal than the distribution of income in nineteenth-century Britain.[22]

What is most important, the system of land tenure, together with slower population growth, restrained the outflow of families from agriculture and from villages, so that urbanisation proceeded at a far slower pace in France than in Britain. Urbanisation and industrialisation can be seen as part of the circular process of economic development and are self-reinforcing. On the supply side, gains from the availability of cheap supplies of labour and externalities associated with the concentration of industry in a narrow geographical compass are well known. Urbanisation also stimulates demand because many of the inputs that go to create and sustain an urban community are industrial commodities supplied by several industries to provide the shelter, heat, light, sanitation systems, roads and transport equipment required for the residents of towns on a scale not needed in the countryside.

Furthermore, urban industry and its associated complex of services created more opportunities for full-time continuous employment for all members of the family (men, women and children). Consequently less labour time remained available to households for the domestic manufacturing of a whole range of products consumed in the home.[23] Thus in Britain continuous and rapid urbanisation expanded demand for processed food as well as factory-made clothing, shoes, furniture and other household utensils; while in France the majority of families engaged for most of the year in agriculture continued to deploy spare or underemployed labour time to make a lot of these things for themselves. Industrial goods made by French factory labour, whatever their quality and price, would therefore have encountered far keener competition from the products made by rural labour within the home than the competition encountered in both the urban and rural markets of the British Isles. In English and Scottish towns workers had less time available to compete with factory labour even if they had wished to use their leisure to supplement wages in that way,[24] while in British villages capitalist agriculture probably harboured less underemployed labour than French family farms. Even by the late eighteenth century specialisation in the villages and small towns of France had not, apparently, proceeded far enough to supersede domestic industry for family consumption. For example, when Markovitch divided his estimate of industrial production for 1781–90 he put industrial autoconsumption of households at 0·7 billion francs, handicraft production at 0·9 billion francs and 'factory output' at 0·9 billion francs.[25] Of course, such domestic manufacturing also survived in England, but throughout the land families seem to have been far more involved in exchange and with market relations than French families. Their famous propensity to truck and barter had encouraged specialisation among producers long before the coming of factories and advanced technology associated with the Industrial Revolution. Factories when they evolved in England competed more directly with specialised workers in the putting out or mercantile system of industry and less with the family economy than they did in France, which prospered, according to Pouthas, up to the revolution of 1848.[26] Markovitch found that 'non industrial forms of organization' (he apparently means enterprises employing fewer than ten workers) still accounted for three-quarters of industrial output in the 1860s.[27]

No doubt emphasis in any explanation for the longer survival of these traditional forms of manufacturing should be placed where it is now placed in histories of French industrialisation, namely upon the segmented nature of the French home market and the relatively low proportion of industrial output sold abroad.[28] Up to the Revolution internal tolls helped to reinforce the isolation of local markets, already strongly protected from outside competition by the facts of geography and the high cost of transport over a terrain two-and-a-half times the size of Britain, a country which in any case was better endowed by nature with rivers, harbours and sea lanes to facilitate the movement of goods from place to place. Partly as a result of the long period of political upheaval associated with the Revolution and Napoleonic Wars, private and public enterprise failed to cover France with a network of canals during the canal age. Railways eventually unified the national market for the products of factory industry and by 1870 had brought the regions of France into competition with one another. Thus between 1845–54 and 1865–74 the output of the transport sector (measured in ton-kilometres) nearly doubled, and almost the whole of this increase can be attributed to railways.[29]

Although an efficient distribution and transport network gives consumers the opportunity of purchasing cheaper factory-made alternatives to the products made by local industries, the extent and speed at which consumers substitute such wares for traditional manufactures depends upon preference patterns and upon such things as design and quality as well as price. As regards price, we must again recall that the progress of mechanisation began at the input end of industrial processing, and machinery proceeded only slowly to take over the process of manufacturing final output. Thus the spectacular reductions in the cost of producing yarn, woven cloth and bar iron were by no means rapidly duplicated over the entire range of manufacturing industry or indeed for some decades in metallurgy and clothing at the finishing end of the iron and textile industries. Price continued, however, to be of prime interest to low-income groups, such as wage earners resident in towns, landless labourers or *manoeuvriers* from villages. While urban wage rates were higher in England, the proportion of consumers with 'middling' incomes may have been larger in France. Presumably that particular social group in both societies cared more about design and quality than wage earners and would be prepared to go on purchasing the more expensive products of traditional industry, even when machine-made substitutes became available.

Traditional small-scale industry can always satisfy local and individual preferences more readily than mechanised industry. It could, for example, cater efficiently for the wishes of families of 'middling' status to differentiate their consumption patterns from the social groups lower down the scale. Working-class tastes and aspirations to quality are, anyway, subject to a stronger budgetary constraint. From most accounts, local and individual preferences for particular styles and types of industrial goods seem to have been highly resilient in France – a discovery that British exporters made after the conclusion of the commercial treaty in 1860 when, according to one observer, they sent to France '*tapis a sujet* with hideous figures and in more hideous colours . . . rolls of the commonest staircase carpets . . . tasteless tissues in silk, cotton and wool, ties which reminded one of Houndsditch'. They 'showed a total ignorance of the market' because 'there is an innate unwillingness to buy bad things merely because they are cheap'.[30] Some historians even condemned French taste for traditional products and their preoccupation with quality as a drag on industrial progress. Conditioned as they were by income distribution, locality and culture, such patterns of consumption seem to have survived longer than they did in Britain where the more skewed distribution of income did little to encourage more subtle forms of differentiated consumption. The British middle class may well have emulated its aristocracy: the masses simply had no means to emulate either. Thus up to the second half of the nineteenth century British industry found an expanding market among social groups more concerned with price and less sensitive to quality, design and the appeal of tradition. Its markets were found on its doorstep among families committed to urban life who had limited funds to spend on manufactures after meeting their food and rent bills. In France such consumers formed a smaller proportion of the home market for organised industry. The rest could afford and demanded more attention to their local or individual needs and preferences.[31]

Paul Bairoch's important new book is concerned to show the relatively small role played by foreign trade in European industrialisation. For this argument we wish simply to observe that external trade operated to reinforce pressures on industry that stemmed from more important variations in patterns of home demand in the two countries. The influence of trade on French industrial development was in any case much slighter. Trafalgar checked whatever aspirations French industry had to capture a greater share of world trade in manufactures from Britain. Thereafter the proportion of industrial output sold abroad remained well below the British ratio.[32] French exports consisted largely of high-quality consumer goods and processed food sold to higher-income groups in Europe, including Britain as the country's best customer. British industry exported a larger share of its output, mainly to countries outside Europe. It found its best markets among consumers at lower ends of the income scale or by supplying the inputs of yarn, bar iron and woven cloth required by foreign industry for local processing and finishing.[33]

At this macro level of generalisation it would be futile to separate and to weight influences from the sides of demand and supply. That is difficult enough for one industry or even at the level of a firm. But not to recognise the demand factor in the long-term development of industry in Britain and France would be myopic. We have been concerned here to bring out some of the ways in which differences in income distribution, in the development of towns and in the relative importance of agriculture and foreign trade in the two economies conditioned the pace and pattern of that development over the nineteenth century. Our reading of industrial history leads us to conclude that whereas in Britain the expansion of urban demand facilitated the progress of larger-scale factory industry, in France the persistence of rural society and more traditional patterns of expenditure acted to constrain the development of factory industry. Consumption patterns in France appear less hospitable to factory industry, and French entrepreneurs found it more difficult to 'impose' their products on traditional markets. Among the more mobile and experimental population of English towns, British entrepreneurs experienced less sales resistance.

6.4   LABOUR SUPPLIES

Now we turn from the influence of demand on commodity mix and specialisation to the supply of labour. Until the last quarter of the nineteenth century the absolute value of industrial production in France remained larger than the comparable total for Britain, but the number of employees classified as industrial workers in Britain already equalled the French industrial work force at the time of Waterloo. Furthermore, between the defeat of Napoleon and the First World War labour employed in industry grew more rapidly in Britain than in France. British technology slowly compensated for the advantages possessed by French industry in its relatively high-value product mix and the quality of its labour force. In order to understand why labour productivity in British industry gradually superseded the average level of labour productivity attained by workers in France it seems helpful to divide industry into two sectors: a factory sector which utilised advanced technology with relatively high ratios of capital to labour, and a 'workshop' or *atelier* sector characterised by smaller-scale and more labour-intensive units of production.

The average level of labour productivity (value added per worker employed) was higher in factory industry. But the gap in productivity between the two sectors should not be exaggerated. Factories were not invariably that much more efficient, at least in the early phase of industrialisation. In a recent article Marglin argued that 'the origin and success of the factory lay not in technological superiority but in the substitution of the capitalists' for the workers' control of the work process and the quality of output. The social function of hierarchical control of production [i.e. the factory] is to provide for the accumulation of capital.'[34] In Marglin's view, factories served basically to maximise profits obtained for their owners by holding down real wages per hour worked, preventing embezzlement and increasing the working day, but they did not necessarily increase output per unit of labour input. Marglin's interesting hypothesis is relevant because commentaries on the British industrial system too often assume that the factory form of industrial organisation was synonymous with optimal efficiency, while commentaries on France often equate backwardness in manufacturing industry with small-scale family firms and the failure to develop types of industrial organisation, as well as technology, thought to be typical of British industry.

There is no need to refine our concepts of factory and workshop sectors because it proved impossible to find comprehensive data on the numbers of workers employed by size of plant or establishment for British industry before the twentieth century. But French statistics going back to the 1840s confirm the prevalence and persistence of small-scale enterprises in France which, in our terms, means that the workshop remained the typical unit for employment in French industry throughout the century. As late as 1896, 36 per cent of the labour force in French manufacturing industry worked in establishments employing less than ten people. German manufacturing establishments seem to have been similar in scale.[35] It really is unfortunate that no comparable data are available for British industry, but the average size of manufacturing establishments was certainly far bigger in the United States – the prototype for large-scale industry. In 1906 the mean number of wage earners employed by firms in American textiles was 67·9, compared to only 5·4 in France. For iron and steel products the means come to 60·2 and 8·1 respectively.[36] Contrasts with British industry are unlikely to be as dramatic, but descriptions of plant size in the two countries suggest that they would be visible, perhaps pronounced, across a wide spectrum of industry. Furthermore, small-scale enterprise is usually held to be one of the major symptoms of backwardness in nineteenth-century France.[37]

However, in the absence of statistical information on the precise degree of inefficiency that might be associated with small-scale establishments in France, we are more disposed to regard the scale of enterprise as adapted to the kind of manufactured goods made there, to the techniques available for such production and, possibly, as a reflection of the insignificance of economies of scale over a wide range of industrial activity for most of the nineteenth century.

This view obtains support from the negative correlation we found between labour productivity on the one hand and the mean size of industrial establishments found in France in 1906. The first step in this regression was to calculate the average number of employees per establishment for fifteen major industries. Next we repeated the calculation for the same fifteen industries listed in the United States Census of Manufactures for 1905. Assuming that the average size of establishments in America came close to the size required for optimal efficiency, we divided the mean size of an establishment for an industry in France by the comparable mean for the United States. For example, Table 6.7 indicates that the average size of a firm in the French textile industry was only 8 per cent of the average-size firm engaged in American textiles. Thus the ratios in column 2 of Table 6.7 are offered as a proxy measure of the degree to which the scale of enterprise in fifteen French industries fell below the scale required for optimal efficiency. Finally, we regressed these ratios upon the average levels of labour productivity for each industry in order to ascertain if there was a direct and significant relationship between optimal scale (as measured) and value added per worker employed for a given industry.

As the notes and numbers for Table 6.7 show, the relationship was, if anything, negative. In other words, industries in France dominated by small-scale enterprise tended to be characterised by higher levels of labour productivity – a result that certainly casts doubt on the presumption that small-scale enterprise was a significant source of inefficiency in French industry. We completed similar exercises for 1840 and 1861–5 but lacked a proxy variable for optimum scale and simply correlated the average size of establishments in fifteen French industries with the average level of labour productivity for these same industries, and again found that industries dominated by small-scale establishments tended to be industries characterised by above-average levels of productivity. We also discovered that manufacturing establishments located in and around Paris were characterised by a scale of employ-

Table 6.7 *Correlation Between Scale and Labour Productivity in French Industry for 1906*

Industry	Scale of establishment (France as % of USA)	Labour productivity in French industry £s
(1)	(2)	(3)
Food	35	158
Textiles	8	91
Wool	56	94
Hosiery	9	85
Cotton	13	174
Iron/steel	13	90
Metallurgy	15	96
Wood	14	43
Leather	7	85
Liquors	50	73
Chemicals	101	156
Bricks and tiles	78	63
Glass	121	28
Other metals	16	65
Paper and printing	155	78

Notes and Sources: The mean size of industrial establishments in France was calculated from: *Résultats statistiques du recensement général de la population*, 1906, vol. 1, part 2 (Paris, 1906). The French figures did not include *isolé* (working on own account). For United States we used: US *Census of Manufactures for 1905*, pp. 544, 554. Labour productivity in French industry was copied from Table 6.3.

The regression: $y = a + bx$

$$n = 15, \text{r}^2 = 0\cdot25$$

ment below that for France as a whole and a level of labour productivity (measured in value terms) above the level attained in similar industries located elsewhere in France.[38]

Although these exercises (particularly correlations for the 1840s and the 1860s) are not a conclusive refutation of the notion that French industry suffered some loss of output because firms operated below optimal scale, they do, nevertheless, indicate that the workshop sector of industry continued to be characterised by high levels of labour productivity right up to the First World War. In the light of this evidence we are disposed to see that sector as dominated by small-scale firms well adapted to a certain product mix and to the technology available to manufacture such products, and catering efficiently for the type of markets served by such industry.

Our description of the factory and workshop sectors of British and French industry is insufficiently supported by statistical evidence to really test many of the observations made in this chapter. Nevertheless, the distinction seems to offer a helpful way to account for the paradoxical fact that labour productivity in British industry only gradually surpassed the productivity levels attained and maintained by workers in French industry. In France the workshop sector began the century with a level of labour productivity well above the British level. Faced with competition from British technology and later from domestic factories in France, workshop industry there adapted and became more differentiated and specialised on products sold to consumers with tastes for style and quality, and incomes to match their demands.[39]

British technology slowly compensated for the traditional advantages possessed by France in the quality of its output and labour force by absorbing an increasing proportion of its labour supply into factory industry. In Britain the worskhop sector came into competition with the factory sooner than it did in France and sections of that sector collapsed fairly quickly, whereas in France it seemed more adaptable and survived within the ambience of the factory. Factories spread more rapidly across British industry, but it took a century of industrialisation before they had absorbed a sufficient share of the industrial labour force to push the average level of productivity up to and above French standards.

There is no way of measuring the speed at which labour in British industry came to be redeployed in factories over the nineteenth century. Clapham's chapters in 'The Early Railway Age' are concerned to emphasise the survival of older and smaller-scale modes of organisation across a broad band of industrial activity up to mid-century.[40] Fong attempted to assess the importance of the factory system for several industries which accounted for about half the work force employed in *manufacturing* industry in 1841. Fong's sample included nearly all industries likely to have been transformed in technique, scale and organisation by the Industrial Revolution. He concluded:

> In the English manufactures in 1840 the factory system had become the prevalent system of industrial organization in textiles such as cotton, woollen, worsted, silk, flax and hemp; in metals such as iron, engine and machine, button screw, steel pen, needle, pin; and in paper, pottery and glass. In other manufactures, in metals such as nail, anchor and chain, clock and watch, cutlery and gun; in clothing products such as lace, ribbon, glove, hat and wearing apparel, the system was making rapid headway, taking second and third place to other industrial systems.[41]

'Other industrial systems' included craftsmen and merchant employers, forms of industrial organisation which probably continued to dominate the rather large wood and furniture industry as well as the sectors mentioned by Fong.

For 1841 we could guess that over half the labour force in manufacturing industry still worked in industries where the factory remained the untypical form of organisation. Twenty years later, according to Booth's figures, some 44 per cent of the industrial labour force of England and Wales manufactured articles from wood, leather and fur, or worked in the building industry or made clothing. Enterprises employing more than ten workers are unlikely to be typical of such activities, or indeed of well-defined branches of metalwork, the processing of food, drink, and tobacco, printing and bookbinding and even some types of shipbuilding and ship repair. From a perusal of Booth's figures there seems to be no difficulty in asserting that as late as 1861 workshops rather than factories remained the dominant form of employment for the majority of Britain's industrial workers.[42]

Thus the productivity gap between British and French industry might be partly explained in terms of a slow growth in the share of the industrial labour force employed in the factory sector. Although that share changed more slowly in France, French industry began with an advantage in the productivity of labour employed in workshop industry. That advantage persisted for several decades because French industry did not absorb labour at anything like the British rate. Between the 1780s and the early twentieth century the British industrial labour force increased by seven times, from 1·2 million to 8·4 million employees, while industrial workers in France increased only 4·5 times (from 1·4 million to 6·3 million).

If we think about nineteenth-century industrialisation in a framework familiar to Ricardo, Malthus and Say (a framework currently employed by the *Annales* school of French historians), the process might be analysed in the traditional manner as a response to demographic pressure.[43] In this 'classical perspective' (or in terms of a whole family of labour absorption models in more contemporary literature on underdevelopment), British industrialisation can be viewed as a response to an increasing supply of urban labour.[44] Supplies of labour for British industry grew more rapidly than in France because population increased at nearly three times the French rate, and also because over time a far higher percentage of the additional supplies of labour made available to the French economy continued to be employed in the agricultural sector. The very different teneurial arrangements that persisted throughout the agricultural regions of France allowed French farms to absorb nearly 3 million extra workers between the 1780s and the beginning of the twentieth century.

Over the same period the total addition of between 6 and 7 million workers to the labour force employed in commodity production was roughly comparable in the two economies. But in Britain the numbers employed in agriculture remained almost constant and British industry provided jobs for an extra 7 million people. But with given rates of investment and with higher ratios of capital to labour, the factory or modern sector of industry could only employ a given fraction of the labour supply potentially available year after year. Several million British workers emigrated in the nineteenth century.[45] The rest found employment either in services or in the workshop sector of industry, which operated with more flexible ratios of capital to labour and possessed greater capacity to utilise the supplies of unskilled workers, who appeared on the labour market decade after decade.

By way of contrast, in France where (despite the far lower level of emigration) the labour force grew more slowly, workers could either move into industry or services or remain on the land. Thus the paradox of the superior productivity of French industry can be interpreted as a reflection of different rates of demographic change and internal migration. In Britain the continuous influx of unskilled labour into the workshop and smaller-scale sector of industry kept average labour productivity from rising, either to the levels attained in the factory sector or up to the standards achieved in large areas of manufacturing in France. At any point of time, possibilities for mechanisation and for the absorption of labour from agriculture and from traditional trades and crafts into factories remained limited. That technical constraint, coupled with a faster-growing supply of labour (and perhaps an inefficiently slow diffusion of the factory system), kept the average level of labour productivity in British industry below the level attained in France until the 1890s.

A convergence of forces eventually narrowed and then eliminated the differential between labour productivity in the two countries.

During the later phase of industrialisation, sometimes referred to as the Second Industrial Revolution and dated from 1873 to 1914, possibilities for substituting capital for labour probably increased. No doubt a full investigation into the relative prices of capital and labour would reveal a greater incentive for the diffusion of methods of production and organisation found to be successful in cotton textiles and other parts of factory industry. In Britain the slower growth of population and internal migration reduced demographic pressure on the urban wage rate and supplies of cheap labour available to industry; but in France the growth rate of the industrial labour force accelerated as agriculture's capacity to absorb labour diminished.[46] As French industry took on more and more workers, labour productivity increased at a far slower rate after 1874 than it had done for the previous four decades. Between 1825–34 and 1865–74 output per worker employed in French industry increased at something like 22 per cent per decade, which may even have been very slightly below the rate of progress achieved by British industry over the same period. Between 1870 and the end of the nineteenth century labour productivity in French industry stagnated, but it increased sharply just before the First World War. In Britain the rate of growth in the productivity of industrial labour also decelerated, but not to the point of stagnation. British industry did not, however, experience the marked upswing in productivity per worker in the decade before the First World War; that upswing restored value added per worker in French industry to an amount which was close to the British level.[47]

Perhaps there is no real paradox: it had simply taken decades for the factory system to triumph – far longer than Ure or Porter imagined and certainly longer than the invidious comparisons between British and French industry found in the tales of travellers and repeated in history books tend to suggest. France in the nineteenth century restrained its fertility, and its people remained in the countryside; while in Britain more people were born in or moved to towns, where they eked out a living in low-productivity occupations in services or traditional manufactures. In contrast to their counterparts in France (the 'poor' who toiled away in their villages), more of the British lower classes lived in the penumbra of a factory system which spread too slowly to raise productivity and to really improve their hard lives.

6.5   CONCLUSIONS

Only more research and detailed comparisons industry by industry will really explain the unorthodox finding that (for most of the nineteenth century) workers in French industry achieved higher levels of productivity than their counterparts in the First Industrial Nation. Nevertheless and despite a tradition of historical writing that begins from the opposite assumption, we are not disposed to regard the estimates of labour productivity presented in Table 4.3 as a statistical illusion. Of course the data should be a lot better, but the differentials seem to be in line with independently measured rates of change in output per worker and with our own crude estimates of capital–labour ratios for British and French industry. They also seem congruent with recent French scholarship on the long-term progress of industry in France, which is periodised as rapid growth in the second half of the eighteenth century interrupted by revolution and war from the American War of Independence to defeat at Waterloo, accelerated growth from 1815–24 to 1855–64, deceleration in the 1860s and 1870s, serious depression from 1883 to 1896, and a very pronounced upswing over several years before the outbreak of war in 1914.[48]

Evidence is sketchy, but we attempted to piece together the elements for an explanation of the 'fact' that labour productivity in British industry lagged behind that of France until the 1890s. At the centre of that tentative explanation is a conception of British and French in-dustrialisation in the nineteenth century as a process of specialisation and labour absorption. There is, of course, nothing original about an approach derived from Adam Smith and classical political economy, but it is a departure, or more accurately a change of emphasis, from recent historiography – more particularly from a body of Anglo-Saxon scholarship which perceives European industrialisation as a diffusion process, with backward or retarded countries on the mainland of Europe slowly adopting techniques of production and forms of business organisation pioneered by the British. That perception is full of insights into industrial development and is certainly a seductive and helpful heuristic device for the organisation of texts in comparative economic history. But history written in this vein becomes an account of mercantilist competition between nations. In the struggle for in-dustrial supremacy there are leaders and followers, and the problem for the historian is to account for the lags in time before retarded nations catch up. Here we summarise in order to capture the spirit of an ap-proach. But even a cursory reading of recent European economic history and typologies of industrialisation should exonerate us from the charge of simplification and reveal how dominated many texts are by the diffusion model and by the British industrial revolution as a paradigm.

We would not question the fact that the prior development and adaptation of certain elements of advanced technology (particularly the steam engine) meant that the British example became a factor in the industrial growth of France, Belgium, Germany and other countries in Europe. There are many features of long-run industrial development that transcend national frontiers and cultural boundaries. Thus over

time throughout Europe and America more and more industrial processes became mechanised, capital deepening proceeded to raise ratios
of capital to labour in industry after industry, enterprises grew larger,
factories replaced workshops and towns took over from villages as the
locus of industrial employment. But in the light of a comparison across
two major countries we are disposed to notice the limitations of an
approach to European industrialisation through the diffusion model –
an approach that seems to gravitate towards adjectives like 'backward'
and 'retarded' and, at its crudest, lapses into the mercantilist jargon
of 'national power'.

Sadly, the characteristic features of long-run industrial progress do
not provide historians with unambiguous indicators for ranking countries along a scale of development at moments of time. Although
industrial efficiency can be defined and assessed wherever an enterprise
or industry happens to be located, neither mercantilist nor technological
pointers to progress are a satisfactory basis for the evaluation of
industrial efficiency. Techniques, scale, location and patterns of organisation and production cannot be judged as backward or advanced in
relation to practices in other countries. As economics teaches, it all
depends on resource endowments, factor prices, product mix, demand
and comparative advantages, which themselves change over time.

Thus an approach to industrial development in different countries
through specialisation, factor supplies and comparative advantage may
bring out the more important elements of diversity in the transition to
industrial society – a diversity that may well be as rich and interesting
as the languages, cultures and political heritage of Europe. That approach will also reveal how the pattern and timing of industrial change
was conditioned by the resources, legal institutions and demographic
experience of each country and each region of Europe. At the same
time, it will be less concerned with leads and lags in the diffusion of
technology, which were, in any case, rather short-lived and perhaps of
marginal significance for overall levels of labour productivity for most
of the nineteenth century.

Turning now to our investigation into productivity levels in British
and French industry, we are conscious of its statistical limitations and
of the difficulty of summing up tendencies that purport to refer to
industry as a whole rather than to particular industries, products and
markets. In statistical language, the observations below relate to modal
products, enterprises and consumers. Above all we are concerned to
bring out broad, but significant, contrasts between Britain and France.
We attempt to remain true to the evidence but hope to find a way through
the welter of detail that informs the voluminous and rich industrial
history of the two nations.

First and foremost, the differential in the productivity of labour employed in British and French industry between 1815 and 1914 was rather slight. Britain's superiority appears to have been persistently and markedly obvious in the mining of mineral ores and coal, and the country's natural advantages spilled over into heat-intensive industries such as metallurgy, bricks, glass and cement. French industry tended to excel at the finishing end of the manufacturing process – in building, engineering, leather goods, some processed foods and some segments of the textile industry, with the important exception of cotton textiles where British efficiency remained obvious for most of the nineteenth century.

A look at the data on product mix and patterns of trade between Britain and France reveals two national industries specialised along lines of comparative advantage, which had developed on the basis of particular resource endowments (especially coal), and fine but significant variations in the patterns of demand. Thus for a wide range of manufactured goods (particularly cotton textiles) British advantages seem to lie more with cheapness than with quality and design, with a basic product rather than a highly finished article. British industry developed by finding markets both at home and abroad among families at lower ends of the income scale who were naturally sensitive to relative prices. In the domestic market the response of entrepreneurs to that kind of demand had been reinforced by accelerated population change, the rapid growth of towns and a more skewed distribution of income; compared, that is, to France, where fertility restraint, the continued predominance of rural industry and peasant agriculture with its reserves of underemployed labour time constrained the ability of French industrialists to sell on the same scale and to the same social groups as their British rivals.

Finally, there is no avoiding the classical preoccupation with supplies of labour and the effects of rather marked contrasts between Britain and France in rates of population growth and internal migration over the nineteenth century. *Ceteris paribus*, differentials in value added per worker employed in industry would change in response to the rate at which each national industry took on additional labour. In Britain, where both population and the industrial work force grew more rapidly than in France, the tendency towards diminishing returns to labour was averted by capital deepening, technical progress and the reallocation of workers into occupations and manufactures where the marginal and average product per worker rose faster than the average for industry as a whole. This is the essence of the first industrial revolution, and the productivity of labour employed in British industry certainly went up at an unprecedented rate. Nevertheless, capital formation and technical and structural change in industry did not proceed fast enough to push the average level of labour productivity above

French standards until later in the nineteenth century. The concentration in some industrial histories on coal, iron and cotton textiles where labour productivity rose far more rapidly than it did in France diverts attention from the full range of industrial employment and tends to exaggerate differences in rates of increase of labour productivity for British and French industry as a whole.

In France the tendency to diminishing returns was weaker because population grew more slowly and agriculture not only retained workers but increased the absolute numbers employed by some 3 million between the Revolution and the First World War. As industrial employment grew, technical and structural changes in France also meant that an increasing share of the work force came to be employed in factories. In this reallocation of the industrial labour force France lagged behind Britain. Its workshops continued to expand and to turn out traditional and high-value products made by skilled labour. Their survival and adaptation compensated for the slower spread of factories. This helped to keep the average level of labour productivity ahead of Britain until the end of the century. Sales overseas reflected, even strengthened, the influence of domestic demand on specialisation and the product mix. In any case, Britain's more successful naval policy over the eighteenth century and victory in the wars from 1793 to 1815 severely restrained any possibilities for export-led industrial development around the Atlantic ports of France.

Only carefully specified and rigorously tested statistical analyses will validate or refute the impressionistic hypotheses being developed here, namely that the techniques of production and the scale and form of industrial organisation found operating in French industry for much of the nineteenth century were in most cases well adapted to the demands that confronted industrialists in that country. Characteristic features of French industrial development, which often emerge in diffusion models as indicators of backwardness, may well, on deeper investigation, turn out to reflect differences in product mix that stem rather more from French resource endowment and market opportunities and rather less from entrepreneurial failure to emulate their successful rivals in Britain.

Value added per worker remained high in France because industry specialised in higher-value products. For such products, differentiated in quality and style, the workshop unit of production, often organised on a family basis, could train skilled labour and cater efficiently for local and other specific demands. In both economies the division of labour between new and older technologies and forms of organisation changed continuously in relation to technological developments over time. British industry responded by concentrating resources upon the production of intermediate goods and basic manufactures – that is, in sectors of processing where opportunities to mechanise production and to organise on a factory basis emerged early in the century. In France, where industry specialised more at the finishing end of the industrial process, old crafts, techniques and workshops not only survived longer, but complemented factory production until they eventually succumbed to the new industrial order later in the century.

We have ventured to express these ideas formally in terms of a model as an appendix to this chapter (Appendix D). There is also an abundance of descriptive evidence and many a quotation in the industrial histories of Britain and France available for adumbration of our hypothesis. But comparisons of productivity industry by industry and firm by firm have yet to be undertaken. Meanwhile, we conclude that adjectives such as 'backward' and 'retarded' should be deployed carefully, if at all, about industry in France and that there is nothing intrinsically para-doxical in the finding that its workers produced more per head than British workers for most of the nineteenth century. The fact reflects contrasts in product mix, in specialisation, in demographic change and rates of internal migration between the two countries. France stuck to the system of property rights in land consolidated by the Revolution, restrained fertility and kept the mass of its population in villages. In Britain the population grew rapidly and became steadily more urban and industrial. But investment and technical change only slowly raised output per worker above French levels. There is no doubt more rapid rates of investment and technical diffusion in France could have maintained the differential in labour productivity beyond 1890. But whether French society or more correctly its business leadership can be categorised as backward, wise or merely indifferent to rapid structural transformation along British lines is a question we leave to our even more speculative conclusions. Marxist and other stage theorists who manage to perceive in economic history some kind of teleological development towards 'full socialism' or 'ages of high mass con-sumption' will continue to see French economic and social development as 'lagging' behind Britain from 1780 to 1914. From the vantage-point of the late twentieth century it seems more difficult to assert that French industry should have emulated the British earlier rather than later. Indeed emulation of British technology and practices across a wide range of industrial activity seems irrelevant to the needs of France for most of the nineteenth century. In any case, what Frenchmen actually did in industry seems to have been accomplished, for the most part, as efficiently as could be expected.

APPENDIX D: A MODEL OF INDUSTRIAL DEVELOPMENT FOR BRITAIN AND FRANCE 1780–1914

The gap in the productivity of the labour force employed in manufactures in Britain and France can be explained in the following manner.

Suppose that, prior to the Industrial Revolution, manufacturing output in the two countries consists of crafts, C. Craftsmen are considered to be equally productive in France and Britain, when they are engaged in producing the same goods. These goods have identical prices in the two countries. There is, however, a range of luxury crafts, C_L, where French products are so differentiated from possible British substitutes as to constitute 'unique goods'. These are crafts with highly priced outputs consumed by a small high-income group of the population. Because of differences in the composition of demand, British craftsmen do not produce comparable products. C_L are crafts where the productivity of labour is high, owing to the amount of human capital invested in skilled labour through apprenticeship systems and other forms of labour training. Now, productivity in manufacturing in France is

$$(1 - b) (Q_L/T_L) + b(Q_Z/T_Z)$$

where Q and T represent output and labour respectively, and b is the proportion of the manufacturing labour force engaged in the Z-sector, that is, in those activities which can be found in Britain as well as in France. Productivity in Britain is

$$q_Z/t_Z = Q_Z/T_Z = q_M/t_M$$

(Throughout, lower-case letters represent Britain and the subscript M refers to entire manufacturing production.) Since we have assumed $Q_L/T_L > Q_Z/T_Z$, the degree by which total manufacturing productivity in France will exceed that in Britain will depend on $(1 - b)$, representing the proportion of the labour force engaged in C_L.

The Industrial Revolution in Britain is characterised by the substitution of capital-intensive technology across a wide range of manufactured activity. The new technology can be summed up as 'the factory', and factories are characterised by a higher average productivity for labour. With the introduction of 'the factory' manufacturing no longer operates under conditions of fixed factor proportions. The isoquant now consists of two technologies. (Here, the 'industrial revolution' is assumed to represent a once-and-for-all introduction of *new* technology. This assumption can be defended by arguing that the actual 'inventions' are really innovations, adapting one principal invention, factory organisation and mechanisation, to particular lines of activity. Thus capital-intensive technology is available from the moment it begins to be used in one line of activity.) The growth path, however, shows that the transition from one vertex to the other was not instantaneous. Although price conditions favoured it, normal imperfections in factor and commodity markets and delays in innovation imply that the transition to the new technology was gradual. Thus the share of factory production increases throughout the period but the factory does not become completely dominant until the end of the century. In this situation, the level of productivity in British industry depends on the relative proportions of the industrial labour force engaged in factories and crafts. In other words,

$$q_M/t_M = (1 - r)(q_Z/t_Z) + r(q_F/t_F)$$

where r is the share of the manufacturing labour force in factories, and q_F and t_F are respectively output and labour in the factory sector. Total productivity in British manufacturing depends on the value of r, or the proportion of the labour force employed in factories, since $q_F/t_F > q_Z/t_Z$.

In France, factory technology, with the same productivity as in Britain, is also adopted to replace the C_Z sector. The C_L sector, however, remains with the same productivity and the same technology. Thus relative productivities in the manufacturing sectors of the two countries will depend on the relative productivities in factory, L- and Z-sectors, and on the proportion of the manufacturing labour force in each, or

$$\frac{P_M}{p_M} = \frac{(1 - b)P_L + b[(1 - v)P_C + vP_F)]}{(1 - r)P_C + rP_F}$$

where v is the proportion of factory labour in the Z-sector in France. A whole range of values can be estimated for b, v and r, and the relative values of P_L, P_C and P_F, to allow this formula to yield the observed results. We believe that, historically, b approaches unity as high-quality craft goods become a smaller component of manufacturing production in France. Both v and r increase, such that by the end of the century, r is very close to unity. In France, however, the speed of transition is not as rapid as in Britain, and at any given time v is smaller than r. Given these behavioural assumptions for the variables, it can be seen that the initial gap will close and that productivity in Britain will increase more rapidly, whatever the relative values of the productivities.

NOTES TO CHAPTER 6

1 W. W. Rostow, *The Stages of Economic Growth* (Cambridge: CUP, 1971), p. 38.
2 P. Deane and W. A. Cole, *British Economic Growth, 1688–1959* (Cambridge: CUP, 1962), pp. 80–1, and an unpublished lecture by F. Crouzet on exports and industrial development in Britain, 1783–1815.
3 Compare F. Crouzet, 'England and France in the Eighteenth Century: A Comparative Analysis of Two Economic Growths' in R. M. Hartwell (ed.), *The Causes of the Industrial Revolution in England* (London: Methuen, 1967) with his 'Wars, Blockade and Economic Change in Europe, 1792–1815'. *Journal of Economic History*, December 1964.
4 D. S. Landes, *The Unbound Prometheus* (Cambridge: CUP, 1970), pp. 142–7; A. Milward and S. B. Saul, *The Economic Development of Continental Europe, 1780–1870* (London: Allen & Unwin, 1973), pp. 270–86.
5 As McCloskey suggests for his comparison between Britain and America: see D. McCloskey, 'International Differences in Productivity, Coal and Steel in America and Britain before World War I' in D. McCloskey (ed.), *Essays on the Mature Economy* (London: Methuen, 1971), pp. 289–95.
6 D. McCloskey, *Economic Maturity and Entrepreneurial Decline* (Cambridge, Mass.: Harvard University Press, 1973).
7 R. C. Allen, 'The Peculiar Productivity History of American Blast Furnaces', *Journal of Economic History*, September 1977, p. 608.
8 W. G. Hoffmann, *British Industry, 1700–1950* (Oxford: Blackwell, 1955), pp. 16–23. See John Wright's critique 'An Index of the Output of British Industry', *Journal of Economic History*, September 1956.
9 C. Booth, 'Occupations of the People of the United Kingdom', *Journal of the Royal Statistical Society*, 1886.
10 See W. Ashworth, 'Changes in Industrial Structure', *Yorkshire Bulletin of Economic and Social Research*, 1965.
11 P. Stearns, 'British Industry through the Eyes of French Industrialists', *Journal of Modern History*, 1965.
12 Calculated from census data cited under Table 6.3.
13 J. H. Clapham, *An Economic History of Modern Britain* (Cambridge: CUP, 1950), pp. 42–51 and ch. 5.
14 P. Mathias, *The First Industrial Nation* (London: Methuen, 1969), chs 5 and 9; C. P. Kindleberger, *Economic Growth in France and Britain, 1851–1950* (Cambridge, Mass.: Harvard University Press, 1964), ch. 8; Ashworth, 'Changes in Industrial Structure'.
15 Calculated from sources cited under Table 6.3.
16 A. Audiganne, *L'industrie contemporaine, ses caractères et ses progrès . . .* (Paris: 1856), cited by Pollard and Holmes, *The Process of Industrialization*, p. 350.
17 Cited by R. E. Cameron, 'Economic Growth and Stagnation in France, 1815–1914' in B. E. Supple (ed.), *The Experience of Economic Growth* (New York: Random House, 1963).
18 P. K. O'Brien, *The Intersectoral Terms of Trade in European Industrialization, 1700–1800* (forthcoming).
19 S. Engerman and P. K. O'Brien, 'Income Distribution in the Industrial Revolution' in D. McCloskey and R. Floud (eds), *The New Economic History of Britain* (to be published by CUP, 1979).
20 P. Mathias and P. K. O'Brien, 'The Economic and Social Burden of Taxes Collected for Central Government in Britain and France, 1715 to 1810', *Journal of European Economic History*, Winter 1976.

21 O'Brien, *The Intersectoral Terms of Trade*.

22 See Chapter 5 above.

23 N. McKendrick, 'Home Demand and Economic Growth; A New View of the Role of Women and Children in the Industrial Revolution' in N. McKendrick (ed.), *Historical Perspectives* (London: Europa Publications, 1974), pp. 153–209.

24 H. Freudenberger and G. Cummins, 'Health Work and Leisure Before the Industrial Revolution', *Explorations in Entrepreneurial History*, (January 1976), pp. 1–4.

25 T. J. Markovitch, 'L'industrie française de 1789 à 1964', *Cahiers de l'ISEA*, AF 4, July 1965, pp. 204–12, and 'Les secteurs dominant de l'industrie française', *Analyse et Prevision*, no. 1 (1966), pp. 161–75.

26 C. H. Pouthas, *La population française dans la première moitié du XIX siècle* (Paris: Presses Universitaires de France, 1956), pp. 198–225.

27 Markovitch, 'Les secteurs', p. 164, and see Landes, *The Unbound Prometheus*, pp. 188–92.

28 Two case studies strongly influenced our views on French industrialisation: C. Fohlen, *L'industrie textile au temps du second empire* (Paris: Plon, 1956), and J. Viat, *L'industrialization de la siderurgie française, 1814–67* (Paris: Mouton, 1967).

29 J. C. Toutain, 'Les transports en France de 1830 à 1965', *Cahiers de l'ISEA*, AF 9, September 1967, pp. 298–304.

30 C. B. Derosne, *Ten Years of Imperialism in France* (London: 1862), pp. 145–50, cited in Pollard and Holmes, *The Process of Industrialization*, pp. 398–9.

31 W. Minchinton, 'Patterns of Demand' in C. M. Cipolla (ed.), *The Fontana Economic History of Europe* (London: Fontana, 1973), vol. 3.

32 P. Bairoch, *Commerce extérieur et développement économique de l'Europe au XIXe siècle* (Paris: Mouton, 1976), pp. 188–9, 193 and 231.

33 ibid., pp. 88 and 94, and his 'Geographical Structure and Trade Balance of European Foreign Trade', *Journal of European Economic History*, Winter 1974, pp. 574–5.

34 S. Marglin, *What Do Bosses Do? The Origins and Functions of Hierarchy in Capitalist Production* (Cambridge, Mass.: Harvard Economics Department, mimeograph, 1971), p. 4.

35 *Résultats statistiques du recensement général de la population* (Paris, 1906), vol 1, part 2, pp. 188–92. For comparisons with Germany see vol. 1, part 3, pp. 48–54.

36 See Table 6.7.

37 T. Kemp, *Economic Forces in French History* (London: Dobson, 1971), p. 287, and D. S. Landes, 'French Entrepreneurship and Industrial Growth in the 19th Century' reprinted in B. E. Supple (ed.), *The Experience of Economic Growth* (New York: Random House, 1963), pp. 340–6

38 The results of this particular statistical exercise will be published as an article. The sources used were: Statistique de la France, *Résultats généraux de l'enquête des années 1861–65* (Nancy, 1873), and *Industrie en 1840–45* (Paris, 4 vols, 1847–52).

39 Very good descriptions of the workshop sector of French industry particularly for workshops located around Paris can be found in L. Chevalier, *La formation de la population parisienne au XIX siècle* (Paris: Presses Universitaires de France, 1940), pp. 73–80 and 110–15. See also B. Gille, *Reserches sur la formation de la grande enterprise capitaliste, 1815–48* (Paris: SEVPEN, 1959).

40 Clapham, *An Economic History*, chs 5 and 10.

41 H. D. Fong, *Triumph of Factory System in England* (Tientsin: Chihli Press, 1930), pp. 4, 5 and 22.

42 Booth, 'Occupations of the People', p. 314.

43 M. Lévy-Leboyer, 'La décélération de l'économie française dans la seconde moitié du XIXᵉ siècle', *Revue d'Histoire Economique et Sociale* (1971), 4, pp. 485–507. See also introduction by the editor and E. Le Roy Ladurie's essay in P. Burke (ed.), *Economy and Society in Early Modern Europe* (London: Routledge, 1972).

44 A recent survey of these models is by W. C. Robinson, 'Types of Disguised Rural Employment and Some Policy Implications', *Oxford Economic Papers*, XXI (1969).

45 Bairoch, *Commerce extérieur*, p. 113.

46 P. Merlin, *L'exode rural* (Paris: Institut National Economique Demographique, Paper 59, 1973), ch. 1.

47 See Table 6.2. But for different estimates see E. H. Phelps-Brown and S. J. Handfield-Jones, 'The Climacteric of the 1890's; A Study of the Expending Economy', *Oxford Economic Papers*, IV (1952).

48 See F. Crouzet, 'French Economic Growth in the Nineteenth Century Reconsidered', *History*, June 1974, pp. 167–79, and papers by Crouzet, Lévy-Leboyer, Marczewski and Roehl cited in notes 21, 22, 24, 25, 26 and 34 to Chapter 1.

Conclusions

Debate on the quality of British and French civilisation is almost as old as their histories as nation states. Countries are prone to evaluate their collective achievements against the attainments of immediate neighbours. Proximity seems to breed rivalry that frequently erupts into armed struggle, but for a hundred years after Napoleon's defeat at Waterloo, competition between England and France took on a more peaceful form. Its goals came to be expressed in economic terms, in the language of growth, productivity and technical progress. Although mercantilists of an earlier era had also used similar criteria to rank the two states, they were largely preoccupied with connections between power and plenty. After the age of democratic revolutions and the transformation in sensibilities wrought by romanticism, perspectives on the purposes of economic growth shifted to bring social welfare into the centre of calculations on the relative merits of different national economies. That shift also occurred in the late eighteenth century because, for the first time in history, technical progress offered masses of people the prospect of higher standards of consumption. The nineteenth century was not a struggle for survival but a race for more, and in an age of materialism states were inevitably judged on how far they satisfied the natural aspirations of their citizens for goods and services. Their rulers and businessmen, their laws and politics, their cultural and moral systems, even family life, came to be evaluated in terms of the capacity of traditional institutions to harness forces making for economic progress. Although the ascetic, the sensitive and the comfortably off might decry the new materialism, they offered no acceptable alternative to its blessings. Most people in most places at most times prefer to eat and drink more food, clothe themselves more elegantly, house and heat themselves more comfortably, travel more easily and enjoy leisure. Above all people wish to consume a greater amount and variety of industrial products. All these material goods can be aggregated into national outputs and averaged into per capita incomes in order to evaluate progress from one generation to another. The same numbers can also be used to assess levels of consumption enjoyed by one national group compared with others. On such scales progress is linear and deprivation is relative. Above all (in Burke's words), 'the age of chivalry had gone', 'that of sophisters, economists and calculators had succeeded', and statistics had entered the debate about British and French civilisation.

Statistics must, however, be placed in context. Throughout the long century of transition to an industrial society, Frenchmen visited England and Englishmen went to France. Many of their published travelogues are merely the tales of ignorant chauvinists, with a more-or-less amusing talent for denigration. But the best of them used their time abroad to reflect seriously on their own as well as the alien society. To aggregate and summarise the complex and qualified views of intelligent men who really made the effort to confront another culture is a little superficial. Nevertheless, there are some discernible and common lines that seem to run through the reactions of Frenchmen as different in character and attitude as Toqueville and Taine, Boutmy and Buret, Sismondi and Say. Their reactions seem, moreover, to persist from the generation of high-minded economists sent to England on official inquiries in the 1820s, through the well-known tour of Leon Faucher in the 1840s to the equally famous studies of the English people by Taine and his pupil Boutmy later in the nineteenth century. In general, what the French admired most was the freedom and the political system enjoyed by their neighbours. 'Great Britain', wrote La Vauguyon in 1817, 'is the classic land of liberty and religious toleration, the two greatest blessings which men can enjoy.'[1]

Of course, they also continued to be impressed by British technology and business methods. But almost without exception they reacted with horror to the living conditions experienced by the working classes in London and the new industrial cities of Leeds, Manchester, Wolverhampton, Glasgow and Liverpool (where the Irish quarters were described by Taine in 1870 as 'the last circle of hell').[2] Smoky, filthy, untidy and indiscriminately built are some of the common adjectives used to describe Britain's urban environment; and dirty, worn, ragged, morally depraved and physically debased are the epithets applied to the denizens of British cities. Ledru-Rollin and Buret admitted, however, that people in France were just as alarmed by the physical and moral debasement of the populations of Mulhouse, Lille, Rouen, Lyons and Paris; but, Ledru-Rollin observed, 'there is nothing in France that can be compared to what we see in the centres of England's producing population'.[3]

When they visited villages, most French travellers appreciated the solid farmhouses, clean stables and byres and orderly layout of Britain's opulent farms. They found agriculture to be a 'true science'. On the other hand, they seldom failed to contrast the conditions of agricultural labourers with the status of those who toiled in the French countryside. As Leon Faucher put it, 'Frenchmen cannot comprehend a state of affairs in which a minority can appropriate to itself the land, better housing and even better air, while relegating to the majority the six feet of space necessary for a bed or a coffin.'[4] Almost all French travellers (even Tocqueville) commented unfavourably on the inequality they observed in England. For example, in 1824 Sismondi returned to France 'convinced that the essential thing for a country and its general well being is *not* the concentration of wealth'.[5] Buret, in his general investigation into poverty, described it as 'leprosy which covers the whole surface of England, the rural population as well as the urban'.[6] To him, the poor in England seemed more miserable than elsewhere in Europe because their condition so contrasted with the advanced state of the economy and the landed gentry among whom a large number of them lived. Taine, who found England better than France at politics, agriculture, manufacturing, the colonisation of distant lands, even at cultivating the mind, preferred three things about his own country: its climate, the distribution of wealth and income, and French family and social life; the last he found more natural, jolly and communicative, largely because of the greater equality established both within the family and between social groups in France.[7]

Travelogues are travellers' tales. However sensitive and educated the tourist, there is no substitute for analysis and measurement. Yet economists need to read such literature, not merely to pick up apt illustrations from the 'unscientific' but often perceptive views of contemporary observers from another culture, but basically because it is salutary to be reminded that there can never be a purely economic view of the history of France and Britain. Politics, culture, manners, morals, leisure and other parts of social and private life are left out of economic history which deliberately and explicitly focuses upon material aspects of civilisation. That perspective should, very properly, remain central to comparisons of developments in Britain and France in an age of materialism, but there are other things. Furthermore, the observations of astute contemporaries helped us to appreciate that the indicators employed in this book to measure the relative achievements of Britain and France in the economic sphere are not unambiguous indicators of social welfare. Of course, economic theory never claimed that estimates of per capita income, real wages, labour productivity and crop yields (however carefully compiled) could be separated from the economic and social systems that generated the outputs upon which the national estimates were based.

Thus, as we read Faucher's and Taine's accounts of British industrial towns, or saw their residents depicted in the art of Gustave Doré, we were forcibly reminded that Britain's output grew faster than the gross national product of France, partly because the location of economic activity shifted more rapidly away from the villages and countryside of

England. Whether they liked it or not, the working people of Britain came to live and work in towns and cities. There the quality of their lives changed. For better or worse is ever debatable because so few left records of how they experienced the transition. Historians will never know if most people truly felt that loss of community, connection and identity,

> Among the close and overcrowded haunts
> of cities where the human heart is sick.

Certainly English poets, from Wordsworth (whose poem 'The Prelude' is quoted above) to Eliot, people of the city 'Huddled between concrete and the sky', have floated images of urban existence that cannot be ignored, however rapid the growth of gross national output.[8]

Yet even in the context of purely statistical inquiry, many of the goods that inflate the level of Britain's output could be defined as products instrumental to an urban system of production, rather than as commodities actually enjoyed by English families. Some percentage of what accountants of national production designate as income is now recognised as payments to offset the distress of urban living. Today in modern America (where industrial cities have improved out of all recognition compared with the century before 1914) the 'disamenities' that so horrified European visitors to English cities, including pollution, congestion, ugliness, noise and insecurity, operate, according to recent estimates by two Yale economists, to depreciate the disposable incomes of American families by about 8 per cent. They go on to comment that if the 'American population were completely urbanized the adjustment would be about one-third of income'.[9] Perhaps estimates on a similar basis could be made for the nineteenth century, and they would surely reveal that the higher incomes paid to families who resided in Britain's industrial cities were earned at a high cost; a cost that was not imposed on the majority of Frenchmen who remained far longer in the countryside.

There is no intention or implication here to deploy an idealised pastoral image of French country life against the squalor of English cities. Such a comparison would require far more research and reflection than we could muster in these preliminary exercises in quantitative history. Still less would we wish to beat the First Industrial Nation with its own rural past. England's agriculture sustained and contributed powerfully to the transition to an industrial economy. In English history town and country seem to be inextricably mixed. Agriculture supplied the urban economy with its food, industrial raw materials and factors of production, capital as well as manpower. Rural families purchased the products of towns.

Yet England's villages can, in a sense, be juxtaposed against its towns to appear (as they so often appear in literary images) as places of repose, honesty and true community. In the transition to industrial society something was lost – by Crabbe's 'poor laborious natives of the place who deplored their fortunes yet sustained their parts'. But in a rural economy one thing mattered above all else: access to the primary instrument of production – land. Over the centuries a system of property rights developed in Britain which had concentrated control over land in the hands of a relatively small group of owners. Within a market context, they determined the forms and terms upon which land could be cultivated and received the lion's share of the surplus generated from the production and sale of agricultural commodities. During the last great waves of enclosure from 1750 to 1835 access to and income from land came to be denied to the vast majority of the rural labour force.

But cries from the afflicted, fulminations from Cobbett, poetic laments for lost pastoral ages of innocence and ease, even sporadic outbreaks of rick burning could not arrest a process that had gone on for centuries. By the General Enclosure Act of 1801, land had been parcelled out in ways that left most people who worked it either in a position of tenant farmers, or with the less enviable status of agricultural labourers. At the same time, the logic and injunctions of a commercialised and efficient system of farming rendered the agricultural institutions of Britain increasingly hostile to redundant labour and inhospitable to the growing numbers of people born in the countryside after 1750. Whatever they felt, however they may have wished to live out their hard lives, millions of landless people simply had to leave the villages for work in the towns.

This same institutional framework which the British had developed for the management of the nation's farmland contributed powerfully to raising the economic efficiency of agriculture and to the creation of a surplus for deployment in the urban economy. Thus, by the late eighteenth century (if not long before) the productivity of workers employed in British agriculture was well above the productivity of those employed on the land of France. Because its system was more hostile to the retention of underemployed labour, land–labour ratios became more favourable in Britain – a country already endowed by nature with soil of a higher quality and better suited to pastoral than to arable farming. With land ownership concentrated, with fields and other instruments of production aggregated into units far larger than modal farms typical of France, Britain's agricultural system possessed undoubted advantages for sustained growth and for the support of structural change. For example, funds could be generated and appropriated more easily for direct investment in agriculture; alternatively, the rents of owners and the profits of their tenant farmers could be diverted through numerous conduits into the urban economy. Such flows encouraged surplus rural labour to migrate and to follow capital into jobs in industry, transport and services. Within agriculture, investment raised ratios of capital to labour and to land. Perhaps the most important component of capital accumulated in the rural economy consisted of animals which supplied higher-value output and power to complement and substitute for labour. Above all, Britain's relatively capital-intensive system of mixed farming operated to maintain and increase the flows of organic fertiliser on to arable land, which raised average yields of grain, potatoes and other field crops.

Across the Channel, its neighbours recognised the superiority of British agriculture. Some even agreed with Arthur Young and appreciated the advantages of its teneurial system. But in France centuries of struggle between king, aristocracy and those who tilled the land culminated in the Revolution of 1789, which gave the peasantry what they had long wanted – full rights of ownership and freedom from the burden of feudal exactions of all kinds. Compared to Britain, France entered the long century to 1914 with a significantly larger agricultural economy in which inequalities in the distribution of land ownership were far less marked. Access to communal and waste land had survived; farms remained smaller. Ratios of capital (particularly animals) to land and labour were significantly lower than in Britain. Above all, the Revolutionary settlement consolidated a teneurial system with a far greater capacity to sustain and retain labour than the more 'capitalist' institutions of Britain's agrarian economy.

Throughout the nineteenth century, output per worker employed in French agriculture remained appreciably and consistently below output per worker employed in British agriculture. In a taxonomic sense this fact alone is sufficient to account for the entire difference in average incomes between the two countries. Some part of the gap in productivity could be attributed to a failure on the part of French farmers to innovate. We are more disposed, however, to see the differential as the product of real constraints on 'peasant' agriculture to save, invest and change the product mix. Agricultural 'backwardness' in France came from the maintenance of high labour densities in the countryside, which inevitably leads to the intensive cultivation of inferior soils and a crop mix dominated by basic foodstuffs. But in France the landless formed a far smaller proportion (in fact a minority) of the rural population and for decade after decade the majority displayed no desire to move off their 'inferior' land into the cities.

This large agrarian sector (often regarded as a 'drag' or 'weight' on progress) certainly conditioned the pace and pattern of industrial development in France along lines that differed from Britain's experience. For example, lower rates of internal migration reduced opportunities for the production and sale of standardised manufactured goods on a large scale. With under-utilised labour time at their disposal, the poor who remained attached to their small plots of land formed a less hospitable market for factory-made goods than the masses of wage earners who resided in English cities. Even those wage-dependent families in French towns who existed on lower real wages had less to spend on anything but necessities. Above the bottom end of the income scale came those middling groups in society with more than the bare minimum available for the purchase of manufactured goods, who were likely to be more sensitive to quality and style than wage earners and *manoeuvriers*. Our impression is that such groups consumed a larger share of the products of French industry than their British counterparts did of the products of their own industry. At present, the state of knowledge on income distribution and class formation in the two countries makes this an untested proposition. But as evidence begins to emerge on the distribution of wealth and income, it supports the observations of French travellers to Britain, who found more remarkable contrasts between wealth and poverty than anything in their own society.[10] Foreign trade operated basically to reinforce the constraints on patterns of production or product mix set by the structure of domestic demand that faced industrialists in Britain and France. At home and abroad, French industry catered *more* for social groups above the lower ends of the income scale. Thus rural and domestic manufacturing continued to compete successfully with factories across a wide band of industry by meeting the particularised wishes of social groups in regional and local markets; markets that were, moreover, protected from internal competition (at least before the spread of railways) by the relatively high cost of internal transport.

Within these 'demand constraints' (which in some fundamental sense can be referred to the survival of a rural economy and the slower pace of structural transformation in France) French industrial output and the productivity of labour grew over the long run at rates that compare favourably with standards set by British industry. Furthermore, our own measurement and reflections upon the overall level of labour productivity in the two sectors prompted us to qualify the picture of French industrialisation that has emerged from the writings of historians, whose views are strongly influenced by diffusion models and stage typologies of economic development. Seen in a context of comparative advantages and specialisation and related to constraints (on the overall importance of foreign trade) set by natural endowments and a long succession of naval defeats over the eighteenth century, the industrialisation of France up to 1914 looks different, and not so grey. Perceptions in this mode are, however, less well defined than they are in other paintings of a technological race between leaders and followers, or 'also rans' – to quote an epithet recently applied to France. In our picture there is more canvas to take in other industries apart from cotton, iron and coal. More colours are used and it becomes altogether more difficult to separate success from failure in the transition to the twentieth century.

Thus it appears that British industry enjoyed benefits from coal and other tractable supplies of mineral ore, that spilled over into metallurgy and other heat-intensive industries. Spinoffs from the early and widespread deployment of a technology based upon cheap supplies of coal exercised an important and persistent influence on the country's industrial development. French industry, denied comparable geological advantages, excelled towards the finishing end of the manufacturing process where its traditional supplies of skilled labour could be used to capture and maintain markets for manufactured commodities of higher-quality finish and design.[11]

Of course, there must have been inefficiency in French industry that stemmed from lags in the adoption of British technology, as well as failures to copy British forms and scale of business organisation. French entrepreneurs certainly passed up some profitable opportunities which pushed the level of industrial output below what it might have been with more rational choices. But, unless and until studies are available to pinpoint such 'irrational' behaviour in the context of the factor prices and market opportunities that faced French businessmen, we are not disposed to believe that their collective failure to adopt better methods *significantly* reduced the level of industrial output in France. Lags in the initial adoption of new technology were not long, and impediments to rapid diffusion earlier in the period can be related more to revolution and war than to the conservatism of the French business elite. France was not an underdeveloped economy shackled with feudal regulations. Decisions from 1780 to 1914 were made in the context of markets for labour, capital and commodities. Tardiness in the diffusion of British technology across French industry cannot be deduced from the continued deployment of particular techniques, the cultural characteristics of businessmen or the scale of industrial enterprise prevalent throughout French industry. Techniques used in France may have been more or less in line with factor prices. The scale of enterprise seems to have been congruent with a certain product mix, itself the outcome of specialisation and comparative advantage; while the family firm found favour not only in France, but also in Britain and elsewhere in Western Europe at the time.[12]

Until the 1890s, on average the productivity of labour employed in French industry remained above British levels, partly because the workshop sector of French industry survived, specialised and adapted to competition from the factory at home and abroad, but also because

British industry absorbed and trained a far greater influx of unskilled labour.

Thus, until the 1870s labour productivity grew at comparable rates in the two countries. Only investment and even more rapid diffusion of the factory system could have increased British industry's capacity to absorb the labour supplies made available to it by population growth and internal migration at even higher levels of output per worker. France experienced its *exode rural* later in the century. At that juncture, as agricultural prices fell and rural handicrafts finally succumbed to competition from factories, families began to leave the countryside in ever-increasing numbers. The urban economy then had to cope with the problems encountered in Britain several decades earlier. Before the upswings in industrial production from 1896 to 1901 and again from 1906 to 1911, labour was only absorbed into French industry at a constant level of output per worker employed; while in Britain the productivity of industrial labour continued to rise, albeit at a slower rate. Output per worker employed by British industry then moved above French levels at a point in time long after the Industrial Revolution began to transform its economy and society.

Why the rural exodus was long delayed in France is not a question we have been able to consider nearly seriously enough in this study. Life for the landless minority who remained in French villages appears in Vidalenc's vivid descriptions for the period 1815–48 as bad as anything experienced by the poor in English agricultural communities.[13] Perhaps, however, the *ménagers* and *journaliers* of France had a shrewd appreciation that their hard lot would not have been really improved by a move to towns. From bits of evidence it seems that their daily wages would not have risen sufficiently to compensate for the disamenities of urban life.[14] Furthermore, French urban industry, characterised by a product mix that demanded more skilled labour, did not offer the same job opportunities as British industry. The recruitment and training of its labour force occurred more on a kin basis and this held down the earnings of proletarian migrants with no family claims on profits or security of employment.

Criticisms of the French economy for its failure to transform structurally imply some irrational prejudice to move away from the countryside by those groups with apparently the most to gain from higher real incomes, a better-quality life and prospects for upward mobility, offered as compensation for uprooting and leaving for the city. Although the choice was there and theirs, the majority of Frenchmen apparently preferred to restrict fertility in order to remain in the countryside. They held fast to the agrarian institutions that the peasantry had fought for during the Revolution, institutions that continued to 'harbour' them during successive revolutions and crises over the nineteenth century.

As we learn more about the social history of French towns and the pace and pattern of internal migration in France, it becomes harder to condemn people's decisions to remain where they were born as irrational. Alternatively (in the comparative spirit of this book), if the structural transformation of the British economy is seen not as a paradigm for Western Europe, but as one path of transition to the twentieth century, the agrarian system of nineteenth-century France ceases to appear as a major impediment to progress and can be perceived as a set of functional institutions which influenced the masses in France to restrain fertility and to remain on the land until the urban economy could provide them with real material comforts and a civilised environment to compensate for the loss of community and a way of life that so many working people seemed reluctant to abandon during the initial stages of industrialisation.

In Britain, with abundant supplies of rural labour, most of the gains from rising yields from land took the form of higher rents and profits obtained by landowners and farmers. Agricultural wage rates rose tardily. Thus population pressure, a relatively slow increase in wages and a very different system of tenure prompted the outflow of people to towns and industries. Most had no real choice but to abandon the ways of their forebears earlier rather than later in the nineteenth century. The new industrial system coped as well as could be expected with the rise in population. In time, material standards of living for the masses certainly improved. The economy of Britain became larger and its State more powerful in international affairs. Total output grew more rapidly than it did in France and by 1914 the population and economic capacities of the two countries were roughly equivalent.

French economic growth suffered more severely from the 'crises of the seventeenth century'. Over the eighteenth century France presumably caught up with Britain, and when Louis XVI summoned the Estates General per capita incomes in the two countries may not have been very far apart. Revolution and war over the next quarter of a century had a more deleterious effect on France than on Britain. Thereafter (1815–1915) commodity output in France increased at a rate that fell below the rate achieved in Britain by around 1 per cent per annum. It is this slower rate of growth in agricultural and industrial output over the nineteenth century that prompted historians to write off and derogate the economic development of France as a story of retardation or relative backwardness. If these adjectives are defined as an unrealised potential for economic growth equivalent to the British rate of advance, then the perspective simply justifies itself. But to escape from tautology, that posited 'unrealised potential' must be located in relation to resources and opportunities available in France itself. External standards, even those set by neighbours and political rivals, excite politicians and stimulate emulation, but may well be irrelevant to the needs and capacities of France.

Several historians have taken this point and attempted to locate an unrealised potential for growth in the country's failure to undertake structural change along British lines. In terms of the composition of commodity output, France did alter the structure of production, but not as rapidly as Britain, where by 1905–13 88 per cent of commodity output was industrial in form, compared to 60 per cent of French output. That degree of dependence on the outside world for food and raw materials seems, however, peculiar to Britain and emanated from the country's status in the world as an imperial power and from an adherence to free trade that may well have contributed to the deceleration of Britain's economic growth from 1873 to 1914. No, the signal distinction of France was to retain such a large share of its labour force employed in agriculture – double the British share from 1815 to 1914. With an average level of productivity in agriculture well below that achieved by industrial workers, it seems that the French economy might have gained (perhaps significantly) from the redeployment of manpower. Unfortunately the 'loss' of output from the posited failure to undertake more structural change is impossible to quantify because it all depends on how productivity in the two sectors might have changed as French workers left the land. Redeployment of labour along British lines would, moreover, have involved a run-down of the agricultural work force and migration to towns at rates that seem beyond the economic and political capacity of the urban economy of France.

Nor can the argument be left there because it is, by implication, a condemnation of the French system of land tenure that harboured labour and retained other resources in the agricultural sector. That system had developed over the centuries in ways that differed markedly from Britain's legal arrangements for the ownership of, and access to, land. Critics of French economic performance sometimes forget that the agrarian institutions of France had been consolidated by the actions of militant peasants during the Revolution. The masses who lived and worked in the countryside displayed little desire for radical changes during the nineteenth century. They remained suspicious of revolutionaries from Paris and other cities who wished to transform the existing system of property rights. The demand for more structural changes either subsumes a demand for agrarian reform imposed from above – a politically untenable policy in nineteenth-century France – or may be an argument in favour of an alternative pattern of institutional development, with a much less egalitarian distribution of land ownership, which would have given France a larger proletariat, a bigger population and a higher level of gross national product. Thus the argument for more structural change seems based on the British paradigm and other stage theories of development that fail to accommodate the 'unobtrusive' industrialisation of France or to explain the long survival there of a village economy, millions of self-employed artisans, workshop production and forms of small-scale enterprise long after they 'should' have passed into history.

France cannot be fitted into a typology of European industrialisation, and its development reminds us that there is more than one way of transition from an agricultural to an industrial economy and from rural to urban society. Nor is it at all obvious that the path of economic development taken by France from 1780 to 1914 was inferior to the vaunted British model. Expressed in per capita terms, the rates of growth of commodity output in the two countries are not so very different. Population growth was, moreover, a real problem for the British economy while earlier restraints on fertility in France owed a good deal to the wider diffusion of land ownership and other property in French society. In British towns and villages the proletariat had little incentive to reduce family size in order to preclude the subdivision of family assets built up over generations. In Britain the birth rate came down only when real prospects for upward mobility occurred rather late in the nineteenth century.

This division of output or its rate of increase by population always invokes the idea that national economic systems should in the end be judged by the standards of consumption and quality of life that they provided for masses of the country's citizens. There may well have been some unrealised potential for higher levels of output and consumption in France, but the majority of Frenchmen displayed no strong desire to realise it by leaving their villages and rural crafts for work in factories and towns. They clung tenaciously to the security provided by land. Millions engaged in industrial production as self-employed artisans (*isolés*) or worked in small-scale family enterprises. Even today this 'dual' structure and dispersed pattern of production distinguishes France from its neighbours: workshops continue to survive in the ambience of factories; the land is parcelled out among small as well as large farmers; self-employed artisans work alongside wage-dependent proletarians. France is still an amalgamation of regions and diverse economies.[15]

Before the First World War contrasts with England were even more marked, and as the two economies moved into the twentieth century convergence was not obvious. In its structure Britain exemplified the classic Marxist paradigm of urban factory industry of capitalists and property-less proletarians. While France? A great deal of its structure remained unclassifiable. But did the 'inefficiencies' of that structure preclude masses of Frenchmen from enjoying the benefits that accrued to masses of their neighbours from the path of development followed by Britain from 1780 to 1914? Our contribution towards answering that very broad question lies basically in the numbers offered for labour productivity and for per capita commodity output. Of course these estimates are far from perfect, but the biases do not by any means run consistently in favour of France. Services have been deliberately left out of the equation, not to make a fetish of commodities but because a good deal of service production was, we believe, instrumental for an urbanised and centralised economic system. We do not expect, on a per capita basis, that the supply of services provided by doctors, teachers, lawyers, entertainers, hospitals, schools, restaurants, hotels and churches added more to the welfare of families in Britain than they did in France. The services that really made a difference were those sold by the British economy to the rest of the world. Thus shipping, banking and other commercial services supplied to foreigners enabled Britain to run a surplus of imported commodities that may have boosted average consumption by something like 15 per cent above the average level in France for most of the nineteenth century. This particular gain can, to some extent, be identified as a pay-off for the nation's investment in naval power and imperial conquest over the previous century. France had also invested heavily in military power. But from Louis XIV to Napoleon French statesmen had a less shrewd appreciation of the potential profit from foreign policy. Most of the resources that they commanded contributed far less towards the long-term welfare of Frenchmen.

A gap of 15 per cent or so is not, however, very wide. Even in measurable material terms, the relative backwardness of France is not so very obvious. Finally, as we remarked earlier, other things, apart from commodity output, come into the appraisal of different kinds of economic system. But conclusions to a statistical exercise are not the place to broaden the discussion into the quality of life offered by the British and French systems over the nineteenth century. French visitors to these shores rarely failed to comment adversely on the conditions of work and habitation experienced by the denizens of Britain's industrial towns. Almost without exception they abhorred the inequalities they found in England's villages. Englishmen also travelled to France and found many of the inefficiencies and signs of relative backwardness mentioned in the literature on the industrial retardation of that country. Arthur Young's condemnation of French agriculture continued to dominate the views of British economists from Porter to McCulloch to Hoskyns. But there is another body of 'Anglo-Saxon' writing on French agriculture and the French economy that is more sceptical about the superiority of Britain's path to the twentieth century and inclined to see a more humane and perhaps a no less efficient transition to industrial society in the experience of France. That tradition includes Morris Birkbeck, Samuel Cobbett, William Thornton and John Stuart Mill. We would like to associate this book with that tradition.[16]

NOTES TO THE CONCLUSIONS

1 Cited in E. Jones, *Les voyageurs français en Angleterre de 1815 à 1830* (Paris: Boccard, 1930), p. 69.
2 H. Taine, *Notes sur l'Angleterre* (Paris: Hachette, 1872), p. 304.
3 A. Ledru-Rollin, *De la decadence de l'Angleterre* (Paris: Escudier Frères, 1850), vol. 2, p. 97, and E, Buret, *De la misère des classes laborieuses en Angleterre et en France* (Paris: Paulin, 1841), vol. 1, pp. 231–41.
4 L. Faucher, *Etudes sur l'Angleterre* (Paris: Guillaume, 1845), p. 46.
5 Jones, *Les voyageurs*, pp. 129–30.
6 Buret, *De la misère*, p. 192.
7 Taine, *Notes sur l'Angleterre*, pp. 390–4. For a summary of Taine's views on England, see F. C. Roe, *Taine et l'Angleterre* (Paris: Librairie Champion, 1923).
8 For a recent and excellent analysis of this literature see R. Williams, *The Country and the City* (London: Chatto & Windus, 1973). The Eliot quotation is from Valerie Eliot, *The Wasteland, A Facsimile* (London: Faber, 1971), p. 43.
9 W. Nordhaus and J. Tobin, 'Is Growth Obsolete?' in *National Bureau of Economic Research*, General Series 96 (New York: Columbia University Press, 1972).
10 Adeline Daumard surveys the research completed and ongoing related to these topics in 'L'histoire de la societé française contemporaine: Sources et methods', *Revue d'histoire Economique et Sociale*, no. 1 (1974).
11 J. R. Harris, 'Industry and Technology in the 18th Century: Britain and France', Inaugural lecture delivered in the University of Birmingham, 1971.
12 Landes has, however, developed another view of family enterprise in E. C. Carter (ed.), *Enterprise and Entrepreneurs in 19th and 20th Century France* (Baltimore: John Hopkins Press, 1976), pp. 43 and 80.
13 J. Vidalenc, *La société française de 1815 à 1848, le peuple des campagnes* (Paris: Rivière, 1970).
14 C. P. Kindleberger, *Economic Growth in France and Britain, 1851–1950* (Cambridge, Mass.: Harvard University Press, 1964), pp. 233–4.
15 For an extremely perceptive analysis of, and explanation for, the dual structure of the French economy, see M. Lévy-Leboyer, 'Innovation and Business Strategies in 19th Century and 20th Century France' in Carter (ed.), *Enterprise and Entrepreneurs*, pp. 88–98.
16 Daniel Heath of Jesus College has written an interesting survey of this literature for his Oxford thesis.

Bibliography of Official Publications

BRITAIN

Board of Agriculture, Agricultural Statistics for 1866, 1879, 1892, 1893 (London).
Agricultural Output of G.B. (London, 1912).
General Report on Enclosures (London, 1808).

Board of Trade:
Report on Wholesale and Retail Prices (London, 1903).
UK Hours and Earnings Inquiry, 1906–07 (London, 1907).
First Census of Production of the United Kingdom, 1907 (London, 1912).

Ministry of Agriculture:
Agricultural land Classification Report, 1966 (London, 1966).
Research Monograph No. 4 (London, 1926).
A Century of Historical Statistics (London, 1968).

Parliamentary Select Committees and Papers:
Select Committee on Banks of Issue, British Parliamentary Papers, 1840 (IV) and 1841 (I).
Select Committee on the Expediency of the Bank Resuming Cash Payments, British Parliamentary Papers, 1819 (IV).
Select Committee on Emigration, British Parliamentary Papers, 1826–7 (V).
Real Values of Exports and Imports, Accounts and Papers, British Parliamentary Papers, 1856 (LVI), 1866 (LXVIII), 1889 (LXXV) and 1906 (CXVII).

FRANCE

Ministère de l'Agriculture:
Récolte des cereals et des pommes de terre (1878).

Ministère du Commerce:
Annales du commerce extérieur 1884, 1886 (1892).

Statistique generale de la France:
Agriculture: Resultats generaux des enquêtes décennales des années 1852, 1862, 1882 et 1892 (1858, 1868, 1887 et 1897).
Agriculture: Statistique agricoles de 1892, 1902, 1912 et 1913 (annuelle 1891–).
Annuaire statistique (annuelle, 1878–).
Industrie en 1840–45 (1847–52).

Industrie: Resultats generaux de l'enquête effectuée dans les années 1861–65 (1873).

Resultats statistique de recensement des industries et professions en 1896 (1900–1901).

Resultats statistiques du recensement de la population, 1901 et 1906 (1906 et 1910).

Index

Say, J. 186
Schumpeter, E. 59n, 66n, 101n
Sérand, E. 143n
Services: and commodity output 29;
and commodity prices 32; definitions
of 29, 30; international services 32,
197; in national accounts 29, 30; and
urbanisation 30, 31; wages in 30
Sexauer, B. 140n
Sismondi 186, 187
Soboul, A. 133, 144n
Stamp, D. 141n
State: and fiscal policy 132; and laissez-
faire 20–1; and land tenure 132–7;
and industry 164
Stearns, P. 182n
Structural Change: in Britain 75, 193,
194; in France 17, 75; and the
composition of national output 92;
definitions of 16, 18; and labour
allocation 90, 92–100, 193–6
Supple, B. 24n, 182n, 183n

Taine, H. 73, 186, 187, 198n
Technology: and its diffusion 18, 160,
191, 192; and economic progress 19,
22; and labour productivity 88; and
structural change 18
Thiers 75
Thompson, F. 144n
Thran, P. 141n
Tisdale, S. 118n
Tobin, J. 198
Tocqueville, A. 73, 139, 145n, 186, 187
Toutain, J. 23, 41, 51n, 52n, 57, 59n, 72n,
77n, 93, 101n, 105n, 120n, 140n, 141n,
142n, 143n, 155, 157n, 183n
Transport 28, 29

Under and Unemployment in Britain
and France 74–5, 138; *See also* labour
input and work force
United States 29, 60, 169, 170
Urban conditions in Britain 73–4, 186–8
Ure, A. 173
Usher, D. 52n

Viat, J. 183n

Vidalenc, J. 193, 198n
Vilar, P. 51n

Wages in Britain: indices of 68, 69; in
industry 147–9, 193; levels 62, 68, 70,
73; money wages 68; real 69; salaries
73, 74; share in GNP 74
Wages in France: indices of 68; in
industry 147–9, 193; levels 62, 68, 70,
73; real 69; salaries 73, 74; share in
GNP 74
Wars: First World 61; Revolutionary
and Napoleonic 60–1, 76, 164, 165,
193
Webb, A. 100n
Weiss, T. 52n
Williams, R. 198n
Wilson, C. 79n
Woodruff, W. 78n
Woolf, S. 144n
Work Force, Britain: composition of
85–6; in commodity production 86–8;
dependency 71–2; and education 89;
employers 70–1; hours worked per
annum 85–6, 124; in industry 173; in
agriculture 173; labour quality 88–9,
124; participation rates 72; self-
employed 70–1; wage earners 70–1;
See also labour productivity *and*
labour input
Work Force, France: in agriculture 102,
173; composition of 85, 86; in
commodity production 86–8; dependency 71–2; and education 39;
employers 70–1; hours worked per
annum 124; in industry 173; labour
quality 88–9, 124; participation rates
72; self-employed 70–1; wage earners
70–1; *See also* labour productivity
and labour input
Wright, J. 25, 51n, 182n
Wrigley, A. 101n
Wordsworth, W. 188

Yamey, B. 52n
Young, A. 43, 53n, 62, 103, 128, 130,
131, 140n, 143n, 144n, 197
Youngson, A. 24n

Printed in the United States
by Baker & Taylor Publisher Services

Printed in the United States
by Baker & Taylor Publisher Services